中央民族大学统筹支持一流大学和一流学科建设过渡性经费资助

美国文化与电影

洪娜 张建青 李佳 编著

American Culture and Movies

中央民族大学出版社
China Minzu University Press

图书在版编目（CIP）数据

美国文化与电影/洪娜，张建青，李佳编著. —北京：中央民族大学出版社，2017. 12

ISBN 978-7-5660-1430-6

Ⅰ. ①美… Ⅱ. ①洪… ②张… ③李… Ⅲ. ①英语—阅读教学—高等学校—教材 ②电影评论—美国 Ⅳ. ①H319. 4：J

中国版本图书馆 CIP 数据核字（2017）第 236633 号

美国文化与电影

编 著 者 洪 娜 张建青 李 佳

责任编辑 李苏幸

封面设计 舒刚卫

出 版 者 中央民族大学出版社

北京市海淀区中关村南大街 27 号 邮编：100081

电话：68472815（发行部） 传真：68933757（发行部）

68932218（总编室） 68932447（办公室）

发 行 者 全国各地新华书店

印 刷 厂 北京盛华达印刷有限公司

开 本 787×1092（毫米） 1/16 印张：22

字 数 380 千字

版 次 2017 年 12 月第 1 版 2017 年 12 月第 1 次印刷

书 号 ISBN 978-7-5660-1430-6

定 价 58.00 元

Contents

Unit One　History

Pre-reading Activities

Answer the following questions before you read this text.

1. How much do you know about Early and Colonial America?

2. What is a frontier? What role does American frontier play in shaping traditional American values?

3. Where and when was the first successful English colony founded?

TEXT A　The Age of Early and Colonial America

Early America

The first Americans crossed the land bridge from Asia and were believed to have stayed in what is now **Alaska** for thousands of years. They then moved south into the land that was to become the United States. They settled along the Pacific Ocean in the Northwest, in the mountains and deserts of the Southwest, and along the Mississippi River in the Middle West.

These early groups are known as **Hohokam, Adenans, Hopewellians, and Anasazi**. They built villages and grew crops. Some built **mounds** of earth in the shapes of **pyramids**, birds, or serpents. Their life **was closely tied to** the land, and their society was **clan-oriented** and **communal**. Elements of the natural world **played an essential part in** their spiritual beliefs. Their culture was **primarily** oral, although some developed a type of **hieroglyphics** to preserve certain texts. **Evidence** shows that there was a good deal of trade among the groups but also that some of their relations were **hostile**.

For reasons not yet completely understood, these early groups disappeared over time and were replaced by other groups of Native Americans, including **Hopi** and **Zuni**, who **flourished**. By the time Europeans reached what is now the United States, about two million native people, maybe more, lived here.

It would be almost 500 more years before other Europeans reached North America and another 100 years after that before **permanent settlements** were established. The first explorers were searching for a sea passage to Asia. Others—**chiefly** British, Dutch, French, and Spanish—came later to claim the lands and riches of what they called the "New World."

The first and most famous of these explorers was **Christopher Columbus** of **Genoa**. His trips were **financed** by Queen Isabella of Spain. Columbus landed on islands in **the Caribbean Sea** in 1492, but he never saw the mainland of the future United States. **John Cabot** of **Venice** came five years later on a **mission** for the king of England. His journey was quickly forgotten, but it provided the basis for British claims to North America.

The 1500s were the age of Spanish exploration in the Americas. **Juan Ponce de León** landed in what is now Florida in 1513. **Hernando De Soto** reached Florida in 1539 and continued as far as the Mississippi River. In 1540, **Francisco Vázquez de Coronado set out** north from Mexico, which Spain had conquered in 1522, in search of the **mythical Seven Cities of Cibola**. He never found them, but his travels took him as far as **the Grand Canyon** in Arizona, as well as into **the Great Plains**.

The first permanent European settlement in what was to become the United States was established by the Spanish in the middle 1500s at St. Augustine in Florida. However, it would not play a part in the formation of the new nation. That story took place in settlements farther north along the Atlantic coast—in Virginia, Massachusetts, New York, and the 10 other areas colonized by a growing tide of immigrants from Europe.

The Colonial Era

The first successful English colony was founded at Jamestown, Virginia, in 1607. A few years later, English **Puritans** came to America to escape religious **persecution** for their opposition to the Church of England. In 1620, the Puritans founded **Plymouth Colony** in what later became Massachusetts. Plymouth was the second permanent British settlement in North America and the first in New England.

In New England the Puritans hoped to build a "city upon a hill" – an ideal community. Ever since, Americans have **viewed** their country **as** a great experiment, a worthy model for other nations to follow. The Puritans believed that government should **enforce** God's **morality**, and they strictly punished **heretics**, **adulterers**, drunks, and **violators** of **the Sabbath**. In spite of their own quest for religious freedom, the Puritans practiced a form of **intolerant moralism**. In 1636 an English **clergyman** named Roger Williams left Massachusetts and founded the colony of **Rhode Island**, based on the principles of religious freedom and separation of church and state, two ideals that were later adopted by **framers** of the U. S. Constitution.

Colonists arrived from other European countries, but the English were far better established in America. By 1733 English settlers had founded 13 colonies along the Atlantic Coast, from **New Hampshire** in the North to Georgia in the South. Elsewhere in North America, the French controlled Canada and Louisiana, which included the vast Mississippi River **watershed**. France and England fought several wars during the 18th century, with North America being drawn into every one. The end of the Seven Years' War in 1763 left England in control of Canada and all of North America east of the Mississippi.

Soon afterwards England and its colonies were in conflict. The mother country **imposed** new taxes, **in part** to **defray** the cost of fighting **the Seven Years' War,** and expected Americans to **lodge** British soldiers in their homes. The **colonists resented** the taxes and resisted the **quartering** of soldiers. Insisting that they could be taxed only by their own colonial **assemblies**, the colonists **rallied** behind the **slogan** "no taxation without representation."

All the taxes, except one on tea, were removed, but in 1773 a group of **patriots** responded by staging **the Boston Tea Party**. **Disguised as** Indians, they boarded British merchant ships and **dumped** 342 **crates** of tea into Boston harbor. This **provoked** a **crackdown** by the British Parliament, including the closing of Boston harbor to shipping. Colonial leaders **convened** the First Continental

Congress in 1774 to discuss the colonies' opposition to British rule. War broke out on April 19, 1775, when British soldiers confronted colonial rebels in **Lexington**, Massachusetts. On July 4, 1776, the Continental Congress adopted a **Declaration of Independence**.

At first the Revolutionary War went badly for the Americans. With few **provisions** and little training, American troops generally fought well, but were outnumbered and overpowered by the British. The turning point in the war came in 1777 when American soldiers defeated the British Army at **Saratoga**, New York. France had secretly been aiding the Americans, but was reluctant to **ally** itself openly until they had proved themselves in battle. Following the Americans' victory at Saratoga, France and America signed treaties of **alliance**, and France provided the Americans with troops and warships.

The last major battle of the American Revolution took place at **Yorktown**, Virginia, in 1781. A combined force of American and French troops surrounded the British and forced their **surrender**. Fighting continued in some areas for two more years, and the war officially ended with **the Treaty of Paris** in 1783, by which England recognized American independence.

(Words: 1104)

New Words

colonial	*adj.* 殖民地的，殖民的
mound	*n.* 堆；高地；坟堆；护堤
pyramid	*n.* 金字塔；角锥体
clan	*n.* 宗族；部落；集团
communal	*adj.* 公共的；公社的
primarily	*adv.* 首先；主要地，根本上
hieroglyphic	*n.* 象形文字；象形文字写的文章 *adj.* 象形文字的；难解的

续表

evidence	*n.* 证据，证明；迹象；明显
hostile	*adj.* 敌对的，敌方的；怀敌意的
flourish	*vi.* 繁荣，兴旺；茂盛；活跃；处于旺盛时期
permanent	*adj.* 永久的，永恒的；不变的
settlement	*n.* 解决，处理；殖民
chiefly	*adv.* 主要地；首先
finance	*n.* 财政，财政学；金融 vt. 负担经费，供给…经费 *vi.* 筹措资金
mission	*n.* 使命，任务；代表团；布道 *vt.* 派遣；向……传教
mythical	*adj.* 神话的；虚构的
Puritan	*adj.* 清教徒的 *n.* 清教徒
persecution	*n.* 迫害；烦扰
enforce	*vt.* 实施，执行；强迫，强制
morality	*n.* 道德；品行，美德
heretic	*adj.* 异端的；异教的 *n.* 异教徒，异端者
adulterer	*n.* 奸夫；通奸者（尤指男人）
violator	*n.* 违背者；违反者；妨碍者
intolerant	*adj.* 无法忍受的；偏狭的
moralism	*n.* 道德主义；格言；教训
clergyman	*n.* 牧师；教士
framer	*n.* 组成者；筹划者
watershed	*n.* （美）流域；分水岭；集水区；转折点
impose	*vt.* 强加；征税；以…欺骗 vi. 利用；欺骗；施加影响
defray	*vt.* 支出；支付
lodge	*n.* 旅馆；门房；集会处；山林小屋 *vi.* 寄宿；临时住宿 *vt.* 提出；寄存；借住；嵌入

续表

colonist	*n.* 殖民者；殖民地居民；移民
resent	*vt.* 怨恨；愤恨；厌恶
quartering	*adj.* 成直角的；四等分的 *n.* 四等分；四分法
assembly	*n.* 装配；集会，集合
rally	*n.* 集会；回复；公路赛车会 *vt.* 团结；集合；恢复健康、力量等 *vi.* 团结；重整；恢复；（网球等）连续对打
slogan	*n.* 标语；呐喊声
patriot	*n.* 爱国者
dump	*vt.* 倾倒；倾卸；丢下，卸下； *vi.* 倒垃圾；突然跌倒或落下；卸货；
crate	*n.* 板条箱；篓 *vt.* 将某物装入大木箱或板条箱中
provoke	*vt.* 驱使；激怒；煽动；惹起
crackdown	*n.* 镇压；（美）制裁；强制取缔；惩罚
convene	*vt.* 召集，集合；传唤 vi. 聚集，集合
provision	*n.* 规定；条款；准备；［经］供应品 *vt.* 供给…食物及必需品
ally	*n.* 同盟国；伙伴；同盟者；助手 *vt.* 使联盟；使联合 vi. 联合；结盟
alliance	*n.* 联盟，联合；联姻
surrender	*n.* 投降；放弃；交出；屈服 *vt.* 使投降；放弃；交出；听任 *vi.* 投降；屈服；自首

Phrases & Expressions

be closely tied to	与……密切相关
play a part in…	在……中起作用
set out	出发

续表

a growing tide of	日益增多的
view…as	把……看作，认为……是
in part	部分地，某种程度上
disguise…as	把……装扮成

Proper Names

Alaska	阿拉斯加州
Hohokam	霍霍坎文化
Adenans	阿戴南斯（美国早期族群）
Hopewellians	霍皮威利安斯（美国早期族群）
Anasazi	阿那萨齐族，早期定居在科罗拉多西南部的族群
Hopi	霍皮语；霍皮人
Zuni	祖尼人；祖尼语
Christopher Columbus	克里斯多弗·哥伦布（意大利航海家）
Genoa	热那亚（意大利西北部港市）
the Caribbean Sea	加勒比海（位于拉丁美洲）
John Cabot	约翰·卡伯特（意大利航海家）
Venice	威尼斯（意大利港市）
Juan Ponce de León	胡安·庞塞·德莱昂（西班牙航海家）
Hernando De Soto	赫尔南多·德索托（西班牙航海家和征服者）
Francisco Vázquez de Coronado	弗朗西斯科·巴斯克斯·科罗纳多（西班牙探险家）
Seven Cities of Cibola	希波拉七城市
the Grand Canyon	科罗拉多大峡谷
the Great Plains	大平原（北美中西部的平原和河谷地区）
Plymouth Colony	普利茅斯殖民地
the Sabbath	安息日
Rhode Island	美国罗得岛州

续表

New Hampshire	新罕布什尔（美国州名）
Lexington	列克星敦市（位于美国肯塔基州）
Saratoga	萨拉托加（美国纽约州东部一个村落）
Yorktown	约克城（美国弗吉尼亚州东南部城镇）

Cultural Notes

1. The Seven Years' War was fought between 1754 and 1763, the main conflict occurring in the seven-year period 1756—1763. It involved most of the great powers of the time and affected Europe, North America, Central America, the West African coast, India, and the Philippines. The two major opponents were Great Britain and France. The war ended with the Treaty of Paris among France, Spain and Great Britain and the Treaty of Hubertusburg among Saxony, Austria and Prussia, in 1763. It was characterized in Europe by sieges and arson of towns as well as open battles with extremely heavy losses; overall, some 900, 000 to 1, 400, 000 people died. The war was successful for Great Britain, which gained the bulk of New France in North America. The Seven Years' War was the last major military conflict fought on the European continent before the outbreak of the French Revolutionary Wars in 1792. For more information, visit https: //en. wikipedia. org/wiki/Seven_ Years%27_ War.

2. The Boston Tea Party (initially referred to by John Adams as "the Destruction of the Tea in Boston") was a political protest by the Sons of Liberty in Boston, on December 16, 1773. The demonstrators, some disguised as American Indians, destroyed an entire shipment of tea sent by the East India Company, in defiance of the Tea Act of May 10, 1773. They boarded the ships and threw the chests of tea into Boston Harbor, ruining the tea. The British government responded harshly and the episode escalated into the American Revolution. The Tea Party became an iconic event of American history, and other political protests such as the Tea Party movement after 2010 explicitly refer to it. For more information, visit https: //en. wikipedia. org/wiki/Boston_ Tea_ Party.

3. The Declaration of Independence is a statement adopted by the Continental Congress on July 4, 1776, which announced that the thirteen American colonies then at war with Great Britain were now independent states, and thus no longer a part of the British Empire. Written primarily by Thomas Jefferson, the Declaration is a formal explanation of why Congress had voted on July 2 to declare independence from Great Britain, more than a year after the outbreak of the American Revolutionary War. The birthday of the United States of America—Independence Day—is celebrated on July 4, the day the wording of the Declaration was approved by Congress. For more information, visit http://www.princeton.edu/~achaney/tmve/wiki100k/docs/United_States_Declaration_of_Independence.html.

4. The Treaty of Paris, signed in Paris by representatives of King George III of Great Britain and representatives of the United States of America on September 3, 1783, ended the American Revolutionary War. This treaty, along with the separate peace treaties between Great Britain and the nations that supported the American cause: France, Spain and the Dutch Republic, are known collectively as the Peace of Paris. Its territorial provisions were "exceedingly generous" to the United States in terms of enlarged boundaries. For more information, visit https://en.wikipedia.org/wiki/Treaty_of_Paris_(1783)

Exercises

Comprehension of the Text

Ⅰ. Answer the following questions according to the passage.

1. What is the major cause of the Seven Years' War?
2. What do you know about the Boston Tea Party?
3. Where did the last major battle of the American Revolution take place?

Vocabulary

Ⅱ. Fill in the blanks with the words given below. Change the form where necessary.

provoke	enforce	mythical	chiefly	intolerant
impose	flourish	permanent	finance	crackdown
convene	resent	violator	mission	hostile

1. Postmodern is just the period which the image culture began to ______.
2. If you try to enforce a culture on others, you may ______internal protests.
3. His ______ to the woman found vent in a sharp remark.
4. They take it for granted that they know more than everyone else, and become narcissistic, proud and ______.
5. This article explains how our ______ hero implemented secure messaging for his vendors and himself.
6. Only true love and compassion for all can bring back ______ prosperity to the human race.
7. We recommend that you ______ this practice rigidly.
8. The ______with tanks and troops showed no signs of easing amid an international outcry over violence against demonstrators.
9. These are not things that we seek to ______ this is who we are.
10. Students should be friendly to others. Violence is strictly forbidden! ____ will be punished according to the university rules and the law.

Translations

Ⅲ. Translate the following sentences into English.

1. 它原本是佛教徒的节日，但现在成为全国人民相互泼水的节日，据说这代表了一种精神洗礼。(be closely tied to)

____

2. 身体健康是老年人保持独立生活能力并且在家庭和社区生活中发挥重要作用的关键所在。(play a part in)

____

3. 联合国环境规划署与海洋保护环境组织共同研究的最新报告指出，日益增加的海洋废弃物问题危害全球的海洋与沙滩。(a growing tide of)

____

4. 我们是否可以继续按计划举行会议，部分地取决于什么时候那种传染病会得到控制。(in part)

____

5. 我们吃着含有有机成分的有机垃圾食品，而因为它贴上有机标志，就伪装成为健康食品。(disguise…as)

____

Ⅳ. Translate the following passage into English.

第一批殖民者17世纪定居在大陆的东海岸，自此就开始了他们的拓荒经历。到了1890年，当西部的最后一片土地也有了定居者后，拓荒经历也随之结束了。美国的边远地区还包括一些相对无人居住的地区，大多分布在美国的西部。相对于居民较多的东部地区，这里的土地更荒凉，生命也更原始。当一个拓荒地区被开拓之后，人们就会开始向西部更远、尚无定居的地方迁移，而且他们迁移时会把当地的美国土著人全部赶走。随着一个接一个定居点的建立，美国人的足迹遍布2700英里宽的整个大陆。他们开始相信，控制所有的土地是命运对他们的安排，最后他们也确实做到了这一点。美国人也曾经给当地的土著人留出了小部分土地，称作“居留地”，但是美国政府违背了自己许下的许多诺言，给整个印第安民族带来了很多灾难。

TEXT B The Road to Independence

Road to Independence

(A) The principles of **liberalism** and **democracy**—the political foundation of the United States—**sprang** naturally **from** the process of building a new society on a virgin land. Just as naturally, the new nation would see itself as different and exceptional. Europe would view it with **apprehension**, or hope.

(B) Britain's 13 North American colonies matured during the 1700s. They grew in population, economic strength, and cultural attainment. They were experienced in self-government. Yet it was not until 170 years after the founding of the first permanent settlement at **Jamestown**, Virginia, that the new United States of America emerged as a nation.

(C) War between Britain and France in the 1750s was fought partly in North America. Britain was victorious and soon initiated policies designed to control and fund its vast empire. These measures **imposed** greater restraints **on** the American colonists' way of life.

(D) **The Royal Proclamation of 1763** restricted the opening of new lands for settlement. **The Sugar Act of 1764** placed taxes on luxury goods, including coffee, silk, and wine, and made it illegal to import rum. **The Currency Act of 1764** prohibited the printing of paper money in the colonies. **The Quartering Act of 1765** forced colonists to provide food and housing for royal troops. And **the Stamp Act of 1765** required the purchase of royal stamps for all legal documents, newspapers, licenses, and leases.

(E) Colonists objected to all these measures, but the Stamp Act sparked the greatest organized resistance. The main issue, in the eyes of a growing number of colonists, was that they were being taxed by a distant **legislature** in which they could not participate. In October 1765, 27 delegates from nine colonies met in New York to coordinate efforts to get the Stamp Act **repealed**. They passed resolutions asserting the individual colonies' right to impose their own taxes.

(F) Self-government produced local political leaders, and these were the men who worked together to defeat what they considered to be oppressive acts of Parliament. After they succeeded, their coordinated campaign against Britain ended. During the next several years, however, a small number of **radicals** tried to keep the controversy alive. Their goal was not accommodation, but independence.

(G) **Samuel Adams** of Massachusetts was the most effective. He wrote newspaper articles and made speeches appealing to the colonists' democratic instincts. He helped organize committees throughout the colonies that became the basis of a revolutionary movement. By 1773, the movement had attracted colonial traders who were angry with British attempts to regulate the tea trade. In December, a group of men **sneaked on** to three British ships in Boston harbor and dumped their cargo of tea overboard.

(H) To punish Massachusetts for the **vandalism**, the British Parliament closed the port of Boston and restricted local authority. The new measures, **dubbed** the Intolerable Acts, backfired. Rather than isolate one colony, they rallied the others. All the colonies except Georgia sent representatives to Philadelphia in September 1774 to discuss their "present unhappy state." It was the first Continental Congress.

(I) Colonists felt a growing sense of frustration and anger over British **encroachment** on their rights. Yet by no means was there **unanimity** of thought on what should be done. Loyalists wanted to remain subjects of the king. Moderates favored compromise to produce a more acceptable relationship with the British government. And revolutionaries wanted complete independence. They began stockpiling weapons and mobilizing forces—waiting for the day when they would have to fight for it.

Revolution

(J) The American Revolution—its war for independence from Britain—began as a small **skirmish** between British troops and armed colonists on April 19, 1775.

(K) The British had set out from Boston, Massachusetts, to seize weapons and **ammunition** that revolutionary colonists had collected in nearby villages. At Lexington, they met a group of Minutemen, who got that name because they were said to be ready to fight in a minute. The Minutemen intended only a silent protest, and their leader told them not to shoot unless fired on first. The British ordered the Minutemen to disperse, and they complied. As they were withdrawing, someone fired a shot. The British troops attacked the Minutemen with guns and **bayonets**.

(L) Fighting broke out at other places along the road as the British soldiers in their bright red uniforms made their way back to Boston. More than 250 "redcoats" were killed or wounded. The Americans lost 93 men.

(M) Deadly clashes continued around Boston as colonial representatives hurried to Philadelphia to discuss the situation. A majority voted to go to war against Britain. They agreed to combine colonial militias into a continental army, and they appointed George Washington of Virginia as commander-in-chief. At the same time, however, this Second Continental Congress adopted a peace resolution urging King George III to prevent further hostilities. The king rejected it and on August 23 declared that the American colonies were in rebellion.

(N) Calls for independence intensified in the coming months. Radical political theorist Thomas Paine helped **crystallize** the argument for separation. In a pamphlet called *Common Sense*, which sold 100,000 copies, he attacked the idea of a **hereditary** monarchy. Paine presented two alternatives for America: continued submission under a tyrannical king and outworn system of government, or liberty and happiness as a self-sufficient, independent republic.

(O) The Second Continental Congress appointed a committee, headed by Thomas Jefferson of Virginia, to prepare a document outlining the colonies' **grievances** against the king and explaining their decision to break away. This Declaration of Independence was adopted on July 4, 1776. The 4th of July has since been celebrated as America's Independence Day.

(P) The Declaration of Independence not only announced the birth of a new nation. It also set forth a philosophy of human freedom that would become a dynamic force throughout the world. It drew upon French and British political ideas, especially those of John Locke in his *Second Treatise on Government*, reaffirming the belief that political rights are basic human rights, and are thus universal.

(Q) Declaring independence did not make Americans free. British forces routed continental troops in New York, from Long Island to New York City. They defeated the Americans at Brandywine, Pennsylvania, and occupied Philadelphia, forcing the Continental Congress to flee. American forces were victorious at Saratoga, New York, and at Trenton and Princeton in New Jersey. Yet George Washington continually struggled to get the men and materials he desperately needed.

(R) Decisive help came in 1778, when France recognized the United States and signed a **bilateral** defense treaty. Support from the French government, however, was based on geopolitical, not ideological, reasons. France wanted to weaken the power of Britain, its long-time adversary.

(S) The fighting that began at **Lexington**, Massachusetts, continued for eight years across a large portion of the continent. Battles were fought from Montreal, Canada, in the north to Savannah, Georgia, in the south. A huge British army surrendered at Yorktown, Virginia, in 1781, yet the war dragged on with inconclusive results for another two years. A peace treaty was finally signed in Paris on April 15, 1783.

(T) The Revolution had a significance far beyond North America. It attracted the attention of Europe's political theorists and strengthened the concept of natural rights throughout the Western world. It attracted notables such as Thaddeus Kosciusko, Friedrich von Steuben, and the Marquis de Lafayette, who joined the revolution and hoped to transfer its liberal ideas to their own countries.

(U) The Treaty of Paris acknowledged the independence, freedom, and sovereignty of the 13 former American colonies, now states. The task of knitting them together into a new nation lay ahead.

(Words: 1250)

New Words

liberalism	*n.* 自由主义；开明的思想或见解
democracy	*n.* 民主，民主主义；民主政治
apprehension	*n.* 理解；恐惧；逮捕；忧惧
legislature	*n.* 立法机关；立法机构
repeal	*n.* 废除；撤销 *vt.* 废除；撤销；废止；放弃；否定
radical	*adj.* 激进的；根本的；彻底的 *n.* 基础；激进分子
vandalism	*n.* 故意毁坏文物的行为；破坏他人财产的行为
dub	*vt.* 配音；轻点；打击；授予称号
encroachment	*n.* 侵入，侵犯；侵蚀
unanimity	*n.* 同意，全体一致

续表

skirmish	*n.* 小冲突，小规模战斗；小争论 *vi.* 进行小规模战斗；发生小争论
ammunition	*n.* 弹药；军火 vt. 装弹药于 vi. 装弹药
bayonet	*n.* 刺刀；卡销 vt. 用刺刀刺 vi. 用刺刀；劈刺
crystallize	*vt.* 使结晶；明确；使具体化；做成蜜饯 *vi.* 结晶，形成结晶；明确；具体化
hereditary	*n.* 遗传类 *adj.* 遗传的；世袭的；世代相传的
grievance	*n.* 不满，不平；委屈；冤情
bilateral	*adj.* 双边的；有两边的

Phrases & Expressions

spring from	起源于，发源（于）……；来自……
impose…on	强制实行，实施
sneak on	潜入

Proper Names

Jamestown	詹姆斯敦（北美洲第一个英国永久殖民地）
The Royal Proclamation of 1763	《1763 年皇家宣言》
The Sugar Act of 1764	《1764 年食糖法案》
The Currency Act of 1764	《1764 年货币法案》
The Quartering Act of 1765	《1765 年驻军法案》
The Stamp Act of 1765	《1765 年印花税法》
Samuel Adams	塞缪尔·亚当斯
Lexington	列克星敦市

Cultural Notes

1. The Royal Proclamation of 1763 was initially issued by King George III in 1763 to officially claim British territory in North America after Britain won the Seven Years War. It is a document that set out guidelines for European settlement of Aboriginal territories in what is now North America. For more information, visit http://indigenousfoundations. arts. ubc. ca/home/government-policy/royal- proclamation – 1763. html

2. The Sugar Act of 1764 was a law that attempted to curb the smuggling of sugar and molasses in the colonies by reducing the previous tax rate and enforcing the collection of duties. It added several products such as hides, skins and potash to the list of enumerated commodities that could be legally exported under the Navigation Acts. For more information, visit http://www. stamp – act – history. com/sugar – act/1764 – april – 5 – sugar – act/

3. The Currency Act of 1764 was a law passed by British Parliament to regulate the issue and legal tender status of paper money in the colonial economy. This act was an extension of the 1751 Currency Act that applied to New England colonies, the 1764 Currency Act applied the same principles to all British colonies in America. For more information, visit http: //www. stamp – act – history. com/timeline/1764 – currency – act/

4. The Quartering Act of 1765 was passed on May 3rd, 1765 and required colonial assemblies to provide housing, food and drink to British troops stationed in their towns with the purpose of improving living conditions and decreasing the cost to the crown. This act was implemented by General Tomas Gage, the commander in chief of North America. Soldiers were to be housed in barracks or empty public buildings and not in private residences. It was the duty of local legislatures to fund the expenses. For more information, visit http://www. stamp – act – history. com/quartering – act/1765 – march – quartering – act/

5. The Stamp Act of 1765 is an act for granting and applying certain stamp duties, and other duties, in the British colonies and plantations in America, towards further defraying the expenses of defending, protecting, and securing the same; and for amending such parts of the several acts of parliament relating to the trade and revenues of the said colonies and plantations, as direct the manner of determining and recovering the penalties and forfeitures therein mentioned. For more information, visit http://avalon.law.yale.edu/18th _ century/stamp _ act_ 1765.asp

Exercises

Comprehension of the Text

Ⅰ. The following 10 statements contain information given in the text. Identify the paragraph from which the information is derived. You may choose a paragraph more than once. Each paragraph is marked with a letter.

1. Britain's 13 North American colonies matured in 1700s.

2. War between Britain and France in the 1750s was fought partly in North America.

3. The Sugar Act of 1764 placed taxes on luxury goods, including coffee, silk, and wine, and made it illegal to import rum.

4. The Quartering Act of 1765 forced colonists to provide food and housing for royal troops.

5. Samuel Adams wrote newspaper articles and made speeches appealing to the colonists' democratic instincts.

6. Moderates favored compromise to produce a more acceptable relationship with the British government.

7. The Second Continental Congress adopted a peace resolution urging King George Ⅲ to prevent further hostilities.

8. In a pamphlet called *Common Sense*, Thomas Paine attacked the idea of a hereditary monarchy.

9. The Declaration of Independence drew upon French and British political ideas, especially those of John Locke in his *Second Treatise on Government*.

10. The Revolution not only attracted the attention of Europe's political theo-

rists, but also strengthened the concept of natural rights throughout the Western world.

Vocabulary

Ⅱ. Fill in the blanks with the words given below. Change the form where necessary.

radical	democracy	hereditary	grievance	liberal
repeal	bilateral	encroachment	crystallize	apprehension
vandalism	dub	impose	coordinate	unanimity

1. Parents should beware of ______their own tastes on their children.
2. We ______ for him at this very sad time.
3. Finally, they passed a law that penalizes private landowners who ______on protected wildlife areas.
4. You must ______the movements of your arms and legs when swimming.
5. We know that personality has a ______component
6. Education is the basis of a ______society.
7. The government has just ______the law segregating public facilities.
8. It reflects real anger and ______about the future.
9. The country needs a period of calm without more surges of ______change.
10. The board ______approved the project last week.

Further Reading

TEXT C The Significance of the American Revolution

The American Revolution had significance far beyond the North American continent. It attracted the attention of a political intelligentsia throughout the European continent. Idealistic notables such as Thaddeus Kosciusko, Friedrich von Steuben, and the Marquis de Lafayette joined its ranks to affirm liberal ideas they hoped to transfer to their own nations. Its success strengthened the concept of natural rights throughout the Western world and furthered the Enlightenment rationalist critique of an old order built around hereditary monarchy and an established church. In a very real sense, it was a precursor to the French Revolution, but it lacked the French Revolution's violence and chaos because it had occurred in a society that was already fundamentally liberal.

The ideas of the Revolution have been most often depicted as a triumph of the social contract/natural rights theories of John Locke. Correct so far as it goes, this characterization passes too quickly over the continuing importance of Calvinist dissenting Protestantism, which from the Pilgrims and Puritans on had also stood for the ideals of the social contract and the self-governing community. Lockean intellectuals and the Protestant clergy were both important advocates of compatible strains of liberalism that had flourished in the British North American colonies.

Scholars have also argued that another persuasion contributed to the Revolution: "republicanism." Republicanism, they assert, did not deny the existence of natural rights but subordinated them to the belief that the maintenance of a free republic required a strong sense of communal responsibility and the cultivation of self-denying virtue among its leaders. The assertion of individual rights, even the pursuit of individual happiness, seemed egoistic by contrast. For a time republicanism threatened to displace natural rights as the major theme of the Revolution. Most historians today, however, concede that the distinction was much overdrawn. Most individuals who thought about such things in the 18th century envisioned the two ideas more as different sides of the same intellectual coin.

Revolution usually entails social upheaval and violence on a wide scale. By these criteria, the American Revolution was relatively mild. About 100,000 Loyalists left the new United States. Some thousands were members of old elites who had suffered expropriation of their property and been expelled; others were simply common people faithful to their King. The majority of those who went into exile did so voluntarily. The Revolution did open up and further liberalize an already liberal society. In New York and the Carolinas, large Loyalist estates were divided among small farmers. Liberal assumptions became the official norm of American political culture—whether in the disestablishment of the Anglican Church, the principle of elected national and state executives, or the wide dissemination of the idea of individual freedom. Yet the structure of society changed little. Revolution or not, most people remained secure in their life, liberty, and property.

(Words: 473)

Questions for discussions

1. What are the main causes of the American Revolution?

2. What influence does the American Revolution have on American society and people?

More to Learn

1. Top Five Causes of the Civil War

- Economic and social differences between the North and the South
- States versus federal rights
- The fight between Slave and Non-Slave State Proponents
- Growth of the Abolition Movement.
- The election of Abraham Lincoln.

http://americanhistory.about.com/od/civilwarmenu/a/cause_civil_war.htm

MOVIES TO SEE (A) Dances with Wolves

Ⅰ. Movie Introduction

Director: Kevin Costner

Starring: Kevin Costner,
Mary McDonnell
Graham Greene

Running time: 180 mins

Released: 1990

Plot: Lt. John Dunbar is dubbed a hero after he accidentally leads Union troops to a victory during the Civil War. He requests a position on the western frontier, but finds it deserted. He soon finds out he is not alone, but meets a wolf he dubs "Two-socks" and a curious Indian tribe. Dunbar quickly makes friends with the tribe, and discovers a white woman who was raised by the Indians. He gradually earns the respect of these native people, and sheds his white-man's ways.

Ⅱ. Excerpts & Expressions

Task 1 Study the underlined sentences and expressions.

1. Native Americans held a meeting about whether they should go to meet John Dunbar.

Kick Bird: He might be a god. Or a white chief with special abilities. That is why we should talk with him.

Wind in His Hair: I do not care for this talk about this white man. Whatever he is, he is not a Sioux and that makes him less. When I hear that more whites are coming, I want to laugh. We took a hundred horses from these people. There was no honor in it. They don't ride well. They don't shoot well. They're dirty. Those soldiers could not even make it through one winter here. And these people are said to flourish? I think they will all be dead soon. I think this fool is probably lost.

Indian 1: Wind in His Hair's words are strong and I have heard them. It's true the whites are a poor race and hard to understand. But make no mistake. The whites are coming. Even our enemies agree on this. So when I see one man alone without fear in our country...I do not think he is lost. I think he may have medicine. I see someone who might speak for all the white people who are coming. I think this is a person with which treaties might be struck.

Indian 2: Kicking Bird is always looking ahead and that is good. But this man cannot cover our lodges or feed our children. He is nothing to us. I will take some men. We will shoot some arrows into this white man. If he truly has medicine, he will not be hurt. If he has no medicine, he will be dead.

Indian 3: No man can tell another what to do. But killing a white man is a delicate matter. If you kill one more are sure to come.

Ten Bears: It's easy to become confused by these questions. It's hard to know what to do. We should talk about this some more. That is all I have to say.

2. Dunbar came to the Indian tribe for the first time

Kicking Bird: We are waiting for you. Now tell him we are glad that he is here.

White woman: You...here...good.

Dunbar: Thank you. I feel good.

Kicking Bird: Ask him why he is at the soldier fort.

White woman: The soldier fort.

Dunbar: Wait. What are your names?

White woman: Our names?

Dunbar: What is his name?

Kicking Bird: He's right. Introductions should come first.

White woman: He...he... kick

Dunbar: Kick?

White woman: More

Dunbar: More kicking?

White woman: kicking. Bird?Bird. Kicking bird.

Dunbar: Kicking Bird. What is he...Is he chief?

White woman: No. A holy man. Holy man.

Dunbar: Your name?

White woman: I don't...

Kicking Bird: How are you called?

Dunbar: Get up? Stand up? Stands? Stands. Your name's Stands?

White woman: Stands. With.

Dunbar: With? Stands with? Fist?

White woman: Yes.

Dunbar: Stands With A Fist? Stands With A Fist. I'm John Dunbar.

White woman: John Dunbar.

Kicking Bird: Dumb Bear.

Dunbar: No. not Dumb Bear.

White woman: Dunbar.

Kicking Bird: Dun...

Dunbar: ...bar. . not Dumb Bear.

Kicking Bird: Dunbar.

3. Dunbar was named "Dances with wolves"by Indians.

Dunbar: Come in, please. Sit down?

Kicking Bird: Yeah.

White woman: Kicking Bird want to know why you want to make war on the Pawnee. They have done nothing to you.

Dunbar: They are Sioux enemies.

Kicking Bird: Only Sioux warriors to go.

Dunbar: Tell him that I have been a warrior, longer than many of the young men who will go on this war party. Tell him (to white woman)

White woman: He said that the Sioux way of being a warrior is not the white way. You are not ready.

Dunbar: I know, I understand. Tell him I cannot learn these ways in camp.

White woman: He also asks that you watch over his family while he is gone. This thing he asks is a great honor for you.

Dunbar: Tell him that I would be happy to watch over his family.

White woman: He thanks Dances With Wolves for coming.

Dunbar: Who is Dances With Wolves?

White woman: It is the name which all the people are calling you now.

Dunbar: Dances With...That's right. That day. Dances with wolves.

Task 2 Work in pairs and play the roles in the expert above.

Ⅲ. Cultural Notes

1. The Sioux are groups of Native American tribes and First Nations peoples in North America. The Sioux comprise three major divisions based on language divisions: the Dakota, Lakota, and Nakota. Today, the Sioux maintain many separate tribal governments scattered across several reservations, communities, and reserves in North Dakota, South Dakota, Nebraska, Minnesota, and Montana in the United States; and Manitoba and southern Saskatchewan in Canada.

2. In the US in the late 1800s and early 1900s buffaloes were hunted for

their skins to make buffalo robes(长袍) and were almost extinct. The smaller numbers of buffalo made life more difficult for the Native Americans, who ate buffalo meat, and this worsened the disagreement between the Native Americans and white men.

Ⅳ. Questions for discussion

1. Was John Dunbar an Indian fighter? What was his purpose of choosing to go to the frontier?

2. When John Dunbar came to the tribe he was given a name Dances-with-wolves, his woman' name was Stands-with-a-fist. Why were they given these names?

3. How did the Indians treat the land and how did they see their role in the world?

4. Why did the lieutenant change his opinion in the end of the movie? What would you do if you were him?

Ⅴ. Movie Review

Task: Write a movie review on ***Dances with Wolves***.

MOVIES TO SEE (B) The Patriot

Movie Introduction

Director: Roland Emmerich

Starring: Mel Gibson
Heath Ledger
Joely Richardson

Running time: 165 mins

Released: 2000

Plot: It is 1776 in colonial South Carolina. Benjamin Martin, a French-Indian war hero who is haunted by his past, now wants nothing more than to live peacefully on his small plantation, and wants no part of a war with the most powerful nation in the world, Great Britain. Meanwhile, his two eldest sons, Gabriel and Thomas, can't wait to enlist in the newly formed "Continental Army." When South Carolina decides to join the rebellion against England, Gabriel immediately signs up to fight...without his father's permission. But when Colonel William Tavington,

British dragoon, infamous for his brutal tactics, comes and burns the Martin Plantation to the ground, tragedy strikes. Benjamin quickly finds himself torn between protecting his family, and seeking revenge along with being a part of the birth of a new, young, and ambitious nation

To Recommend More Movies

❖ *Gone with the Wind* (1939)
❖ *The Civil War* (1990)
❖ *Gettysburg* (1993)
❖ *Pearl Harbor* (2001)
❖ *Cold Mountain* (2003)

Unit Two Geography

Pre-reading Activities

Answer the following questions before you read this text.

1. How much do you know about the American geography?
2. What is the typical climate of the United States?
3. Can you list the top 10 cities in America according to the number of population?

TEXT A American Geography

The United States is located in central North America, is located in the Western Hemisphere, also includes the **territory** north of Alaska and **the Pacific Northwest Central Hawaii islands**. The north and the Canadian **border**, south through **the Gulf of Mexico, West Pacific,** east **the Atlantic**. The coastline of 22680 kilometers. Major area **belongs to temperate continental climate**, the southern **subtropical climate**, western **coastal** area **distribution** has a temperate climate with **Mediterranean climate**. In the Northern Plains (Central Plains) with large temperature difference, **Chicago** in January the average temperature of -3 DEG C, July 24 **DEG C**; the Gulf of Mexico in January the average temperature of 11 degrees C, July 28 C. The **nadir** for **the Death Valley** (Death Valley, - 86m), the highest point is mount Mckinley (**Mount Mckinley**, 6198 meters).

Americans often **speak of** their country as one of several large regions. These regions are cultural units rather than governmental units—formed by history and geography and shaped by the economics, literature and **folkways** that all the parts of a region share.

What makes one region different from another? Within several regions, language is used differently and there are strong dialects. There are also differences in outlook and attitude **based on** geography. A region's **multicultural heritage as well as** distinct **demographic** characteristics like age and occupation also make regions different and special.

The United States is a varied land of forests, deserts, mountains, high flat lands and **fertile** plains. The country lies mostly in the **temperate zone** but there is a very wide range of climate variations. The continental United States **stretches** 4,500 kilometers from the Atlantic Ocean on the east to **the Pacific Ocean** on the west. It borders Canada on the north and reaches south to Mexico and the Gulf of Mexico. The United States covers a total area of 9 million square kilometers (including Alaska and **Hawaii**). Alaska is the largest in area of the 50 states, and **Texas** is the second largest.

From the **Appalachian Mountains** in the East to the **Rocky Mountains** in the West, the center of the country is **drained** by **the Mississippi** and **Missouri Rivers** and their branches. The Mississippi is one of the world's great rivers; it was known to Native Americans as the "father of waters". Water from the source of its main branch, the Missouri River, flows about 6,400 kilometers from the northern Rocky Mountains to the mouth of the Mississippi in the Gulf of Mexico. On a **topographic map** of the United States, the mountains look like **jagged masses**, the plains like **vast**, open flat spaces, and the rivers like **meandering** threads. Today, highways, railways and **transcontinental** aircraft **criss-cross** the land, making travel easy. But only a few generations ago, the **topographic features** on the map represented great dangers and difficulties.

Today's visitors, riding over a good road in the **Cascade Mountains** in the west coast states of **Oregon** and **Washington,** may see marks on the rocks made by ropes where pioneer settlers painfully lowered their horses and **wagons** down **cliffs** to reach the fertile river valley far below. In the **Sierra Nevada Mountains** of **California**, the main route now runs through a mountain pass which was once too narrow for a wagon to go through. Pioneer families reaching that pass had to **take** their wagons **apart** piece by piece, carry them through, and then **reassemble** them on the other side. In 1848, pioneers who crossed the continent made the trip in 109 days—if they were fortunate and strong. Today a **New York** family can drive by car to **San Francisco** in less than a week.

People who visit the United States sometimes wonder how the states got their names. Some of the most interesting names came from **American Indian** languages.

For example, **Illinois** was named for the Indians who used to live in that part of the country. In their language, Illinois means "Brave Men". **Connecticut** means "At the Long River Mouth"in the language of the Indians who used to live there.

Twenty-five of the states have Indian names, but other names were taken from different languages. **Georgia** and **Pennsylvania** have names which were taken from the **Latin language**. **Florida** and **Colorado** were named by **Spanish** people. States like **New Hampshire** and **New Jersey** were named after places in England.

The two newest states have names which did not come from any of those languages. Hawaii got its name from a word in the Hawaiian language which means "homeland". Alaska was named by the **Russians**, from whom Alaska was bought in 1867.

(Words: 768)

New Words

territory	*n.* 领土，领域；范围；地域；版图
border	*n.* 边境；边界；国界 *vt.* 接近；与…接壤；在…上镶边 *vi.* 接界；近似
coastal	*adj.* 沿海的；海岸的
distribution	*n.* 分布；分配
nadir	*n.* 最低点；最底点；［天］天底
folkway	*n.* 民风；社会习俗；习惯

续表

multicultural	*adj.* 多种文化的；融合或具有多种文化的
heritage	*n.* 遗产；传统；继承物；继承权
demographic	*adj.* 人口统计学的；人口学的
fertile	*n.* 肥沃；多产 *adj.* 富饶的，肥沃的；能生育的
stretch	*n.* 伸展，延伸 *vt.* 伸展，张开 *vi.* 伸展 *adj.* 可伸缩的
drain	*n.* 排水；下水道，排水管；消耗 *vt.* 喝光，耗尽；使流出；排掉水 *vi.* 排水；流干
jagged	*adj.* 锯齿状的；参差不齐的
mass	*n.* 团，块；群众，民众；大量，众多；质量 *adj.* 群众的，民众的；大规模的，集中的 *vt.* 使集合 *vi.* 聚集起来，聚集
vast	*n.* 浩瀚；广阔无垠的空间 *adj.* 广阔的；巨大的；大量的；巨额的
meandering	*n.* 漫步；漫谈；［建］曲径 *adj.* 曲折的；聊天的；漫步的
transcontinental	*adj.* 横贯大陆的；大陆那边的
criss-cross	*adj.* 纵横交错的；十字形的；n. 十字号
wagon	*vt.* 用运货马车运送货物 *n.* 货车，四轮马车
cliff	*n.* 悬崖；绝壁
reassemble	*vt.* 重新装配；重新召集 *vi.* 重新集合

Phrases & Expressions

belong to	属于
speak of	谈到；论及
base on	以…为基础；基于
as well as	也；和…一样
temperate zone	[气象] 温带
topographic map	[测] 地形图；等高线图
topographic features	地形要素
take apart	拆开；剖析；粗暴对待

Roper Names

the Pacific Northwest Central Hawaii islands	太平洋西北地区中心的夏威夷岛
the Gulf of Mexico	墨西哥湾（位于北美东南部边缘）
West Pacific	西太平洋
the Atlantic	大西洋
temperate continental climate	[气候] 温带大陆性气候
subtropical climate	[气候] 亚热带气候
Mediterranean climate	地中海气候
Chicago	芝加哥（美国中西部城市）
DEG C	摄氏度
the Death Valley	死谷（美国西南部一地区，是世界最低和最干旱的地区之一）
Mount Mckinley	麦金利山
the Pacific Ocean	太平洋（等于 the Pacific）
Hawaii	夏威夷岛；夏威夷（美国州名）
Texas	德克萨斯州（美国州名）
Appalachian Mountains	阿巴拉契亚山脉

续表

Rocky Mountains	落基山脉
the Mississippi	密西西比河
Missouri River	密苏里河
Cascade Mountains	喀斯喀特山脉
Oregon	俄勒冈州（美国州名）
Washington	华盛顿（美国州名）
Sierra Nevada Mountains	内华达山脉（位于美国加州）
California	加利福尼亚州（美国州名）
New York	纽约
San Francisco	旧金山（美国城市）
American Indian	美洲印第安人
Illinois	伊利诺伊州（美国州名）
Connecticut	康乃迪克州（美国州名）
Georgia	乔治亚州（美国州名）
Pennsylvania	宾夕法尼亚州（美国州名）
Latin language	拉丁语
Florida	佛罗里达州（美国州名）
Colorado	科罗拉多州（美国州名）
Spanish	西班牙人；西班牙语
New Hampshire	新罕布什尔州（美国州名）
New Jersey	新泽西州（美国州名）
Russian	俄语；俄国人

Cultural Notes

1. The Gulf of Mexico is an ocean basin largely surrounded by the North American continent. It is bounded on the northeast, north, and northwest by the Gulf Coast of the United States, on the southwest and south by Mexico, and on the southeast by Cuba. The U. S. states of Texas, Louisiana, Mississippi, Alabama, and Florida border the Gulf on the north, which are often referred to as the "Third Coast"in comparison with the U. S. Atlantic and Pacific coasts, or sometimes the "south coast", in juxtaposition to the great lakes region being the "north coast". For more information, visit http: //en. wikipedia. org/wiki/Gulf_ of_ Mexico.

2. Mediterranean climate is one typical of the Mediterranean Basin and is a particular variety of subtropical climate. The lands around the Mediterranean Sea form the largest area where this climate type is found, but it also prevails in much of California, in parts of Western and South Australia, in southwestern South Africa, sections of Central Asia, and in central Chile. For more information, visit http: //en. wikipedia. org/wiki/Mediterranean_ climate.

3. Death Valley is a desert valley located in Eastern California's Mojave Desert, the lowest, driest, and hottest area in North America. Death Valley's Badwater Basin is the point of the lowest elevation in North America, at 282 feet (86m) below sea level. This point is 84. 6 miles (136. 2 km) east—southeast of Mount Whitney, the highest point in the contiguous United States with an elevation of 14, 505 feet (4, 421m). Death Valley's Furnace Creek holds the record for the highest reliably reported air temperature in the world, 134 °F (56. 7 °C) on July 10, 1913. For more information, visit http: //en. wikipedia. org/wiki/Death_ Valley.

Exercises

Comprehension of the Text

Ⅰ. Answer the following questions according to the passage.

1. What climate does the American area distribution belong to?

2. What makes one region different from another in America according to the test?

3. Which river is known to Native Americans as the "father of waters"?

Vocabulary

Ⅱ. Fill in the blanks with the words given below. Change the form where necessary.

territory	coastal	distribution	folkway	multicultural
heritage	fertile	stretch	drain	jagged
mass	vast	cliff	transcontinental	reassemble

1. But there are no signs, yet, of any ________celebration.

2. With the effective of zone, the language, consuetude, ________ and circumstance with the folk music attached are quite different.

3. The message implied in the logo of Shanghai World Expo is that the Chinese people wish to host an exposition of global and ________convergence.

4. All of our cultural ________which is useful should be inherited, but in a critical way.

5. We suggest you ________ by touching your toes for at least 30 seconds before you make the attempt.

6. The family helped her win the ________majority of votes in the province in the 2004 presidential election.

7. She says that the goods and services provided by nature—like clean air, rain or ________ soils—should not be taken for granted.

8. I scowled at his perfect face. His eyes were light again today, a deep, golden honey color. Then I had to look down, to __________ my now-tangled thoughts.

9. The two sides continued to dispute the ownership of the ________.

10. The principle of _________ in socialist society is "from each according to his ability"and "to each according to his work".

Translations

Ⅲ. Translate the following sentences into English.

1. 这就是他要求学生们做的：从以下四个选项中选取问题，"读者如何才能成为好读者"——"读者应该是书友会的成员"。(belong to)

____

2. 他说，“但如果我们谈到人权问题和中国所发生的事情，要记得这类事情在很多其他国家也在发生”。(speak of)

____

3. 然而，这种合作必须建立在信任、协商、平等和互利的基础上，必须从事实出发，而不是依凭推论。(base on)

____

4. 必须告诫人们的是：地球不仅是他们的家园，也是他们的孩子和所有后代的家园，还是其他所有的植物和动物的家园。(as well as)

____

5. 有一天，她就等她父母离开家，以便能拆开电视机，并赶在他们回来之前把它装好。(take apart)

____

Ⅳ. Translate the following passage into English.

纵观整个历史，美国人一直是一个迁移的民族。早期的移民者必须长途跋涉才能抵达新大陆，他们一到达就沿着东岸定居，但却不满足于长居那里，冒险家和商人旅行至未知的西部地区。稍后，移民也向西迁移去开发这些新地区。由于向西迁移，美国人最后占据了整块新大陆——从大西洋到太平洋。即使到今天，美国人似乎仍然无法在一地久居。根据研究，美国人平均每五年要搬一次家。

TEXT B Houston

(A) Houston is the fourth-largest city in the United States of America and the largest city within the state of Texas. As of the 2006 U. S. **Census** estimate, the city has a population of 2.2 million within an area of 600 square miles (1,600km^2). Houston is the seat of Harris County and the economic center of the Houston—Sugar Land—**Baytown metropolitan** area—the sixth-largest metropolitan area in the U. S. with a population of 5.6 million.

(B) The fourth-largest city in the US is a **sprawling metropolis** of **highrises** malls and parking lots. Hot, **humid** and flat, Houston may not be Texas' **premier** destination, but it has much to offer, including great museums, beautiful parks, a **hip** young population and a variety of excellent excursions.

(C) The days when cows and oilmen **roamed** the streets of Houston are long gone. Houston **dominates** southeastern Texas, **thanks to** a **historic** commitment to growth **typical of** the **Lone Star state**, characterized by a lack of zoning and other planning **restrictions, resulting in** a sprawling, confusing city.

(D) Downtown Houston, the original business center, is a **thicket** of highrises **interspersed with** parking lots, ringed by **elevated freeways**. The streets can seem surprisingly empty during the day, with **nary** a **pedestrian** to be found braving the hot and **shimmering sidewalks**. But the people are there. In a variation of a **post-apocalyptic** nightmare, most downtown buildings are linked by air-conditioned underground **pedestrian tunnels lined with** shops and restaurants.

(E) After dark, the area is **sparsely populated** above and below ground, though some life can be found around the new baseball stadium and in the north end's nightclub district. Major neighborhoods include Houston Heights, an **affluent**, quiet residential area north of downtown, **overlooking** the Buffalo Bayou; **Montrose**, the center of Houston's **gay** scene, with a **funky** mix of shops, restaurants, galleries and **tattoo parlors** a few blocks southwest of downtown.

(F) Houston got its start in 1836, when brothers Augustus and John Allen **set up** a **trading post** on the Buffalo Bayou, a river that now **meanders** through the heart of the city. The Allens named their new holding Houston **in honor of General Sam Houston**, who had just defeated the Mexican Army at **San Jacinto**. The coming of the railroad **boosted** the economy in the 1860s and 1870s, but the real **prosperity** was still around the corner.

(G) It was the 1901 discovery of oil at nearby Spindletop that put Houston on the road to riches. The city's only **obstacle to** growth was its **sweltering** summer heat, but beginning in the 1930s, the widespread **availability** of air conditioning made massive downtown development a reality.

(H) Beginning in the 1950s, downtown **underwent** wave after wave of skyscraper construction. **Hand in hand** with the building **boom** was a craze to **raze**: dozens of older commercial and residential buildings were leveled and turned into parking lots for the growing army of office workers. **NASA's Mission Control**

Center opened a few miles from Houston in 1963, and six years later the city's name became the first word ever spoken by a human being on the surface of the moon.

(I) Throughout the 1970s, Houston's fortunes continued **skyward**. When oil reached a **barrel** in 1981, Houston was **awash** in money as scores of happy Texans got rich quick; four years later, the price of oil **plummeted** to **single digits** and Houstonians got poor even faster. **Glitzy** but empty high rises stood next to giant construction holes that had to be filled back in when the financing **ran out**.

(J) In the 1990s, Houston's economy **diversified** as the city rode the general economic boom that swept the US. In 1997, Houston elected its first black mayor, Lee Brown. The following year, Houston was **drenched** by a **torrential** downpour and **menaced** by **tornadoes**. The flood waters were strong enough to **sweep** houses **off** their foundations. Several people were killed and large areas of the city remained under water for days.

(K) Houston's economy has a broad industrial base in the energy, manufacturing, **aeronautics**, transportation, and **health care** sectors; only New York City is home to more **Fortune 500 headquarters** in the city limits. Commercially, Houston **is ranked as** a **gamma** world city, and the area is a leading center for building oilfield equipment. **The Port of Houston** ranks first in the United States in international **waterborne tonnage** handled and second in total **cargo** tonnage handled. The city has a multicultural population with a large and growing international community. It is home to many cultural institutions and exhibits—attracting more than 7 million visitors a year to the Houston Museum District. Houston has an active visual and **performing arts** scene in the Theater District and is one of few U. S. cities that offer **year-round** resident companies in all major performing arts.

(Words: 785)

New Words

Census	*n.* 人口普查，人口调查 *vt.* 实施统计调查
metropolitan	*n.* 大城市人；大主教；宗主国的公民 *adj.* 大都市的；大主教辖区的；宗主国的
sprawling	*adj.* 蔓生的，不规则地伸展的
metropolis	*n.* 大都市；首府；重要中心
highrise	*n.* 高层建筑
humid	*adj.* 潮湿的；湿润的；多湿气的
premier	*n.* 总理；首相 *adj.* 第一的；最初的
hip	*n.* 臀部；蔷薇果；忧郁 *adj.* 熟悉内情的；非常时尚的
roam	*n.* 漫步，漫游；流浪 *vt.* 在…漫步，漫游；在…流浪 *vi.* 漫步，漫游；流浪
dominate	*vt.* 控制；支配；占优势；在…中占主要地位 *vi.* 占优势；处于支配地位
historic	*adj.* 有历史意义的；历史上著名的
restriction	*n.* 限制；约束；束缚
thicket	*n.* ［林］灌木丛；丛林；错综复杂
elevated	*adj.* 提高的；高尚的；严肃的；欢欣的
freeway	*n.* 高速公路
nary	*adj.* 连…也没有的
pedestrian	*n.* 行人；步行者 *adj.* 徒步的；缺乏想象力的
shimmering	*adj.* 闪烁的；微微发亮的
sidewalk	*n.* 人行道
post-apocalyptic	*n.* 后启示录

续表

affluent	*n.* 支流；富人 *adj.* 富裕的；丰富的；流畅的
overlook	*vt.* 俯瞰；远眺；忽视 *n.* 眺望；忽视
gay	*n.* 同性恋者 *adj.* 快乐的；放荡的；艳丽的
funky	*adj.* 时髦的；畏缩的；恶臭的
tattoo	*n.* 文身 *vt.* 刺花纹于 *vi.* 刺花样
parlor	*n.* 客厅；会客室；业务室 *adj.* 客厅的
meander	*n.* 漫步；曲流（常用复数） *vt.* 漫步；蜿蜒缓慢流动 *vi.* 漫步；漫谈
boost	*n.* 推动；帮助；宣扬 *vt.* 促进；增加；支援 *vi.* 宣扬；偷窃
prosperity	*n.* 繁荣；成功
sweltering	*adj.* 闷热的；热得难受的
availability	*n.* 可用性；有效性；实用性
undergo	*vt.* 经历；经受；忍受
boom	*n.* 隆隆声；繁荣；吊杆 *vt.* 使兴旺；发隆隆声 *vi.* 急速发展；发隆隆声
raze	*vt.* 夷为平地；破坏；消除；拆毁
skyward	*adj.* 向上的；向着天空的 *adv.* 向上；朝天空
barrel	*n.* 桶；枪管；炮管 *vt.* 把…装入桶内 *vi.* 快速移动

续表

awash	*adj.* 被浪冲打的；与水面齐平的；充斥的
plummet	*vi.* 垂直落下；（价格、水平等）骤然下跌 *n.* ［测］铅锤；坠子
glitzy	*adj.* 炫目的；闪光的；耀眼的
diversify	*vt.* 使多样化，使变化；增加产品种类以扩大
drench	*n.* 滂沱大雨；浸液 *vt.* 使湿透；给（牲畜）灌药
torrential	*adj.* 猛烈的；汹涌的；奔流的
menace	*n.* 威胁；恐吓 *vt.* 威胁；恐吓 *vi.* 恐吓；进行威胁
tornado	*n.* ［气象］龙卷风；旋风；暴风；大雷雨
aeronautics	*n.* 航空学；飞行术
headquarters	*n.* 总部；指挥部；司令部
gamma	*n.* 微克；希腊语的第三个字母
waterborne	*adj.* 水运的；水传播的；由水浮起的
tonnage	*n.* 吨位，载重量；船舶总吨数，排水量
cargo	*n.* 货物；船货
year-round	*adj.* 整年的；一年到头的

Phrases & Expressions

thanks to	由于，幸亏
typical of	是…的典型特征
result in	导致，结果是
intersperse with	用…点缀
pedestrian tunnel	人行地道
line with	按照，与…一致；沿着…排列
sparsely populated	人口稀少，人口稀疏

续表

set up	建立；装配；开业；竖立
trading post	商栈；交易站
in honor of	向…致敬，向…表示敬意；为庆祝…
obstacle to	对…的障碍
hand in hand	手拉手地；联合
single digits	个位数
run out	用完；耗尽；跑出；到期；伸向
sweep off	扫去；大量清除
health care	卫生保健
rank as	把…看作
performing arts	表演艺术

Proper Names

Baytown	贝城（美国城市）
Lone Star state	德克萨斯州的别名
Montrose	蒙特罗斯
General Sam Houston	休斯顿将军
San Jacinto	圣哈辛托（美国德克萨斯州县名）
NASA's Mission Control Center	美国国家航空航天局任务控制中心
Fortune 500	财富 500 强（指《财富》杂志每年评出的全美国 500 家最大的企业）
The Port of Houston	休斯敦口岸

Cultural Notes

1. NASA The National Aeronautics and Space Administration (NASA) is the United States government agency responsible for the civilian space program as well as aeronautics and aerospace research. For more information, visit http://en. Wikipedia. org/wiki/ National_ Aeronautics_ and_ Space_ Administration.

2. Fortune 500 The Fortune Global 500, also known as Global 500, is an annual ranking of the top 500 corporations worldwide as measured by revenue. The list is compiled and published annually by Fortune magazine. For more information, visit http://en. wikipedia. org/wiki/Fortune_ Global_ 500.

Exercises

Comprehension of the Text

Ⅰ. The following 10 statements contain information given in the text. Identify the paragraph from which the information is derived. You may choose a paragraph more than once. Each paragraph is marked with a letter.

1. Montrose is the center of Houston's gay scene, with a funky mix of shops, restaurants and galleries.

2. In 1836, brothers Augustus and John Allen set up a trading post on the Buffalo Bayou and Houston got its start.

3. It made massive downtown development a reality because of the widespread availability of air conditioning in the 1930s.

4. Lee Brown was elected as the first black mayor in Houston in 1997.

5. Houston has a multicultural population with a large and growing international community.

6. Houston has a population of 2. 2 million within an area of 600 square miles.

7. The Port of Houston ranks first in the United States in international waterborne tonnage handled and second in total cargo tonnage handled.

8. Because of the growing army of office workers, dozens of older commercial and residential buildings were leveled and turned into parking lots.

9. Surprisingly, the streets in downtown Houston can seem empty during the day, with nary a pedestrian to be found braving the hot and shimmering sidewalks.

10. Houston went on the road to riches because of the 1901 discovery of oil

at nearby Spindletop.

Vocabulary

Ⅱ. Fill in the blanks with the words given below. Change the form where necessary.

metropolis	humid	dominate	elevated	historic
overlook	boost	prosperity	availability	undergo
glitzy	diversify	menace	cargo	year-round

1. This is a ______ opportunity for our institutions and the peoples of the world.

2. Many of them are intentionally out of reach, either by price or ________.

3. But when people have enough calories they need to ______ towards vegetables, pulses and meat.

4. No one nation can or should try to ________ another nation.

5. This ______ his confidence and increased his intelligence.

6. While swimming pool weather is restricted to the summer months, the starry sky will be there ________.

7. As global climate warms, these birds are pushed higher and higher up the mountain in search of the cool, ___________ conditions they need to survive.

8. There can be no durable development and ________ without peace.

9. The idea is that you have an ________ desk where you can stand rather than sit.

10. I ______ any hardship to master this art in the shortest time.

Further Reading

TEXT C Philadelphia

Although it's dear to the hearts of America's flag-wavers, there's a lot more to Philly than the Liberty Bell and Independence Hall. Yet, despite the support of patriots and the cappuccino set, the "City of Brotherly Love" has long been the butt of jokes by WC Fields and other laugh-a-minute types.

When the insults finally soaked in—just in time for America's bicentennial in 1976—the city began renovating. Philadelphia now enjoys recognition as a major cultural center with world-class museums, performing arts centers and some stunning architecture.

In March 1681, England's King Charles II granted William Penn a charter to a parcel of land west of the Delaware River. Charles dubbed the area "Penn" in honor of William's father, with Penn the Younger adding "-sylvania", meaning "woodlands". Brimming with pacifist Quaker idealism, Penn regarded his colony as a "holy experiment" and ensured as its governor and proprietor that its laws respected religious freedom and liberal government. Penn chose Philadelphia as the capital of Pennsylvania in 1682, optimistically naming it after the Greek for "brotherly love". A survivor of London's Great Fire of 1666, he made sure the city's design included a grid system with wide streets, not the narrow, winding maze that caused so much havoc in England's capital. This format was to become the inspiration for most American cities.

Philadelphia quickly grew to become the second largest city (after London) in the British empire, before ceding that title to New York City. Opposition to British policy in the colonies became seated in the city, where colonial leaders would meet to plan their course of action. The result was the Declaration of Independence, and in 1790 Philadelphia became the temporary capital of the new United States before Washington DC got the job in 1800. The US Constitution was drawn up and first read here in 1786. Often led by the multitalented Benjamin Franklin, Philadelphia became a center for developments in the world of arts and science.

Between 1793 and 1820, Philadelphia suffered five yellow-fever epidemics, which killed thousands but led to the construction of the US's first city water system. Philadelphia's fortunes declined in the 19th century, as New York took over as the nation's cultural, commercial and industrial center. Philly never regained the stature of its early years, despite continued cultural and educational innovation, commerce and shipbuilding, and a brief boom let following WWII.

During the mid - 20th century, like many American cities, Philadelphia watched much of its middle class forsake the city for the suburbs. The 1970s saw Philly grapple with inner city tensions, typified by the firefights between the police and the paramilitary MOVE group. However, by 1976, lavish plans for the nation's bicentennial had inspired a citywide cleanup and renovation campaign—a restoration that continues today—and the city is now consistently rated among the nation's "best" in national polls of lifestyle and character.

The Philadelphia Museum of Art is among the largest art museums in the United States. It has collections of more than 227, 000 objects that include "world-class holdings of European and American paintings, prints, drawings, and decorative arts". The Main Building is visited by more than 800, 000 people annually, and is located at the west end of Philadelphia's Benjamin Franklin Parkway.

Other museum sites include the Rodin Museum, also located on the Benjamin Franklin Parkway; the Ruth and Raymond G. Perelman Building, across the street from the Main Building; and historic houses in Fairmount Park. The Perelman Building opened in 2007, and houses some of the more popular collections, as well as the Museum's library, with over 200, 000 books and periodicals, and 1.6 million other documents.

The museum is closed on Mondays, and the basic entrance price is $20, with various concessions. The museum holds a total of about 25 special exhibitions every year, including touring exhibitions arranged with other museums in the United States and abroad. Some have an extra charge for entrance.

(Words: 653)

Questions for discussions

1. When did Philadelphia quickly grow to become the second largest city?

2. What is visited by more than 800, 000 people annually, and is located at the west end of Philadelphia's Benjamin Franklin Parkway?

3. How many special exhibitions are held in the museum every year?

More to Learn

1. Appreciate the song of "Streets Of Philadelphia"

Streets Of Philadelphia

Bruce Springsteen

I was bruised and battered and I couldn't tell
What I felt
I was unrecognizable to myself
I saw my reflection in a window I didn't know
My own face
Oh brother are you gonna leave me
Wast in away
On the streets of Philadelphia

I walked the avenue till my legs felt like stone
I heard the voices of friends vanished and gone
At night I could hear the blood in my veins
Black and whispering as the rain
On the streets of Philadelphia

Ain't no angel gonna greet me
It's just you and I my friend
My clothes don't fit me no more
I walked a thousand miles
Just to slip the skin

The night has fallen, I'm lyin'awake
I can feel myself fading away

So receive me brother with your faithless kiss
Or will we leave each other alone like this
On the streets of Philadelphia

MOVIES TO SEE (A) The Day After Tomorrow

Ⅰ. Movie Introduction

Director: Roland Emmerich

Starring: Dennis Quaid
Jake Gyllenhaal
Ian Holm
Emmy Rossum
Sela Ward
Dash Mihok

Running time: 124mins

Released: 2004

Plot: *The Day After Tomorrow* takes a big-budget, special-effects-filled look at what the world would look like if the greenhouse effect and global warming continued at such levels that they resulted in worldwide catastrophe and disaster, including multiple hurricanes, tornadoes, tidal waves, floods and the beginning of the next Ice Age. At the center of the story is a paleoclimatologist (a scientist who studies the ways weather patterns changed in the past), Professor Jack Hall, who tries to save the world from the effects of global warming while also trying to get to his son, Sam, who was in New York City as part of a scholastic competition, when the city was overwhelmed by the chilling beginnings of the new Ice Age. In addition to all of the other challenges Dr. Hall faces, he's also going against the flow as humanity races south to warmer climes, and he's nearly the only ongoing north.

Ⅱ. Classic Scenes

Task 1 Study the underlined sentences and expressions in the following classic scenes.

1. In Conference On Global Warming, New Delhi

Professor Hall: We found evidence of a cataclysmic climate shift, which occurred 10,000 years ago. The concentration of these natural greenhouse gases in the ice cores indicates that runaway warming pushed Earth into an ice age which lasted two centuries.

Participant A: I'm confused. I thought your were talking about global warming, not an ice age.

Professor Hall: Yes, it is a paradox, but global warming can trigger a cooling trend. Let me explain. The Northern Hemisphere owes its climate to the North Atlantic Current. Heat from the sun arrives at the equator and is carried north by the ocean. But global warming is melting the polar ice caps and disrupting this flow. Eventually it will shut down. And when that occurs, there goes our warm climate.

Participant B: Excuse me. When do you think this could happen, professor? when?

Professor Hall: I don't know. Maybe in 100 years, maybe in 1000. But what I do know is that if we do not act soon, our children and grandchildren will have to pay the price.

Vice President: And who's going to pay the price of the Kyoto Accord? It would cost the world's economy hundreds of billions of dollars.

Professor Hall: With all due respect, Mr. Vice President, the cost of doing nothing could be even higher. Our climate is fragile. At the rate we're burning fossil fuels and polluting the environment, the ice caps will soon disappear.

Vice President: Professor Hall, our economy is every bit as fragile as the environment. Perhaps you should keep that in mind before making sensationalist claims.

Professor Hall: Well, the last chunk of ice that broke off was about the size of Rhode Island. Some people might call that pretty sensational.

2. In J. D's Dad's place before the flood attacks New York.

Larua: Wow. You live here?

J. D: It's my dad's place. He's kind of never around, so...

Sam: Where is he?

J. D: Skiing in Europe with my stepmom.

Larua: Is this you and your brother? (point to the picture)

J. D: Yeah, that's when we took a bike trip together.

Brian: It's been raining like this for three days now.

TV News: It's a mob scene here at Grand Central Station. Over half the platforms are flooded and service has been suspended on all trains. With planes still grounded and trains now out of service...

Larua: That's bad news for the...

J. D: Victor's coming to pick me up. You guys want a ride to train station?

Brian: Not anymore.

TV News: In Nova Scotia earlier today the ocean rose by 25 feet in a matter of seconds. What we have feared for the past few days has indeed happened. The cold front moving from the Arctic has created an enormous storm system in Canada which, incredible as it sounds, looks more like a tropical hurricane...

J. D: I gotta go pick up my little brother. Do your guys want a ride?

Laura: Where is he?

J. D: He's in a boarding school in Philadelphia.

TV News: If this system moves south, we could see a wind-driven storm surge threaten the entire Eastern Seaboard.

Sam: Okay, bye.

J. D: Victor's stuck in traffic over on Fifth Avenue. It'll be easier to head out of town if we meet him over there.

Brian: You mean walk?

J. D: No, not in this.

Sam: We should take the stairs.

J. D: We're on the top floor.

Laura: I guess we're walking. Maybe we should just stay here.

Police: I think the young lady is right.

Sam: No, we need to get home.

3. Storm is coming

Police: All right, everybody. Quiet down. When was the last time anyone got a signal on a cell phone?

Person A: I got through to my cousin in Memphis an hour ago. They've being evacuated to the south.

Police: We should get moving too. The water is frozen over enough to walk on. We should get going before the snow gets too deep. Everyone, wrap yourselves up as fast as you can.

Sam: We shouldn't go.

J. D: Why not, Sam? Everyone's leaving.

Sam: When I talked to my dad, he told me to stay inside. The storm will kill anybody in it.

Laura: Then you have to say something.

Sam: I know.

Sam: Excuse me, Sir, you're making a mistake.

Police: What? Listen, we're all scared, but we've got no choice.

Sam: That's not it.

Police: Get ready to go.

Sam: If these people go outside, they will freeze to death!

Police: Okay, what is this nonsense?

Sam: It's not nonsense. All right? Look, this storm is gonna get worse. The people caught outside will freeze to death.

Person B: where are you getting this?

Sam: My dad's a climatologist. He works for the government.

Person B: What do we do?

Sam: We stay inside, we deep warm, and we wait it out.

Police: The snow is getting deeper by the minute. We'd be trapped here without food, supplies...

Sam: It's a risk, yeah.

Police: An unnecessary risk.

Sam: No, no. It's not.

Police: We've wasted enough time talking. Come on. Let's go.

Sam: Look, look. Just book for a second.

Police: Come on, everybody.

Sam: This storm is gonna get bad. It's gonna get really, really bad. You've not gonna be able to survive it. Believe me. Sir, please just stay. Just stay. Just don't ...

Task 2 Work in pairs or groups and play the roles in one of your favorite scenes.

Ⅲ. Cultural Notes

1. Ice Age: An ice age is a period of long-term reduction in the temperature of Earth's surface and atmosphere, resulting in the presence or expansion of continental and polar ice sheets and alpine glaciers.

https://en.wikipedia.org/wiki/Ice_age

2. Rhode Island: Rhode Island was one of the British colonies. It was called Rhode Island or Rhode Island and Providence Plantations. The Colony of Rhode Island and Providence Plantations was one of England's original Thirteen Colonies established on the east coast of North America bordering the Atlantic Ocean. After the American Revolution, it became the State of Rhode Island and Providence Plantations.

https://en.wikipedia.org/wiki/Colony_of_Rhode_Island_and_Providence_Plantations

Ⅳ. Questions for discussion

1. What are the themes involved in this film?
2. Can you give an explanation of greenhouse effect?
3. When the storm is coming, what should we do?

Ⅴ. Movie Review

Task: Write a movie review on *The Day After Tomorrow*.

MOVIES TO SEE (B) Yellowstone—Winter

Ⅰ. Movie Introduction

Director: Peter Firth

Starring: re_ symbol_ FilmPlayer

Running time: 49 mins

Released: 2009

Plot: Yellowstone National Park, established by the U. S. Congress and signed into law by President Ulysses S. Grant on March 1, 1872, is a national park located primarily in the U. S. state of Wyoming, although it also extends into Montana and Idaho. Yellowstone, widely held to be the first national park in the world, is known for its wildlife and its many geothermal features, especially Old Faithful Geyser, one of the most popular features in the park. It has many types of ecosystems, but the subalpine forest is dominant.

To Recommend More Movies

❖ *The Yellowstone—Summer* (2009)

❖ *The Yellowstone—Autumn* (2009)

❖ *2012* (2009)

❖ *The Choir Boys* (2004)

❖ *The Great Debaters* (2007)

Unit Three Government and Politics

Pre-reading Activities

Answer the following questions before you read this text.

1. How much do you know about American government?

2. How are the powers distributed between the three branches of American government?

3. Is the federal electoral system always effectively working?

TEXT A U. S. Government: A Brief Introduction

Government

The United States' system of government was established in 1789, based on the world's first written **constitution** (1787). The Constitution designed a system of checks and balances that would protect Americans against **excessive** central power. It separated the government into three branches—**executive**, **legislative**, and **judicial**—and balanced power between the federal government and the individual states.

One of the theoretical **pillars** of the United States Constitution is the idea of "**checks and balances**" among the powers and responsibilities of the three branches of American government. For example, while the legislative (Congress) has the power to create law, the executive (President) can **veto** any legislation—an act which, in turn, can be **overridden** by Congress. The President nominates judges to the nation's highest judiciary authority (Supreme Court), but those nominees must be approved by Congress. The Supreme Court, in its turn, has the power to **invalidate** as "unconstitutional" any law passed by the Congress.

A **Bill of Rights** (added to the Constitution in 1791) protects individual liberties from the long arm of government. Considered one of the **cornerstones** of American democracy, it includes the right to free speech, the right to bear arms, and the right not to **incriminate** oneself.

The ever-shifting distribution of powers between the different branches of government is a constant source of controversy. **Applying** the sometimes **ambiguous** words of the 200 – year-old Constitution to today's societal challenges provides job security for constitutional scholars and Supreme Court justices alike. Yet few would dispute that the document is remarkable in having **articulated** the values and aspirations of **successive** generations of Americans since 1788.

The Executive

The executive branch of government **consists of** a president and a vice president (who are elected "on the same ticket" for four years), and a cabinet **composed of** the heads (or secretaries) of the fifteen executive departments. The president serves as head of state and head of armed forces, and is restricted to a maximum of two elected terms in office.

The Legislature

The **bicameral** legislative branch of government (Congress) comprises two houses: the 100 – member Senate, and the 435 – member House of Representatives. The number of congressmen and women elected to the House of Representatives from each state is based on its population. Members serve two-year terms. In the Senate, each state is represented by two members. Senators serve six-year terms, with one-third of the seats being up for election every two years.

The Judiciary

The judicial branch of government is headed by the Supreme Court of nine judges, who are **appointed** for life by the president. The highest court in the land, it is the final **arbiter** in determining the constitutionality of legislative and executive actions and maintaining the balance between state and federal institutions.

The States

With the passage of time, the **delicate** balance of power has **shifted away from** the states, as the role of central government has steadily expanded. The individual states still retain significant administrative and policy-making **autonomy**, however.

The visitor can be baffled by the wide variance in state laws, with everything from drinking age to **capital punishment** being **adjudicated** by geography. Most states replicate the federal structure, each having its own constitution, a chief executive (the governor), a bicameral state congress, and a judiciary.

The state governments tend to have the greatest influence over most Americans' daily lives. **The Tenth Amendment** prohibits the federal government from exercising any power not **delegated** to it by the States in the Constitution; as a result, states handle the majority of issues most relevant to individuals within their **jurisdiction**. Because state governments are not authorized to print currency, they generally have to raise revenue through either taxes or bonds. As a result, state governments tend to impose severe budget cuts or raise taxes any time the economy is **faltering**.

Political Parties

The "winner take all" electoral structure favors a two-party system. Democrats tend to be more **liberal** than Republicans, and believe in a stronger role for government. They **countenance** higher taxes to pay for social programs. Regarded as "the party of the people," the Democratic party has particular **appeal to** ethnic minorities and women.

Considered to be more socially **conservative** and pro free enterprise than the Democrats, the Republican party favors state rights and strengthening the armed forces. Republicans count a strong following among the middle class, business interests, and the farming community.

By European standards, both are fairly **centrist** and party lines are frequently crossed when voting on legislation. In fact, politicians often demonstrate more loyalty to the agenda of their home constituents than that of their party. Another significant feature of the political scene is the special interest groups that **lobby** politicians to influence their policy decisions.

Federal Electoral System

Presidential elections are held every four years, on the first Tuesday in November. The **inauguration** of the winning candidate is held on the following January 20.

Confusing to many outsiders, technically the president is elected not by universal **suffrage** but by a 538 – member electoral college. How does this work? Each state has a number of electoral-college votes, **proportionate** to the size of its population. When people vote for a presidential candidate, they are actually instructing their state electoral college to cast their votes for that candidate. The candidate who receives the most votes is awarded that state's entire **allocation** of electoral-college votes. The presidency is awarded to the candidate who receives a majority of the nation's 538 electoral-college votes.

One **repercussion** of the 2000 election, in which **George W. Bush** lost the popular vote but won the presidency, has been to **focus attention on** whether this system truly expresses the will of the people.

(Words: 935)

New Words

constitution	*n.* 建立，组成；体格；构成方式；宪法
excessive	*adj.* 过度的，极度的；过分的
executive	*n.* 总经理；行政部门；[计算机] 执行指令 *adj.* 执行的；管理的；政府部门的
legislative	*adj.* （关于）立法的；立法决定的；有权立法的，用以立法的；立法机构的 *n.* 立法权；立法机关
judicial	*adj.* 司法的；法庭的；明断的；公正的
pillars	*n.* 柱，台柱，顶梁柱；墩，柱脚；（组织、制度、信仰等的）核心
veto	*n.* 否决权，否认权；行使否决权；否决理由 *vt.* 否决，不同意；不批准，禁止
override	*vt.* 推翻，无视；践踏；优先于
invalidate	*vt.* 使无效；使作废；证明…错误；使站不住脚
cornerstones	*n.* 奠基石；基础；最重要部分；柱石
incriminate	*vt.* 使（某人）显得有罪，牵连，归罪于；控告；归咎于

续表

ambiguous	*adj.* 含糊的，不明确的；引起歧义的
articulate	*adj.* 发音清晰的；善于表达的；有关节的 *vt.* 清晰地发（音）；言语表达；（用关节）连接
successive	*adj.* 连续的，相继的；继承的，接替的
bicameral	*adj.* 两院制的
appoint	*vt*. 任命，委派；约定，指定
arbiter	*n.* ［法］仲裁人，裁决者；权威人士，主宰者
delicate	*adj.* 微妙的；熟练的；纤弱的；易损的
autonomy	*n.* 自治，自治权；自主权；自治国，社区，或集团等；人身自由
adjudicate	*vt.* 判决，宣判；当…的评判员（或裁判员、仲裁人） *n.* 判决，宣判；裁判员
replicate	*vt.* 复制，复写；重复，反复；折转；［生］复制 *adj.* 复制的；折叠的；［植］折转的 *n.* 复制品
delegate	*n.* 代表，代表团成员 *vt.* 委派代表；授权给
jurisdiction	*n.* 司法权；管辖权；管辖范围；权限
falter	*vi.* （嗓音）颤抖；支吾其词；蹒跚；摇晃 *n.* 支吾，结巴；踌躇，不稳；摇晃；颤抖
liberal	*n.* 自由主义者；自由党党员 *adj.* 开明的；自由的；慷慨的；不拘泥的
countenance	*n.* 表情；脸，面孔；赞同，支持；鼓励 *vt.* 表示赞同；嘉奖；宽恕
conservative	*n.* 保守的人；（英国）保守党党员，保守党支持者 *adj.* 保守的；（英国）保守党的；（式样等）不时新的
centrist	*n.* （政治上的）中立派；温和派 *adj.* 温和派的
lobby	*n.* 门厅，大厅；休息室；游说团；投票厅 *vi.* 为了支持或抵制某项特定目标游说 *vt.* 对…进行游说；陈情（试图努力影响某人采取有利行动）

续表

inauguration	*n.* 就职；就职典礼；开始；开创
suffrage	*n.* （政治性选举的）选举权，投票权
proportion-ate	*adj.* 成比例的；相称的；适当的 *vt.* 使…成比例；使相称；使相当；使适应
allocation	*n.* 配给，分配；分配额（或量）；划拨的款项；拨给的场地
repercussion	*n.* 弹回，返回；反响，影响

Phrases & Expressions

checks and balances	三权分立，权力制衡
apply…to…	适用于；运用
consist of	由…组成；包括
compose of	由…构成
shift away from	从…转向…；转变
capital punishment	死刑
appeal to	向…投诉；向…呼吁；对…有吸引力
focus attention on	集中精力、关注、焦点在…

Proper Names

Bill of Rights	人权法案
The Tenth Amendment	第10项修正案
George W. Bush	乔治W. 布什

Cultural Notes

1. Bill of Rights A bill of rights, sometimes called a declaration of rights or a charter of rights, is a list of the most important rights to the citizens of a country. The purpose is to protect those rights against infringement from public officials and private citizens. The term "bill of rights" originates from England, where it refers to the Bill of Rights 1689 enacted by Parliament following the Glorious Revolution, asserting the supremacy of Parliament over the monarch, and listing a number of fundamental rights and liberties. For more information, visit https://en. wikipedia. org/wiki/Bill_ of_ rights

2. The Tenth Amendment The Tenth Amendment (Amendment X) to the United States Constitution, which is part of the Bill of Rights, was ratified on December 15, 1791. It expresses the principle of federalism, which undergirds the entire plan of the original Constitution, by stating that the federal government possesses only those powers delegated to it by the Constitution. All remaining powers are reserved for the states or the people. In drafting this amendment, its framers had two purposes in mind: first, as a necessary rule of construction; and second, as a reaffirmation of the nature of the federal system. For more information, visit https://en. wikipedia. org/wiki/Tenth_ Amendment_ to_ the_ United_ States_ Constitution

3. George W. Bush George Walker Bush (born July 6, 1946) is an American politician and businessman who served as the 43rd President of the United States from 2001 to 2009, and the 46th Governor of Texas from 1995 to 2000. For more information, visit https://en. wikipedia. org/wiki/George_ W. _ Bush

Exercises

Comprehension of the Text

Ⅰ Answer the following questions according to the passage.

1. What system is employed to protect Americans against excessive central power?

2. Can you give a specific example to illustrate the principle of "checks and balances"?

3. What are the strengths and weaknesses in American political landscape?

Vocabulary

Ⅱ. Fill in the blanks with the words given below. Change the form where necessary.

excessive	veto	ambiguous	articulate	successive
delicate	autonomy	delegate	lobby	proportionate
inauguration	faltering	liberal	conservative	appoint

1. This agreement is very ________ and open to various interpretations.
2. Gun control advocates are ________ hard for new laws.
3. The majority of Scots favor an __________ Scotland involving devolution or complete independence.
4. The government is devising a plan to ________ prisoners held in detention camps.
5. When the chairman of Campbell's retired, McGovern was named as his __.
6. The Prime Minister has the power to dismiss and _______ senior ministers.
7. A ____________ amount of time was devoted to one topic, so let's cut it short and get down to business.
8. Their marriage is a __________ balance between traditional and contemporary values.
9. She was always very _____________ dressed when we went out.
10. Managers are also accused of paying themselves ________ high salaries.

Translations

Ⅲ. Translate the following sentences into English.

1. 提前搞清楚什么规章适用于你的情况。(apply to)

____

2. 健康饮食应由新鲜的水果和蔬菜构成。(consist of)

____

3. 能源安全还将推动中国从煤炭和石油转向其他能源。(shift away)

____

4. 他将呼吁国家延长领取失业救济金的时限。(appeal to)

____

5. 此次会议可能有助于将关注焦点放在经济上。(focus attention on)

____

Ⅳ. Translate the following passage into English.

最高法院法官的道德判断近日已成为重要议题。当法官像政客一样行事时，法院便不能维持其作为法律守护者的合法性。但在某些情况下，法官的行事方式依然损害了法院独立、公正的声誉。比如，大法官安东宁·斯卡利亚便现身政治活动。这种行为降低了法院裁定被视作公正判断的可能性。导致这一问题的部分原因是法官不受道德规范的制约。至少，法院自身应该服从那些适用于联邦司法系统其余部门的行为规范。这一事件及其他类似事件提出了一个问题：法院和政治之间是否还存有界限。

TEXT B The American Two-party System

(A) No one now living in the United States can remember when the contest began between the **Democratic** and the **Republican** parties. It has been going on for more than a century, making it one of the oldest political **rivalries** in the world.

(B) The American political system is a **classical** example of the two-party system. When we say that we have a **two-party system** in the United States we do not mean that we have only two parties. Usually about a dozen parties **nominate** presidential **candidates**. We call it a two-party system because we have two large parties and a number of small parties, and the large parties are so large that we often forget about the rest. Usually the small parties collectively **poll** less than 5 per cent of the vote cast in national elections.

(C) The democratic and Republican parties are the largest and most competitive organizations in the American **community**. They organize the **electorate** very simply by maintaining the two-party system. Americans almost **inevitably** become Democrats or Republicans because there is usually no other place for them go to. Moreover, because the rivalry of these parties is very old, most Americans know where they belong in the system. As a consequence of the **dominance** of the major parties, most elected officials are either Republicans or Democrats. **Attempts** to **break up** this old system have been made in every presidential election in the past one hundred years, but the system has survived all **assaults**.

(D) How does it happen that the two-party system is so strongly **rooted in** American politics? The explanation is probably to be found in the way elections are conducted. In the United States, unlike countries with a **parliamentary** system of government, we elect not only the President, but a large number of other officials, about 800,000 of them. We also elect **congressmen** from single-member districts. For example, we elect 435 members of the **House of Representatives** from 435 districts (there are a few exceptions), one member for each district. **Statistically**, this kind of election favors the major parties. The system of elections makes it easy for the major parties to maintain their dominant position, because they are likely to win more than their share of the offices.

(E) One of the great consequences of the system is that it produces majorities automatically. Because there are only two competitors in the running, it is almost inevitable that one will receive a majority. Moreover, the system tends slightly to **exaggerate** the victory of the winning party. This is not always true, but the strong **tendency** to produce majorities is built into the system.

(F) In over 200 years of **constitutional** history, Americans have learned much about the way in which the system can be managed so as to make possible the peaceful **transfer** of power from one party to the other. At the level of presidential elections, the party **in power** has been **overturned** by the party **out of power** nineteen times, almost once a decade. In the election of 1860, the political system **broke down**, and the **Civil War**, the worst disaster in American history, resulted. Our history justifies our confidence in the system but also shows that it is not **foolproof**.

(G) The second major party is able to survive a **defeat** because the statistical tendency that exaggerates the victory of the winning party operates even more strongly **in favor of** the second party against the third, fourth, and fifth parties. As a result, the defeated major party is able to maintain a **monopoly** of the opposition. The advantage of the second party over the third is so great that it is the only party that is likely to be able to overturn the party in power. It is able, therefore, to attract the support of everyone seriously opposed to the party in power. The second party is important as long as it can monopolize the movement to **overthrow** the party in power, because it is certain to **come into power** sooner or later.

(H) Another consequence of the two-party system is that whereas minor parties are likely to **identify themselves with** special interests or special programs and thus take extreme positions, the major parties are so large that they tend to be **moderate**. Evidence of the moderation of the major parties is that much business is conducted across party lines. What happens when the Democrats control one house of Congress and the Republicans control the other? About the same volume of **legislation** is passed as when one party controls both houses, although some important legislation is likely to be blocked temporarily. It is possible to **carry on** the work of the government even when party control is divided because party differences are not fundamental.

(Words: 784)

New Words

rivalry	*n.* 竞争，对抗，对立；竞争行为，对抗行为
classical	*adj.* 古典的，经典的；传统的；第一流的 *n.* 古典音乐
nominate	*vt.* 提名…为候选人；任命；挑选；指定
candidate	*n.* 候选人；报考者；申请求职者；攻读学位者
poll	*n.* 民意调查；投票选举；投票数；头部 *vt.* 得到（一定数目的）选票；对…进行调查；修剪 *vi.* 投票；做民意调查
community	*n.* 社区；社会团体；共同体；［生态］群落
electorate	*n.* 选民（全体）；选举区；［史］选帝侯的爵位［领土］
inevitably	*adv.* 不可避免地，自然而然地；必然地，无疑的

续表

dominance	*n.* 优势；支配；统治；优性
attempt	*vt.* 试图；尝试 *n.* 进攻；尝试，冲击
assault	*n.* 攻击；袭击，进攻；威胁，殴打；侵犯人身 *vt.* 袭击；强暴；使（感官）难受 *vi.* 发起攻击；动武
parliamentary	*adj.* 议会的，国会的；议会制度的；根据议会的
congressmen	*n.* 国会议员
statistically	*adv.* 统计上地，统计地
exaggerate	*vt. &vi.* 夸张；（使）扩大；（使）增加
tendency	*n.* 倾向，趋势；（话或作品等的）旨趣，意向；性情；癖好
constitutional	*adj.* 宪法的，符合宪法的；本质的；体质上的；保健的
transfer	*n.* 转移；调动；换乘；（运动员）转会 *vt.* 使转移；使调动；转让（权利等）；让与 *vi.* 转让；转学；转乘；转会（尤指职业足球队）
overturn	*vt. & vi.* （使）翻倒 *vt.* 使垮台，推翻；撤销（判决等） *n.* 推翻，垮台；瓦解；灭亡，毁灭
foolproof	*adj.* （方法、计划、系统等设计得）万无一失的，肯定成功的
defeat	*vt.* 击败，战胜；挫败；［法］宣告无效，作废 *n.* 战胜；失败；［法］废除
monopoly	*n.* 垄断；专卖；垄断者；专利品
overthrow	*vt.* 打倒，推翻；使屈服，征服；使瓦解；撞倒 *n.* 推翻，打倒；打翻；倾倒；［棒］投得过高的球
moderate	*adj.* 有节制的；稳健的，温和的；适度的，中等的 *vt.* 使和缓；主持；节制 *vi.* 变缓和；做主持人
legislation	*n.* 立法，制定法律；法律，法规

Phrases & Expressions

break up	结束；（使）破碎；放假；（使）散开
be root in	深植于…
in power	当权的，在朝的
out of power	丧失权利的；在野的
break down	出故障，坏了
in favor of	赞成［支持］（某人或某事物）；以…取代；有利于
come into power	（开始）掌权，上台，执政
identify oneself with	参加到…中
carry on	经营；〈非正〉继续进行;争吵;吵闹

Proper Names

Democratic party	民主党
Republican party	共和党
House of Representatives	众议院
Civil War	美国内战

Cultural Notes

1. Democratic party and Republican party The Democratic Party is one of the two major contemporary political parties in the United States, along with the Republican Party to its right. Tracing its origins back to Thomas Jefferson's and James Madison's Democratic-Republicans, the modern-day Democratic Party was founded around 1828, making it the world's oldest active party. The Republican Party, commonly referred to as GOP (abbreviation for Grand Old Party), is one of the two major contemporary political parties in the United States, the other being its historic rival, the Democratic Party. For more information, visit https://en.wikipedia.org/wiki/Democratic_Party_(United_States) and. https://en.wikipedia.org/wiki/Republican_Party_(United_States)

2. House of Representatives The United States House of Representatives is one of the two houses of the United States Congress (a bicameral legislature). It is frequently referred to as The House. The other house is the Senate. The major power of the House is to pass federal legislation that affects the entire country, although its bills must also be passed by the Senate and further agreed to by the U. S. President before becoming law. For more information, visit https://en. wikipedia. org/wiki/United_ States_ House_ of_ Representatives.

3. Civil War The American Civil War, widely known in the United States as simply the Civil War as well as other sectional names, was a civil war fought from 1861 to 1865 to determine the survival of the Union or independence for the Confederacy. Among the 34 states in January 1861, seven Southern slave states individually declared their secession from the United States and formed the Confederate States of America. The Confederacy, often simply called the South, grew to include eleven states, and although they claimed thirteen states and additional western territories, the Confederacy was never diplomatically recognized by a foreign country. The states that remained loyal and did not declare secession were known as the Union or the North. The war had its origin in the fractious issue of slavery, especially the extension of slavery into the western territories. After four years of combat, which left over 600, 000 Union and Confederate soldiers dead and destroyed much of the South's infrastructure, the Confederacy collapsed and slavery was abolished. Then began the Reconstruction and the processes of restoring national unity and guaranteeing civil rights to the freed slaves. For more information, visit https://en. wikipedia. org/wiki/American_ Civil_ War.

Exercises

Comprehension of the Text

Ⅰ. The following 10 statements contain information given in the text. Identify the paragraph from which the information is derived. You may choose a paragraph more than once. Each paragraph is marked with a letter.

1. There are a number of minor parties in the U. S. besides the two major ones.

2. Americans enjoy a constitutional history of more than 200 years.

3. The contest between the Democratic and the Republican parties has lasted so long that it is impossible for anyone living to remember when it started.

4. The defeated major party can still be put in a favorable position in the opposition.

5. It is highly possible for minor parties to participate in special interests and special programs and take extreme positions.

6. As a result of old rivalry of these parties, Americans have developed a better understanding of where their positions are in the system.

7. It is not always the case that the success of the winning party will receive more emphasis in the system.

8. The President as well as the majority of other officials comes into being from general election.

9. The fact that there are no fundamental party differences makes the work of the government carry on.

10. An extreme condition when the political system collapsed in America is during the Civil War.

Vocabulary

Ⅱ. Fill in the blanks with the words given below. Change the form where necessary.

classical	nominate	candidate	community	inevitably
dominance	assault	statistically	exaggerate	tendency
transfer	overturn	foolproof	monopoly	moderate

1. Sheila admitted that she did sometimes ________ the demands of her job.

2. He accused his opponents of wanting to ________ the government.

3. Government _______ show the largest drop in industrial output for ten years.

4. The defeat had ____________ consequences for British policy.

5. The Socialists united behind their probable presidential ________ , Michel Rocard.

6. Trendy teachers are denying children the opportunity to study ________ texts.

7. In 1974 the Justice Department sued AT & T for attempting to ________ the telephone industry.

8. Being even ________ overweight increases your risk of developing high blood pressure.

9. The attack is one of a series of savage sexual ________ on women in the university area.

10. The growth of such vigilante gangs has worried ________ leaders, police and politicians.

Further Reading

TEXT C House of Cards

With its thirteen episodes released all at once, Season Two of *House of Cards* has proven no less a hit than its first season as the game of power continues in the American political TV thriller.

House of Cards is an American political drama series developed and produced by Beau Willimon. It is an adaptation of a previous BBC miniseries of the same name which is based on the novel by Michael Dobbs.

Set in the present day Washington, D. C. , *House of Cards* is the story of Francis Underwood, an ambitious Democrat from South Carolina's 5th congressional district and the House Majority Whip. Following his assistance in ensuring the election of President Garrett Walker, Underwood is informed by Chief of Staff Linda Vasquez that the existing agreement to appoint his Secretary of State will not be honored. Furious at Walker's betrayal, Underwood and his wife Claire, an environmental activist, begin seeking out pawns in a protracted political war against Walker. Soon brought into the fray are troubled Congressman Peter Russo and Zoe Barnes, a young political reporter for the *Washington Herald* newspaper.

The series has a huge, loyal fan base. Average Joes who enjoy a well-written story and superb acting have binge-watched the show, which has also taken the real-life Washington by storm.

Obama Likes *House of Cards*

President Obama has made no secret of the fact he's a big fan of the Netflix series *House of Cards*.

But the commander in chief said he wishes real-world Washington worked in the same "ruthlessly efficient" manner it does in the hit show, which stars Kevin Spacey as the cunning congressman and top political power-broker Frank Underwood.

During a meeting with top CEOs, Mr. Obama asked a Netflix executive whether he brought "advance copies" of the show's second season, before comparing actual D. C. with the fictional version depicted on screen.

"I wish things were that ruthlessly efficient," Mr. Obama said of the political landscape seen in *House of Cards*.

Of Kevin Spacey's character—who manipulates other lawmakers and top officials on a daily basis, allowed a fellow congressman to die from carbon dioxide poisoning and cheats on his wife regularly, among other questionable behavior—Mr. Obama said: "This guy's getting a lot of stuff done."

Netflix executives also reportedly asked Mr. Obama to do a cameo appearance in the show. It's unclear whether he'll accept the invitation.

Entertains with Power Game

With the politician rising to power, plot twists happening one after another keep viewers on the edge of their seats. And this may help explain why *House of Cards* has also found a large audience outside of the U. S. despite that it requires some level of understanding of American politics. In China, the show has been streamed millions of times on Sohu. com, which purchased exclusive rights to the show in mainland China.

If you have watched the show, you may wonder whether Washington in reality is as it's depicted on the show. According to Missouri Senator Claire McCaskill, *House of Cards* is "highly entertaining fiction but not very realistic."

Realistic or not, the show has done an excellent job in keeping viewers entertained, and will likely continue to do so when it returns with the third season next year.

Memorable Lines from the Show

A person's character isn't determined by how he or she enjoys victory, but rather how he or she endures defeat.

There are two kinds of pains, sort of pain that makes you strong, or useless pain, sort of pain that's only suffering.

After all, we are nothing more or less than what we choose to reveal.

Take a step back. Look at the bigger picture. One bite at a time. That's how you devour a whale.

Power is a lot like real estate. It's about location, location, location. The closer you are to the source, the higher you property value.

(Words: 643)

Questions for discussions

1. In your understanding, what is the core value displayed from the show?
2. Do you think it is morally correct for a politician to achieve his political ambition through illegal means?
3. What inspiration can you draw from the show?

More to Learn

1. Appreciation

Politics

By W. B. Yeats

"In our time the destiny of man presents its meaning in political terms."

-Thomas Mann

How can I, that girl standing there,

My attention fix
On Roman or on Russian
Or on Spanish politics?
Yet here's a traveled man that knows
What he talks about,
And there's a politician
That has read and thought,
And maybe what they say is true
Of war and war's alarms,
But O that I were young again
And held her in my arms!

MOVIES TO SEE (A) Lincoln

I. Movie Introduction

Director: Steven Spielberg

Starring: Daniel Day-Lewis
Sally Field
David Strathairn
Tommy Lee Jones

Running time: 150mins

Released: 2012

Plot: *Lincoln* is a 2012 historical film about the final four months of Lincoln's life, focusing on the president's efforts in January 1865 to have the Thirteenth Amendment to the United States Constitution (which abolished slavery) passed by the United States House of Representatives, while the American Civil War nears its end. As the Civil War continues to rage, America's president struggles with continuing carnage on the battlefield as he fights with many inside his own cabinet on the decision to emancipate the slaves. For more information, visit http://www.imdb.com/title/tt0443272/.

Ⅱ. Classic Scenes

Task 1 Study the underlined sentences and expressions in the following classic scenes.

1. Abraham Lincoln pounds his hand on a table as his cabinet squabbles

Abraham Lincoln: I can't listen to this anymore. I can't accomplish a goddamn thing of any worth until we cure ourselves of slavery and end this pestilential war! I wonder if any of you or anyone else knows it. I know! I need this! This amendment is that cure! We've stepped out upon the world stage now. Now! With the fate of human dignity in our hands. Blood's been spilled to afford us this moment now! Now! Now! And you grouse so and heckle and dodge about like pettifogging Tammany Hall hucksters!

2. Last lines, from Second Inaugural speech

Abraham Lincoln: Fondly do we hope, fervently do we pray, that this mighty scourge of war may speedily pass away. Yet, if God wills that it continue until all the wealth piled by the bondsman's two hundred and fifty years of unrequited toil shall be sunk, and until every drop of blood drawn with the lash shall be paid by another drawn with the sword, as was said three thousand years ago, so still it must be said "the judgments of the Lord are true and righteous altogether. "With malice toward none, with charity for all, with firmness in the right as God gives us to see the right, let us strive on to finish the work we are in, to bind up the nation's wounds, to care for him who shall have borne the battle and for his widow and his orphan, to do all which may achieve and cherish a just and lasting peace among ourselves and with all nations.

3. At the beginning of the movie, on the battlefield

Pvt. Harold Green: Some of us was in the Second Kansas Colored. We fought the rebs at Jenkins' Ferry last April, just after they'd killed every Negro soldier they captured at Poison Springs. So at Jenkins' Ferry, we decided weren't taking no reb prisoners. And we didn't leave a one of ' em alive. The ones of us that didn't die that day, we joined up with the 116th U. S. Colored, sir. From Camp Nelson Kentucky.

Abraham Lincoln: What's your name, soldier?

Pvt. Harold Green: Private Harold Green, sir.

Cpl. Ira Clark: I'm Corporal Ira Clark, sir. Fifth Massachusetts Cavalry. We're waiting over there. We're leaving our horses behind, and shipping out with the 24th Infantry for the assault next week on Wilmington.

Abraham Lincoln: How long have you been a soldier?

Cpl. Ira Clark: Two year, sir.

Abraham Lincoln: Second Kansas Colored Infantry, they fought bravely at Jenkins' Ferry.

Pvt. Harold Green: That's right, sir.

Cpl. Ira Clark: They killed a thousand rebel soldiers, sir. They were very brave. And making three dollars less each month than white soldiers.

Pvt. Harold Green: Us 2nd Kansas boys, whenever we fight now we...

Cpl. Ira Clark: Another three dollars subtracted from our pay for our uniforms.

Pvt. Harold Green: That was true, yes sir, but that changed...

Cpl. Ira Clark: Equal pay now. Still no commissioned Negro officers.

Abraham Lincoln: I am aware of it, Corporal Clark.

Cpl. Ira Clark: Yes, sir, that's good you're aware, sir. It's only that...

Pvt. Harold Green: You think the Wilmington attack is gonna be...

Cpl. Ira Clark: Now that white people have accustomed themselves to seeing Negro men with guns, fighting on their behalf, and now that they can tolerate Negro soldiers getting the same pay-in a few years perhaps they can abide the idea of Negro lieutenants and captains. In fifty years, maybe a Negro colonel. In a hundred years-the vote.

Abraham Lincoln: What will you do after the war, Corporal Clark?

Cpl. Ira Clark: Work, sir. Perhaps you'll hire me.

Abraham Lincoln: Perhaps I will.

Cpl. Ira Clark: But you should know, sir, that I get sick at the smell of bootblack, and I cannot cut hair.

Abraham Lincoln: I've yet to find a man who could cut mine so it'd make any difference.

Pvt. Harold Green: You've got springy hair for a white man.

Abraham Lincoln: *[chuckling]* I do. My last barber hanged himself. *[Green laughs]* And the one before that. Left me his scissors in his will.

4. In the cabinet's office

Abraham Lincoln: Thunder forth, God of War.

Edwin Stanton: We'll commence our assault on Wilmington from the sea… Why is this burned? Was the boy playing with it?

Abraham Lincoln: It got took by a breeze several nights back.

Edwin Stanton: This is an official War Department map!

William Seward: And the entire cabinet's waiting to hear what it portends.

Gideon Welles: A bombardment. From the largest fleet the Navy's ever assembled.

Abraham Lincoln: Old Neptune, shake thy hoary locks.

Gideon Welles: Fifty-eight ships are underway, of every tonnage and firing range.

Edwin Stanton: We'll keep up a steady barrage. Our first target is Fort Fisher. It defends Wilmington port.

James Speed: A steady barrage?

Edwin Stanton: A hundred shells a minute. Till they surrender.

William Fessenden: Dear God.

Abraham Lincoln: Wilmington's their last open seaport. Therefore…

Edwin Stanton: Wilmington falls, Richmond falls after.

William Seward: And the war…is done.

John Usher: Then why, if I may ask are we not concentrating the nation's attention on Wilmington? Why, instead, are we reading in the Herald that the anti-slavery amendment is being precipitated on the House floor for debate—because your eagerness, in what seems an unwarranted intrusion of the Executive into Legislative prerogatives, is compelling it to its…to what's likely to be it's premature demise? You signed the Emancipation Proclamation, you've done all that can be expected—

James Speed: The Emancipation Proclamation's merely a war measure. After the war the courts will make a meal out of it.

John Usher: When Edward Bates was Attorney General, he felt confident in it enough to allow you to sign—

James Speed: Different lawyers, different opinions. It frees slaves as a military exigent, not in any other—

Abraham Lincoln: I don't recall Bates being any too certain about the legality of my Proclamation, just it wasn't downright criminal. Somewhere's in between. Back when I rode the legal circuit in Illinois, I defended a woman from Metamora named Melissa Goings, 77 years-old. They said she murdered her husband, he was 83. He was choking her and she grabbed a hold of a stick of firewood and fractured his skull and he died. In his will he wrote: ' I suspect she has killed me. If I get over it, I will have revenge. ' No one was keen to see her convicted, he was that kind of husband. I asked the prosecuting attorney if I might have a short conference with my client. And she and I went into a room in the courthouse, but I alone emerged. The window in the room was found to be wide open. It was believed the old lady may have climbed out of it. I told the bailiff right before. I left her in the room she asked me where she could get a good drink of water, and I told her Tennessee. Mrs. Goings was seen no more in Metamora. Enough justice had been done; they even forgave the bondsman her bail.

John Usher: I'm afraid I don't see—

Abraham Lincoln: I decided that the Constitution gives me war powers, but no one knows just exactly what those powers are. Some say they don't exist. I don't know. I decided I needed them to exist to uphold my oath to protect the Constitution, which I decided meant that I could take the rebel's slaves from them as property confiscated in war. That might recommend to suspicion that I agree with the Rebs that their slaves are property in the first place. Of course I don't, never have, I'm glad to see any man free, and if calling a man property, or war contraband, does the trick... Why I caught at the opportunity. Now here's where it gets truly slippery. I use the law allowing for the seizure of property in a war knowing it applies only to the property of governments and citizens of belligerent nations. But the South ain't a nation, that's why I can't negotiate with'em. If in fact the Negroes are property according to law, have I the right to take the rebels' property from'em, if I insist they're rebels only, and not citizens of a belligerent country? And slipperier still: I maintain it ain't our actual Southern states in rebellion but only the rebels living in those states, the laws of which states remain in force. The laws of which states remain in force. That means, that since it's states' laws that determine whether Negroes can be sold as slaves, as property-the Federal government doesn't have a say in that, least not yet then Negroes in those states are slaves, hence property, hence my war powers allow me to confiscate'em as such. So I confiscated'em. But if I'm a respecter of states' laws, how then can I legally free'em with my Proclamation, as I done, unless I' m cancelling states' laws? I felt the war demanded it; my oath demanded it; I felt right with myself; and I hoped it was legal to do it, I'm hoping still. Two years ago I proclaimed these people emancipated-"then, hence forward and forever free." But let's say the courts decide I had no authority to do it. They might well decide that. Say there's no amendment abolishing slavery. Say it's after the war, and I can no longer use my war powers to just ignore the courts' decisions, like I sometimes felt I had to do. Might those people I freed be ordered back into slavery? That's why I'd like to get the Thirteenth Amendment through the House, and on its way to ratification by the states, wrap the whole slavery thing up, forever and aye. As soon as I'm able. Now. End of this month. And I'd like you to stand behind me. Like my cabinet's most always done. As the preacher once said, I could write shorter sermons but once I start I get too lazy to stop.

John Usher: It seems to me, sir, you're describing precisely the sort of dictator the Democrats have been howling about.

James Speed: Dictators aren't susceptible to law.

John Usher: Neither is he! He just said as much! Ignoring the courts? Twisting meanings? What reins him in from, from...

Abraham Lincoln: Well, the people do that, I suppose. I signed the Emancipation Proclamation a year and a half before my second election. I felt I was within my power to do it; however I also felt that I might be wrong about that; I knew the people would tell me. I gave'em a year and a half to think about it. And they re-elected me. And come February the first, I intend to sign the Thirteenth A-mendment.

Task 2 Work in pairs or groups and play the roles in one of your favorite scenes.

Ⅲ. Cultural Notes

1. *Tammany Hall*: Tammany Hall, also known as the Society of St. Tammany, the Sons of St. Tammany, or the Columbian Order, was a New York City political organization founded in 1786 and incorporated on May 12, 1789, as theTammany Society. It was the Democratic Party political machine that played a major role in controlling New York City and New York State politics and helping immigrants, most notably the Irish, rise up in American politics from the 1790s to the 1960s. For more information, visit https://en.wikipedia.org/wiki/Tammany_Hall.

2. *Second Kansas Colored*: The United States Colored Troops (USCT) were regiments in the United States Army composed of mainly African-American (colored) soldiers, although non-African Americans people of color such as Pacific Islanders, Asian Americans and Native Americans also fought under USCT regiments. They were first recruited during the American Civil War, and by the end of that war in April, 1865, the 175 USCT regiments constituted about one-tenth the manpower of the Union Army. For more information, visit https://en.wikipedia.org/wiki/United_States_Colored_Troops.

3. *Emancipation Proclamation*: The Emancipation Proclamation was a presidential proclamation and executive order issued by President Abraham Lincoln on January 1, 1863. In a single stroke, it changed the federal legal status of more than 3 million enslaved persons in the designated areas of the South from "slave" to "free". It had the practical effect that as soon as a slave escaped the control of the Confederate government, by running away or through advances of federal troops, the slave became legally free. Eventually it reached and liberated all of the designated slaves. It was issued as a war measure during the American Civil War, directed to all of the areas in rebellion and all segments of the executive branch (including the Army and Navy) of the United States. For more information, visit

https: //en. wikipedia. org/wiki/Emancipation_ Proclamation.

4. *The Thirteenth Amendment*: The Thirteenth Amendment (Amendment XIII) to the United States Constitution abolished slavery and involuntary servitude, except as punishment for a crime. In Congress, it was passed by the Senate on April 8, 1864, and by the House on January 31, 1865. The amendment was ratified by the required number of states on December 6, 1865. On December 18, 1865, Secretary of State William H. Seward proclaimed its adoption. It was the first of the three Reconstruction Amendments adopted following the American Civil War. For more information, visit https: //en. wikipedia. org/wiki/Thirteenth_ Amendment_ to_ the_ United_ States_ Constitution.

Ⅳ. Questions for discussion

1. What are the roles of black people in American history?

2. What is the significance of the Emancipation Proclamation?

3. Do you think that President Abraham Lincoln attributed part of his political success to his sense of humor?

Ⅴ. Movie Review

Task: Write a movie review on Lincoln.

MOVIES TO SEE (B) The Campaign

Ⅰ. Movie Introduction

Director: Jay Roach

Starring: Will Ferrell, Zach Galifianakis, Jason Sudeikis

Running time: 97 mins

Released: 2012

Plot: North Carolina's district 14 is about to elect a new Congressman. Cam Brady (D-Hammond) is running unopposed for a fifth consecutive term. After an affair and a massive scandal that follows, Brady's approval rating drops to the point where the billionaire Motch brothers find a candidate to replace him. They choose Marty Huggins (R-Hammond), the son of a famous republican, to run against Brady. This has the media interested as it could tip the scales with a slim majority in the House. As the campaign escalates, Brady constantly shoots himself in the foot, winning the approval and disapproval of the media. Will Marty Huggins trump Cam Brady, or will Cam Brady prevail and go on to yet another term?

To Recommend More Movies

- ❖ *White House Down* (2013)
- ❖ *Fahrenheit 9/11* (2004)
- ❖ *Crash* (2004)
- ❖ *Broken City* (2013)
- ❖ *Argo* (2012)

Unit Four Economy

Pre-reading Activities

Answer the following questions before you read this text.

1. What is the dominant position of American economy?
2. How much do you know about American economy?
3. Can you list the top 10 businesses in America?

TEXT A Economy of America

The United States entered the 21st century with an economy that was bigger, and by many measures more successful, than ever. Though the United States held less than 5 percent of the world's population, it **accounted for** more than 25 percent of the world's economic output. In the 1990s, the American economy recorded the longest **uninterrupted** period of expansion in its history. A wave of technological **innovations** in computing, **telecommunications**, and the biological sciences were **profoundly** affecting how Americans work and play.

The United States remains a "market economy". Americans continue to believe that an economy generally operates best when decisions about what to produce and what prices to **charge for** goods are made through the **give-and-take** of millions of independent buyers and sellers, not by government or by powerful private interests.

Besides believing that free markets promote economic efficiency, Americans **see** them **as** a way of promoting their political values as well—especially, their **commitment to** individual freedom and political **pluralism** and their opposition to **undue** concentrations of power. The American belief in "free enterprise" has not **precluded** a major role for government, however. Americans **at times** have **looked**

to government to break up or **regulate** companies. That appeared to be developing so much power that they could **defy** market forces. They have **relied on** government to address matters the private economy overlooks, from education to protecting the environment. And despite their **advocacy** of market principles, they have used government at times to **nurture** new industries, and at times even to protect American companies from competition.

THE BUSINESS OF AMERICA

Agriculture, mass production, the labor movement, and the economic system "The business of America," President **Calvin Coolidge** said in 1925, "is business". This **formulation** is actually **cannier** than it may appear. **Substitute "preoccupation"** for the first "business", and you have a **capsule** summary of the **entrepreneurial** spirit behind America's prosperity. This chapter examines agriculture, the first American industry; the American style of mass production; the labor movement; and the nation's economic system.

A NATION OF FARMERS

Agriculture in the United States has changed **dramatically** over the last 200 years. At the time of the **American Revolution** (1775 – 83), 95 percent of the population **was engaged in** farming. Today that figure is less than 2 percent. Although individuals or families own 85 percent of all farms in the United States, they own only 64 percent of the farmland. The remainder is owned by corporations, large and small, and farming and its related industries have become big business-"**agribusiness**". Yet for all the changes, agriculture is a constant in American life, and the food produced is safe, **abundant**, and **affordable**.

Early in American history, farmers **set the tone** for the rest of the nation. Farmers have never been as **self-sufficient** as myth would have it, dependent as they are on the **uncertainties** of weather and the marketplace. **Nonetheless**, they have exhibited an individualism and an **egalitarianism** admired and **emulated** by the rest of society.

As settlement advanced from east to west, U. S. agriculture attained a richness and variety **unmatched** in most other parts of the world. This is true still today, in large part **owing to** the quantity of land and the generosity of nature. Only in a relatively small portion of the western United States is rainfall so limited that deserts exist. Elsewhere, rainfall **ranges from** modest **to** abundant, and rivers and underground water allow for **irrigation** where needed. Large stretches of level or gently rolling land, especially in the Midwest, provide ideal conditions for large-scale agriculture.

In most sections of the United States, land was too abundant and labor too scarce for the English system—in which a landed **gentry** owned vast estates and most farmers were **tenants**—to take hold. North American agriculture came to be based on **a multitude of** family farms. Moreover, these farms tended to be **scattered** and isolated, **rather than clustered around** villages, thus **enhancing** the farmer's individualism and **self-reliance**.

Readiness to **embrace** new technology has been characteristic of American farmers, and throughout the 19th century one new tool or invention followed another in rapid **succession**. For example, the **scythe** and **cradle** replaced the **sickle** for harvesting grain, then **gave way to** Cyrus McCormick's mechanical reaper in the 1830s. By the time of the American Civil War (1861 – 65), machines were taking over the work of **haying**, **threshing**, **mowing**, **cultivating**, and planting—and, in doing so, **spurring** big increases in productivity.

Another factor in the rise of agricultural output was the rapid flow of settlers across the Mississippi River in the late 19th century. The federal government promoted the internal migration in several ways, including the **Homestead Act**. **Enacted** in 1862, the act **perpetuated** the existing pattern of small family farms by offering a "**homestead**" of 65 hectares to each family of settlers for a **nominal** fee.

For a time inventions and pro-farming policies were almost too successful. Overproduction became a serious problem after the Civil War. With demand unable to **keep pace with** supply, the prices farmers received for their products fell. The years from the 1870s until about 1900 were especially hard for the American farmer.

(Words: 856)

New Words

uninterrupted	*adj.* 不间断的；连续的
innovation	*n.* 创新，革新；新方法
telecommunication	*n.* 电讯；［通信］远程通信；无线电通讯
profoundly	*adv.* 深刻地；深深地；极度地
pluralism	*n.* 多元主义；多元论
undue	*adj.* 过度的，过分的；不适当的
preclude	*vt.* 排除；妨碍；阻止
regulate	*vt.* 调节，规定；控制；管理；校准
defy	*n.* 挑战；对抗 *vt.* 藐视；公然反抗；挑衅
advocacy	*n.* 主张；拥护；辩护
nurture	*n.* 养育；教养；营养物 *vt.* 养育；鼓励；培植；熏陶
formulation	*n.* 构想，规划；公式化；简洁陈述
canny	*adj.* 精明的，谨慎的；节约的
substitute	*n.* 代用品；代替者 *vt.* 代替 *vi.* 替代
preoccupation	*n.* 全神贯注，入神；当务之急；关注的事物
capsule	*adj.* 压缩的；概要的 *n.* 胶囊 *vt.* 压缩；简述
entrepreneurial	*adj.* 企业家的；创业者的
dramatically	*adv.* 戏剧地；引人注目地
agribusiness	*n.* 农业综合企业
abundant	*adj.* 丰富的；充裕的；盛产的
affordable	*adj.* 负担得起的
uncertainty	*n.* 不确定；不可靠

续表

nonetheless	*adv.* 尽管如此；但是；然而
egalitarianism	*n.* 平等主义；平均主义
emulate	*n.* 仿真；仿效 *vt.* 仿真；模仿
unmatched	*adj.* 无与伦比的；不相配的；无匹敌的
irrigation	*n.* 灌溉；冲洗
gentry	*n.* 人们（多用贬义）；贵族们
tenant	*n.* 承租人；房客；佃户；居住者 *vt.* 租借（常用于被动语态）
scattered	*adj.* 分散的；散乱的
enhance	*vt.* 提高；加强；增加
self - reliance	*n.* 自我依赖
readiness	*n.* 敏捷，迅速；准备就绪
embrace	*n.* 拥抱 *vt.* 拥抱；信奉；包含 *vi.* 拥抱
succession	*n.* 连续；继位；继承权
scythe	*n.* 长柄大镰刀 *vt.* 用大镰刀割
cradle	*n.* 摇篮；发源地；发祥地；支船架 *vt.* 抚育；把…放在摇篮内；把…搁在支架上
sickle	*n.* 镰刀
reaper	*n.* 收割者；收割机；收获者
hay	*n.* 干草 *vt.* 把草晒干 *vi.* 割草晒干
thresh	*n.* 打谷 *vt.* 推敲；打谷；反复做 *vi.* 打；打谷；颠簸

续表

mow	*n.* 草堆；谷堆 *vt.* 割草；收割庄稼 *vi.* 割草；收割庄稼
cultivate	*vt.* 培养；陶冶；耕作
spur	*n.* 鼓舞；刺激；马刺；山坡 *vt.* 激励；鞭策；给…装踢马刺 *vi.* 骑马疾驰；给予刺激
enact	*vt.* 颁布；制定法律；扮演
perpetuate	*adj.* 长存的 *vt.* 使不朽；时永存；保持
homestead	*n.* 宅地；家园；田产
nominal	*n.* ［语］名词性词 *adj.* 名义上的；有名无实的

Phrases & Expressions

account for	对…做出解释；对…负有责任；（比例）占
charge for	索价，要价；为…收费
give-and-take	妥协；互让；意见交换
see…as	把…看作
commitment to	恪守承诺；投入
at times	有时；偶尔
look to	注意；指望；照看
rely on	依靠，依赖
be engaged in	参与；从事于；忙于
set the tone	定调子
self-sufficient	自给自足的；极为自负的；过于自信的
owing to	由于；因为
range from…to	从…到…变动
be based on	根据；以…为基础

续表

a multitude of	大批的；众多的
rather than	而不是；宁可…也不愿
cluster around	簇拥；仅仅环绕；聚集
give way to	给…让路
keep pace with	并驾齐驱；保持同步；跟上

Proper Names

Calvin Coolidge	卡尔文·柯立芝（前美国总统）
American Revolution	美国独立战争
Homestead Act	（美）宅地法

Cultural Notes

1. American Revolution The American Revolution was a political upheaval that took place between 1765 and 1783 during which colonists in the Thirteen American Colonies rejected the British monarchy and aristocracy, overthrew the authority of Great Britain, and founded the United States of America. For more information, visit http://en.wikipedia.org/wiki/American_ Revolution.

2. American Civil War The American Civil War, widely known in the United States as simply the Civil War as well as other sectional names, was a civil war fought from 1861 to 1865 to determine the survival of the Union or independence for the Confederacy. Among the 34 states in January 1861, seven Southern slave states individually declared their secession from the United States and formed the Confederate States of America. The Confederacy, often simply called the South, grew to include eleven states, and although they claimed thirteen states and additional western territories, the Confederacy was never diplomatically recognized by any foreign country. The states that remained loyal and did not declare secession were known as the Union or the North. The war had its origin in the fractious issue of slavery, especially the extension of slavery into the western territories (Territories are organized areas that could potentially become states.). After four years of combat, which left over 600, 000 Union and Confederate soldiers dead and destroyed much of the South's infrastructure, the Confederacy collapsed and slavery was abolished. Then began the Reconstruction and the processes of restoring national unity and guaranteeing civil rights to the freed slaves. For more information, visit http: //en. wikipedia. org/wiki/American_ Civil_ War.

3. Homestead Acts The Homestead Acts were several United States federal laws that gave an applicant ownership of land, typically called "homestead", at little or no cost. In the United States, this originally consisted of grants totaling 160 acres (65 hectares, or one-quarter section) of in appropriated federal land within the boundaries of the public land states. An extension of the Homestead Principle in law, the United States Homestead Acts were initially proposed as an expression of the "Free Soil"policy of Northerners who wanted individual farmers to own and operate their own farms, as opposed to Southern slave-owners who could use groups of slaves to economic advantage. For more information, visit http: // en. wikipedia. org/wiki/Homestead_ Acts.

Exercises

Comprehension of the Text

Ⅰ Answer the following questions according to the passage.

1. How many populations does the United States hold in the world and how much economic output does it account for of the world?

2. What do Americans see as a way of promoting their political values as well besides believing that free markets promote economic efficiency?

3. Who set the tone for the rest of the nation early in American history?

Vocabulary

Ⅱ. Fill in the blanks with the words given below. Change the form where necessary.

uninterrupted	profoundly	regulate	overlook	advocacy
nurture	substitute	dramatically	abundant	nonetheless
stretch	unmatched	enhance	succession	cultivate

1. Not only have we overcome them all, Buffett pointed out, but our standard of living has increased ______—nearly seven fold in the last century.

2. Parents want to know the best way to ________ and raise their child to adulthood.

3. Employing these methods, we ______ our understanding of the data.

4. This film will make every Chinese rethink ______.

5. We must try our best to ______ our expenditure.

6. ______, it has added enormous processing capacity because of the effectiveness of its new hardware and software.

7. There was a dispute about the rightful _________ to the throne.

8. Our country has a vast territory and _________ resources.

9. She is seeking a _______ for the very man whose departure made her cry.

10. To reduce tobacco use, we are now moving from ______ to a scaling up of interventions.

Translations

Ⅲ. Translate the following sentences into English.

1. 如我开始所说的，对于当今卫生领导层来说，分担责任、团结一致以及保证公平和社会公正是最重要的一些品质。(commitment to)

____

2. 如果他们知道自己的努力对公司的影响是多么重要时，他们会以他们从事的工作为自豪。(be engaged in)

____

3. 由于贪污，这个公司的经理已被撤职查办。(owing to)

____

4. 因此，“中产阶级”这个术语涵盖了众多的差异。(a multitude of)

____

5. 俄罗斯的道路是出了名的危险，司机也很少给行人让道。(give way to)

____

Ⅳ. Translate the following passage into English.

失业率减幅在 2015 年下降得可能不会那样的迅速，据经济学家所言，特别是如果更多的人进入劳动力市场由于更容易找到工作。尽管如此，和 2014 年相似的大量招聘和录用将会使低的失业率数据显得更加的可信。Faucher 说：“在 2015 年年底我们的失业率大致会处在 5% 到 5.5% 之间，而且会让我们更加实际地感受到这一点”。

TEXT B Wall Street

(A) Wall Street is a 0.7 – mile-long (1.1 km) street running eight blocks, roughly northwest to southeast, from **Broadway** to South Street on the East River in Lower Manhattan in the financial district of New York City. Over time, the term has become a **metonym** for the financial markets of the United States as a whole, the American financial sector (even if financial firms are not physically located there), or **signifying** New York-based financial interests.

(B) Wall Street is the home of the **New York Stock Exchange**, the world's largest stock exchange by overall average daily **trading volume** and by total market **capitalization** of its listed companies. Several other major exchanges have or had headquarters in the Wall Street area, including **NASDAQ**, the New York Mercantile Exchange, the New York Board of Trade, and the former American Stock Exchange. **Anchored** by Wall Street, New York City has been called the world's principal financial center, only **rivaled** by the City of London & **Canary Wharf** in London.

(C) Finance professor Charles R. Geisst wrote that the exchange has become "**inextricably intertwined** into New York's economy". Wall Street pay, **in terms of** salaries and bonuses and taxes, is an important part of the economy of New York City, the tri-state metropolitan area, and the United States. In 2008, after a

downturn in the stock market, the decline meant $18 billion less in **taxable income,** with less moneyavailable for "apartments, furniture, cars, clothing and services". A **falloff** in Wall Street's economy could have "**wrenching** effects on the local and regional economies".

(D) Estimates vary about the number and quality of financial jobs in the city. One estimate was that Wall Street firms employed close to 200,000 persons in 2008. Another estimate was that in 2007, the financial services industry which had a $70 billion profit became 22 percent of the city's **revenue**. Another estimate(in 2006) was that the financial services industry **makes up** 9% of the city's work force and 31% of the tax base. An additional estimate (2007) from Steve Malanga of the Manhattan Institute was that the securities industry accounts for 4.7 percent of the jobs in New York City but 20.7 percent of its wages, and he estimated there were 175,000 securities-industries jobs in New York (both Wall Street area and midtown) paying an average of $350,000 annually.

(E) Between 1995 and 2005, the sector grew at an annual rate of about 6.6% annually, a respectable rate, but that other financial centers were growing faster. Another estimate (2008) was that Wall Street provided a fourth of all personal income earned in the city, and 10% of New York City's tax revenue. The city's securities industry, **enumerating** 163,400 jobs in August 2013, continues to form the largest segment of the city's financial sector and an important economic engine, accounting in 2012 for 5 percent of private sector jobs in New York City, 8.5 percent (US $3.8 billion) of the city's tax revenue, and 22 percent of the city's total wages, including an average salary of US $360,700.

(F) The seven largest Wall Street firms in the 2000s (decade) were **Bear Stearns**, **JPMorgan Chase**, **Citigroup Incorporated**, **Goldman Sachs**, **Morgan Stanley**, **Merrill Lynch** and **Lehman Brothers**. During the **recession** of 2008-10, many of these firms went out of business or were bought up at fire sale prices by other financial firms. In 2008, Lehman filed for bankruptcy, Bear Stearns was bought by JP Morgan Chase forced by the U.S. government, and Merrill Lynch was bought by Bank of America in a similar **shot-gun** wedding. These failures marked a **catastrophic downsizing** of Wall Street as the financial industry goes through **restructuring** and change. Since New York's financial industry provides almost one-fourth of all income produced in the city, and accounts for 10% of the city's tax revenues and 20% of the state's, the downturn has had huge repercussions for government treasuries.

(G) New York's mayor Michael Bloomberg reportedly over a four-year period **dangled** over $100 million in **tax incentives** to persuade Goldman Sachs to build a 43-story headquarters in the financial district near the destroyed World Trade Center site. In 2009, things looked somewhat gloomy, with one analysis by the Boston Consulting Group suggesting that 65,000 jobs had been permanently lost because of the downturn. But there were signs that Manhattan property prices were **rebounding** with price rises of 9% annually in 2010, and bonuses were being paid once more, with average bonuses over $124,000 in 2010.

(Words: 737)

New Words

metonym	*n.* 换喻中所使用的词或短语
signify	*vt.* 表示；意味；预示 *vi.* 有重要性；要紧；冒充内行
capitalization	*n.* 资本化；资本总额；大写
anchored	*adj.* 固定的；抛锚的 *vt.* 固定；抛锚；主持（anchor 的过去式）
rival	*n.* 对手；竞争者 *adj.* 竞争的 *vt.* 与…竞争；比得上某人 *vi.* 竞争
inextricably	*adv.* 逃不掉地；解不开地；解决不了地
intertwined	*adj.* 缠绕的；错综复杂的
downturn	*n.* 衰退（经济方面）；低迷时期
falloff	*n.* 下降，减少；分开；减退

续表

wrench	*vt.* 扭伤；猛扭 *vi.* 扭伤；猛扭
revenue	*n.* 税收，国家的收益；收入
enumerating	*n.* 枚举
recession	*n.* 衰退；不景气；后退；凹处
shot-gun	*n.* 鸟枪法
catastrophic	*adj.* 灾难的；悲惨的；灾难性的，毁灭性的
downsizing	*n.* 精简，裁员；缩小规模
restructuring	*n.* 调整；改组；重建
dangle	*vt.* 使摇晃地悬挂 *vi.* 摇晃地悬挂着
rebound	*vt.* 使弹回 *vi.* 回升；弹回

Phrases & Expressions

trading volume	交易额
in terms of	依据；按照；在…方面；以…措辞
taxable income	[税收] 应纳税的所得
makes up	组成；补足；化妆；编造
tax incentives	[税收] 捐税鼓励

Proper Names

Broadway	百老汇（美国纽约市戏院集中的一条大街）
New York Stock Exchange	[金融] 纽约证券交易所
NASDAQ	美国纳斯达克
Canary Wharf	金丝雀码头；伦敦金融区
Bear Stearns	贝尔斯登（美国投资银行）
JPMorgan Chase	摩根大通公司
Citigroup Incorporated	花旗集团公司（金融公司，总部设于美国）

续表

Goldman Sachs	高盛投资公司
Morgan Stanley	摩根士丹利投资公司
Merrill Lynch	美林证券公司（财富 500 强公司之一，总部所在地美国，主要经营证券经纪）
Lehman Brothers	雷曼兄弟（美国第四大投资银行，现在已破产）

Cultural Notes

1. New York Stock Exchange The New York Stock Exchange (NYSE), sometimes known as the "Big Board", is an American stock exchange located at 11 Wall Street, Lower Manhattan, New York City, New York. It is by far the world's largest stock exchange by market capitalization of its listed companies at US $19.69 trillion as of May 2015. The average daily trading value was approximately US $169 billion in 2013. For more information, visit http://en.wikipedia.org/wiki/New_York_Stock_Exchange.

2. NASDAQ The NASDAQ Stock Market, commonly known as the NASDAQ (currently stylized as Nasdaq), is an American/Canadian stock exchange. It is the second-largest exchange in the world by market capitalization, behind only the New York Stock Exchange. The exchange platform is owned by The NASDAQ OMX Group, which also owns the OMX stock market network and several other US stock and options exchanges. For more information, visit http://en.wikipedia.org/wiki/NASDAQ.

Exercises

Comprehension of the Text

Ⅰ. The following 10 **statements contain information given in the text. Identify the paragraph from which the information is derived. You may choose a paragraph more than once. Each paragraph is marked with a letter.**

1. Wall Street plays an important role in the United States according to sala-

ries and bonuses and taxes.

2. An estimate in 2008 was that Wall Street provided 25% of all personal income earned in the city, and 10% of New York City's tax revenue.

3. New York's mayor persuaded Goldman Sachs to build a 43 – story headquarters near the destroyed World Trade Center site in the financial district.

4. Wall Street is the world's largest stock exchange with average daily trading volume and total market capitalization of its listed companies.

5. Wall Street firms employed about 200,000 persons in 2008 according to one estimate.

6. The securities industry in New City continues to form the largest segment of the city's financial sector in 2013.

7. These failures, such as Lehmans' bankruptcy, Bear Stearns bought by JP Morgan Chase and so on, marked a catastrophic downsizing of Wall Street as the financial industry goes through restructuring and change in 2008.

8. Wall Street has become a metonym of the financial markets and the American financial sector in the United States as a whole.

9. In 2008, the United States has a decline in taxable income because of the downturn in the stock market.

10. New York City has been called the world's principal financial center, only rivaled by the City of London & Canary Wharf in London.

Vocabulary

Ⅱ. Fill in the blanks with the words given below. Change the form where necessary.

signify	capitalization	anchored	rival	inextricably
intertwined	downturn	wrench	revenue	recession
catastrophic	restructuring	repercussion	dangle	rebound

1. When your ______ is your enemy, you should first of all get to understand him.

2. We want to develop as many treatments as we can, and we can only do that if we have ______.

3. You don't have as much time to recover from the market ______, but you're not without options

4. They're ______ like balls of loose twine.

5. Economists at Goldman Sachs believe that mainland China's market ____ will rise to $41 trillion by 2030 from $5 trillion now.

6. Love has various lodgings; the same word does not always ______ the same thing.

7. He insisted negotiations on the aid were "well on track" and that there was "no question about ______" Greek debt.

8. When will the US economy ______ from the collapse of the tech bubble in 2001?

9. As an author, libraries are the place you go to meet your readers, the centre of their community, and to lose this service would be ______.

10. If drinking and smoking seem ______ linked, perhaps it's because in the brain's pleasure centre they actually are.

Further Reading

TEXT C The Recovery of U. S. Economy

WASHINGTON (Market Watch)—The U. S. economy finally got a big jolt of energy in 2014 after the lamest recovery since World War II. And 2015 is shaping up to be an even better year.

Here are five things consumers and investors can count on (probably) in 2015:

The economy will grow 3% for the first time in 10 years.

The U. S. is set to add nearly 3 million jobs in 2014—the biggest increase since 1999. The burst in job creation, expected to continue in 2015, is sure to fuel consumer spending. So, too, will a plunge in gasoline prices that's given households extra cash to spare on other goods and services. See: Americans saved $14 billion as gasoline prices declined in 2014.

The pickup in consumption in turn will entice businesses to hire and invest more to keep up with rising sales. The result: The U. S. is likely to grow more than 3% for the first time since 2005.

Bernard Baumohl, chief global economist of the Economic Outlook Group, said he is even more optimistic. "The next two years could be the best two we have seen in at least a decade, "he said. "There is clearly a lot of evidence the economy is gaining a lot of momentum."

Perhaps the biggest domestic threat to the 3% growth scenario would be a surprisingly swift hike in interest rates, but from all indications a dovish Federal Reserve is unlikely to take aggressive action in 2015.

One of the main shackles on the economy over the past four years has been stagnant wages. Hourly earnings have risen an average of 2% annually—just two-thirds of the long-term U. S. average.

Yet that's finally about to change. With hiring up and unemployment falling, businesses will have to go the extra mile for employees or risk losing sales to competitors because they lack enough staff to boost production.

"Everywhere I go business owners are seeing an increase in demand, "said Gus Faucher, senior economist at PNC Financial Services. "Businesses will have to raise wages to attract or maintain workers."

Businesses are already responding: Job openings in November hit the second highest level in 14 years. In another telltale sign, people are quitting jobs at the fastest rate in five years. Research shows that people who quit one job for another typically do so because they are offered higher pay.

The unemployment rate has plunged over the past three years to 5. 8% from 8. 6%, but almost nobody, including the Federal Reserve, thinks the labor market is really that healthy.

Some 18. 1 million people, for example, want a good full-time job but can't find one, an unusually high number 5 1/2 years into a recovery. And despite a sharp decline in the number of people out of work six months or longer, that figure is still higher than at any time before the 2007 – 09 recession.

The unemployment rate probably won't fall quite as rapidly in 2015, according to economists, especially if more people enter the labor force because jobs are easier to find. Yet another large spate of hiring similar to the gain in 2014 would make the low unemployment rate more believable.

"By the end of next year we will be at the point where the unemployment rate is between 5% and 5.5%, and it will truly feel legitimate," Faucher said.

Inflation (and deflation) won't rear its ugly head Surging oil production—along with slower global growth—has caused the price of petroleum to collapse from more than $100 a barrel last summer to barely $50 a barrel at the end of 2014. The effect has been to reverse an uptick in U. S. inflation earlier in the year.

Perhaps just as important, stable or falling prices will boost the inflation—adjusted pay of U. S. workers and gives them more bang for their buck. "It's an unambiguous positive for household demand," said Neil Dutta, head of economics at Renaissance Macro Research. "People will have more money to spend."

While oil prices may rebound in 2015, they almost certainly won't return to $100 a barrel any time soon, barring a geopolitical crisis in a major petroleum-producing region. So the gift will keep giving this year and further feed an accelerating U. S. recovery.

Faster growth should also dispel worries about another Fed bogeyman: deflation, or falling prices. "It's impossible to have deflation in an economy growing 3% -plus and adding the most jobs since the 1990s," Baumohl said.

The U. S. will perform well even if the rest of the world doesn't.

(Words: 751)

Questions for discussions

1. What do you know the five things consumers and investors can count on in 2015 in US economy?

2. What does it refer to according to the job openings in November hit the second highest level in 14 years in the United States?

3. How will the oil prices keep giving this year and further feed an accelera-

ting American recovery?

More to Learn

1. U. S. Ten Main Financial Groups

Rockefeller Financial Group	洛克菲勒财团
Morgan Financial Group	摩根财团
First National City Bank Financial Group	第一花旗银行财团
Du Pont Financial Group	杜邦财团
Boston Financial Group	波士顿财团
Mellon Financial Group	梅隆财团
Cleveland Financial Group	克利夫兰财团
California Financial Group	加利福尼亚财团
Chicago Financial Group	芝加哥财团
Texas Financial Group	德克萨斯财团

MOVIES TO SEE (A) Wall Street

I. Movie Introduction

Director: Oliver Stone

Starring: Michael Douglas
Charlie Sheen
Daryl Hannah
Martin Sheen

Running time: 126 mins

Released: 1987

Plot: Bud Fox is a Wall Street stockbroker in early 1980's New York with a strong desire to get to the top. Working for his firm during the day, he spends his spare time working on an angle with the high-powered, extremely successful (but ruthless and greedy) broker Gordon Gekko. Fox finally meets with Gekko, who takes the youth under his wing and explains his philosophy that "Greed is Good". Taking the advice and working closely with Gekko, Fox soon finds himself swept into a world of "yuppies", shady business deals, the "good life", fast money, and fast women; something which is at odds with his family including his estranged father and the blue-collared way Fox was brought up.

Ⅱ. Classic Scenes

Task 1 Study the underlined sentences and expressions in the following classic scenes.

1. Bud Fox and His father was in a pub

Bud Fox: Nice to see you're in such a good mood, Dad. Did Mom give you fish for dinner? You smoke too much. How often you gotta go to the hospital to realize?

Dad: Leave me alone. It's the only thing that makes me feel good. Spaghetti! Your mother still makes lousy spaghetti.

Bud Fox: It's pasta now. Spaghetti's out of date.

Dad: So am I. You want a beer? Billie Bring a Molson Lite for the kid!

So. You look like you've grown another inch, but you don't look so hot, Buddy. You're gonna get bags under your eyes.

Bud Fox: Yeah, I had a tough day. Some jerk DK'd me. I gotta cover his loss.

Dad: Speak English.

Bud Fox: DK: Didn't know who I was when the options he bought took a bath. Bastard reneged on me!

Dad: I told you not to get into that racket. You coulda been a doctor or a lawyer. If you'd stayed at Bluestar, you coulda been a supervisor now instead of being a salesman.

Bud Fox: Dad, how many times I gotta tell you I am not a salesman? I'm an account executive. Soon I'm moving into investment banking.

Dad: You ask strangers for money. You're a salesman.

Bud Fox: Dad, it takes time. You gotta build a client list. I can make more money in one year as a broker than in five at this airline.

Dad: I don't get it, kid. You borrow money to go to NYU. First year out, you make 35 grand. You made 50 grand last year, and can't pay off your loans. Where does it go?!

Bud Fox: Dad, 50K does not get you to first base in the Big Apple. I got 40% in taxes, 15 grand for rent. I got school loans, car loans, food, that's three bills a month. I need suits...

Dad: Come back home and live rent free instead of that roach-infected place. $ 50,000! Jesus Christ! The whole world's off its rocker! I make $ 47,000 last year. That's before taxes.

Bud Fox: That's Queens, Dad! A 5% mortgage and you rent the top room. I gotta live in Manhattan to be a player. There is no nobility in poverty any more, Dad. One day you'll be proud of me. You'll see!

Dad: It's yourself you gotta be proud of, Huckleberry. How much you need?

Bud Fox: Can you spare 300? I'll pay you back next month, I promise.

Dad: I don't know if I got that much on me.

Bud Fox: Not in here, please.

Dad: It adds up. 300 here, 200 there. Your brother... I always say money's something you need in case you don't die tomorrow. Right, Carl?

Carl: How you doing?

Bud Fox: How's work treating you?

Dad: Damn mandatory drug test. They're driving us craze. I got flagged for my blood pressure pills. Can you believe that? The good news is we had a meeting with the controller about some union business. Remember the accident last year and the investigation? The FAA is gonna rule it was a manufacturing error in the door-latch mechanism. I knew it. I kept telling them it wasn't maintenance. It's the greedy manufacturers in Cincinati.

Bud Fox: That's great.

Dad: This gets us out from under suspension. We can go for those new routes to Pittsburgh and Boston. We'll compete with the big guys.

Bud Fox: To Bluestar. As your broker, all I can advise is you hold on to that stock.

Dad: What stock? Are you kidding?

Bud Fox: Are you sure about this thing?

Dad: What?

Bud Fox: The FAA announcement.

Dad: Sure, I'm sure. Look at me. You got that mischievous look in your eye, Buddy. You used to smile like that when you were a kid sleeping. It's true. Just like that.

2. In the Office of Mr Gekko

Bud Fox: How do you do, Mr Gekko? I'm Bud Fox.

Mr Gekko: So you say. Nice to meet you. Hope you're intelligent. Where did you get these?

Bud Fox: I got a connection at the airport.

Mr Gekko: So what's on your mind, Kemo Sabe? Why am I listening to you? I gotta monitor my blood pressure, so don't upset me.

Bud Fox: No, no, Sir.

Mr Gekko: In 45 seconds, the microprocessor computers your systolic and diastolic pressure. Got an LCD read-out, cost-effective... Less than one visit to a doctor.

Bud Fox: I just wanna let you know I've read all about you at NYU Business. I think you're a genius. I've always dreamed of one thing and that's to do business with a man like you.

Mr Gekko: What firm you with?

Bud Fox: Jackson Steinem.

Mr Gekko: They're going places. Good junk-bond department. You are the financing on that Jansen investment?

Bud Fox: Yeah. I'm working on some other interesting stuff.

Mr Gekko: Cosmetic company, by any chance? Are you twelfth man on the deal team? Last to know?

Bud Fox: I can't tell you that, Mr Gekko.

Mr Gekko: So what you got for me, Sport?

Bud Fox: Chart breakout on Whitewood-Young Industries. Explosive earnings. A 30% discount from book. Great cash flow. Couple of 5% holders.

Mr Gekko: It's a dog.

Bud Fox: Strong management.

Mr Gekko: It's a dog, pal. What else you got besides connections at the airport?......What else you got?

Bud Fox: Terafly. Analysts don't like it. I do. The break-up value is twice the market price. This deal finances itself. You sell off two divisions......

Mr Gekko: Not bad for a quant, but that's a dog with different fleas. Come on, pal. Tell me something I don't know. It's my birthday. Surprise me.

Bud Fox: Blue star.

Mr Gekko: What?

Bud Fox: Bluestar Airlines.

Mr Gekko: Rings bell somewhere. So what?

Bud Fox: It's a comer. So medium-body jets. 300 pilots. Flies to Florida, Canada, uh, Northeast, the Caribbean. Great slots in major cities.

Mr Gekko: I don't like airlines. Lousy unions.

Bud Fox: Well, there was a crash last year. They just got a favorable ruling on a lawsuit. Even the plaintiffs don't know about it.

Mr Gekko: Well, how do you know about it?

Bud Fox: I just know. The decision should clear the way for new planes and routes. There's only a small float. You should grab it. Good for a five-point pop.

......

Mr Gekko: Interesting. Got a card?

Bud Fox: Home number's on the back.

Mr Gekko: Bud Fox, I look at a hundred deals a day. I choose one.

Bud Fox: I hope to hear from you, sir.

Mr Gekko: Thanks for the cigars.

3. Mr Gekko's speech in the conference of the Stockholders in Teldar Paper

Well, I appreciate the opportunity you're giving me, Mr Cromwell... as the single largest shareholder in Teldar Paper, to speak. We are not here to indulge in fantasy, but in political and economic reality. America... America has become a second-rate power. Its trade deficit and its fiscal deficit are at nightmare proportions. In the days of the free market, when our country was a top industrial power there was accountability to the stockholder. The Carnegies, the Mellons, the men that built this great empire, made sure of it because it was their money at stake. Today, management has no stake in the company! All together, these men sitting up here own less than 3% of the company. And where does Mr Cromwell put his $ 1,000,000 salary? Not in Teldar stock. He owns less than 1%. You own the company. That's right, you, the stockholder. And you are all being royally screwed over by these bureaucracy with their steak lunches, their fishing trips, their corporate jets and golden parachutes. ......Teldar Paper, Mr Cromwell, has 33 different vice presidents, each earning over $ 200,000 a year. Now, I have spent the last two months analyzing what all these guys do. And I still can't figure it out. One thing I do know is that our paper company lost $ 110m last year. And I'll bet half of that was spent in all the paperwork between all these vice presidents. The new law of evolution in corporate America seems to be...survival of unfit test. Well, in my book you either do it right, or you get eliminated. In the last seven deals that I have been involved with there were 2.5m stockholders who have made a pre-tax profit of $ 12 billion. Thank you. I am not a destroyer of companies. I am of liberator of them! The point is, ladies and gentlemen. The greed, for lack of a better word is good. Greed is right. Greed works. Greed clarifies, cuts through and captures the essence of the evolutionary spirit. Greed, in all of its forms greed for life, for money, for love, knowledge has marked the upward surge of mankind. And greed, you mark my words, will not only save Teldar Paper but that other malfunctioning corporation called the USA. Thank you very much.

Task 2 Work in pairs or groups and play the roles in one of your favorite scenes.

Ⅲ. Questions for discussion

1. What are the themes involved in this film?
2. How did you understand the word "greed" according to the film?
3. Can you make a description of Bud Fox?

Ⅳ. Movie Review

Task: Write a movie review on *Wall Street*.

MOVIES TO SEE (B) Pirates of Silicon Valley

Ⅰ. Movie Introduction

Director: Martyn Burke

Starring: Anthony Michael Hall
Noah Wyle
Wanda Christine
Michael Chieffo

Running time: 95 mins

Released: 1999

Plot: *Pirates of Silicon Valley* is a 1999 original TNT film directed by Martyn Burke. It stars Noah Wyle as Steve Jobs and Anthony Michael Hall as Bill Gates. Spanning the years 1971—1997, the film is based on Paul Freiberger and Michael Swaine's book Fire in the Valley: The Making of The Personal Computer. It explores the impact of the rivalry between Jobs (Apple Computer) and Gates (Microsoft) on the development of the personal computer.

To Recommend More Movies

- ❖ *Trading Places* (1983)
- ❖ *The Secret of My Success* (1987)
- ❖ Other People's Money (1991)
- ❖ Barcelona (1994)
- ❖ Jerry Maguire (1996)
- ❖ *Boiler Room* (2000)
- ❖ *The Corporation* (2003)
- ❖ *In Good Company* (2004)

Unit Five Arts

Pre-reading Activities

Answer the following questions before you read this text.

1. Do you enjoy pop music? Can you give a brief introduction to an album that you love?

2. What do you know about Grammy Award, which is usually called the Oscar in the music industry?

3. Who is your favorite pop singer and why?

TEXT A Lady Gaga, a Star Surrounded by Controversy

Stefani Joanne Angelina Germanotta, better known by her stage name Lady Gaga, is an American pop singer and songwriter. Gaga has been influenced by rock artists such as **David Bowie** and **Queen**, as well as pop music artists such as **Madonna**, **Britney Spears** and **Michael Jackson**. The Queen's song "Radio Ga Ga" inspired her stage name, "Lady Gaga." She commented: "I **adored Freddie Mercury** and Queen had a hit called *Radio Ga Ga*. That's why I love the name…Freddie was unique—one of the biggest personalities in the whole of pop music." **In response to** the comparisons between herself and Madonna, Gaga stated: "I don't want to sound **presumptuous**, but I've made it my goal to revolutionize pop music. The last revolution was launched by Madonna 25 years ago."

Gaga has a vocal range of a **contralto**. Her vocals have drawn frequent comparison to those of Madonna and **Gwen Stefani**, while the structure of her music is said to **echo** classic 1980s pop and 1990s Euro pop. While reviewing her **debut** album *The Fame*, *The Sunday* Times asserted: "In combining music, fashion, art and technology, Gaga **evokes** Madonna, Gwen Stefani." Similarly, The Boston Globe commented that she draws "obvious inspirations from Madonna to Gwen Stefani…in her girlish but **sturdy** pipes and **bubbly** beats." Though her **lyrics** are said to lack intellectual stimulation, "she does manage to get you moving and **grooving** at an almost effortless pace." Music critic Simon Reynolds wrote.

Gaga has identified fashion as a major influence. She considers **Donatella Versace** her **muse**. Gaga has her own creative production team which she handles personally. The team creates many of her clothes, stage **props**, and **hairdos**. "When I'm writing music, I'm thinking about the clothes I want to wear on stage. It's all about everything altogether—performance art, pop performance art, and fashion. For me, it's everything coming together and being a real story that will bring back the super-fan. I want the imagery to be so strong that fans will want to taste and lick every part of it." Gaga's **outre ensembles** brought performance art into mainstream.

Critical reception of Gaga's music, fashion sense and **persona** are mixed. Her status as a role model, **trailblazer** and fashion icon is **by turns** affirmed and denied. Gaga's albums have received mostly positive reviews, with critics pointing out her unique place in pop music. Her role as a self-esteem **booster** for her fans is also **lauded**, as is her role in **breathing** life **into** the fashion industry. Her performances are described as "highly entertaining and innovative"; in particular, the **blood-spurting** performance of "*Paparazzi*" at the 2009 **MTV Video Music Awards** was described as "eye-popping" by MTV. She continued the "blood soaked" theme in *The Monster Ball Tour*, in which she wears a **revealing** leather **corset** and is "attacked" by a performer dressed in black who **gnaws** on her throat, causing "blood" to spurt down her chest, after which she lies "dying" in a pool of blood. Her performances of that scene in Manchester, England, **triggered** protests from family groups **in the aftermath of** a local tragedy, in which a taxi driver had murdered 12 people. "What happened in Bradford is very fresh in people's minds and given all the violence which happened in Cumbria just hours earlier, it was insensitive," said Lynn Costello of Mothers Against Violence. Chris Rock later defended her **flamboyant**, **pro-**

vocative behavior. "Well, she's Lady Gaga," he said, "She's not 'Lady Behave Yourself.' Do you want great behavior from a person named Gaga? Is this what you were expecting?" She later returned to the 2010 MTV Video Music Awards wearing a dress **supplemented** by boots, a purse and a hat—each **fabricated** from the flesh of a dead animal. The dress, named by *Time* magazine's Fashion Statement of 2010 and more widely known as the "meat dress", was made by an Argentinean designer and received divided opinions—evoking the attention of worldwide media but **invoking** the **fury** of animal rights organizations. Gaga, however, later denied any intention of causing disrespect to any person or organization and wished for the dress to be interpreted as a statement of human rights.

Contrary to her outre style, *The New York Post* described her early look as like "refugee from **Jersey Shore**" with "big black hair, heavy eye makeup and tight, revealing clothes." Towards the end of 2008, comparisons were made between the fashions of Gaga and fellow recording artist **Christina Aguilera** that noted similarities in their styling, hair, and make-up. Aguilera stated that she was "completely unaware of Gaga" and "didn't know if it was a man or a woman." Gaga released a statement in which she welcomed the comparisons due to the attention providing useful publicity, saying, "She's such a huge star and if anything I should send her flowers, because a lot of people in America didn't know who I was until that whole thing happened. It really **put** me **on the map** in a way."

Besides her career in music, Gaga has enhanced her reputation as a **philanthropist** who has contributed to various charities and **humanitarian** works. Gaga held a concert of *The Monster Ball Tour* following the 2010 Haiti earthquake and dedicated it to the country's reconstruction relief fund. This concert donated any received revenue to the relief fund while, in addition, all profits from sales of products on Gaga's official online store were donated. After the earthquake and **tsunami** hit Japan on March 11, 2011, Gaga designed a bracelet, of which, all of the money generated went to Japanese relief efforts.

In view of Lady Gaga's influence on modern culture and her rise to global fame, sociologist of the University of South Carolina since the Spring of 2011 organizes a course titled "Lady Gaga and the Sociology of the Fame" **with the objective of unraveling** "sociologically relevant **dimensions** of the fame of Lady Gaga **with respect to** her music, videos, fashion, and other artistic endeavors".

(Words: 1095)

New Words

adore	*vt.* 敬爱；崇拜
presumptuous	*adj.* 自以为是的，冒失的
contralto	*n.* 女低音
echo	*vt.* 与……相似
debut	*n.* （表演者或运动员的）首次登台，初次露面；（歌手的）首次录音
evoke	*vt.* 唤起，引起
sturdy	*adj.* 结实的，强壮的
bubbly	*adj.* 气泡的；兴奋的
lyric	*n.* 歌词
groove	*vi.* 跟着音乐节奏跳舞
muse	*n.* （给画家、诗人或音乐家带来灵感的）女神，创作女神
prop	*n.* 演出道具
hairdo	*n.* （女子的）发式，发型
outre	*adj.* 奇特的，怪异的
ensemble	*n.* 全套服装
persona	*n.* 人物角色，伪装的外表
trailblazer	*n.* 先驱，创始人
booster	*n.* 有正面效果的事物；起推动作用的事物
laud	*vt.* 称赞，赞扬
blood-spurting	*adj.* 喷血的
revealing	*adj.* 透露真情的；袒胸露肩的
corset	*n.* （妇女为衬托身体的）紧身胸衣

续表

gnaw	*vt.* 咬，啃
trigger	*vt.* 引发，引起
flamboyant	*adj.* 引人注目的，炫耀的，时髦的
provocative	*adj.* 挑衅的，煽动的
supplement	*vt.* 增补，补充
fabricate	*vt.* 制造，制作
invoke	*vt.* 引起，唤起，激发（感情或景象）
fury	*n.* 狂怒，暴怒
philanthropist	*n.* 慈善家
humanitarian	*adj.* 人道主义的，博爱的
tsunami	*n.* 海啸
unravel	*vt.* 揭开，揭示
dimension	*n.* 方面，特征

Phrases & Expressions

in response to	对……做出反应
by turns	轮流地，交替地
breathe…into…	将（生气、信心或兴奋）注入；为…带来
in the aftermath of…	……的后果，余波是……
contrary to…	与……相反
put somebody on the map	使某人出名，使负盛名
in view of…	鉴于……，基于……
with the objective of…	以……为目标
with respect to…	关于……，谈到……

Proper Names

Stefani Joanne Angelina Germanotta	斯蒂芬妮·乔安妮·安吉丽娜·杰尔马诺塔
David Bowie	大卫·鲍伊

续表

Queen	皇后乐队
Madonna	麦当娜
Britney Spears	"小甜甜" 布兰妮·斯皮尔斯
Michael Jackson	迈克尔·杰克逊
Freddie Mercury	弗雷迪·莫库里
Gwen Stefani	格温·史蒂芬尼
Donatella Versace	多那泰拉·范思哲
MTV Video Music Awards	美国 MTV 音乐电视大奖
Jersey Shore	泽西海滩
Christina Aguilera	克里斯蒂娜·阿奎莱拉

Cultural Notes

1. Stefani Joanne Angelina Germanotta Stefani Joanne Angelina Germanotta, known professionally as Lady Gaga, is an American singer, songwriter, actress and record producer. For more information, visit https://en.wikipedia.org/wiki/Lady_ Gaga.

2. David Bowie David Bowie was an English singer, songwriter and actor. He was a figure in popular music for over five decades, regarded by critics and musicians as an innovator, particularly for his work in the 1970s. For more information, visit https://en.wikipedia.org/wiki/David_ Bowie.

3. Queen Queen are a British rock band that formed in London in 1970. Their classic line-up was Freddie Mercury (lead vocals, piano), Brian May (lead guitar, vocals), Roger Taylor (drums, vocals), and John Deacon (bass guitar). Queen's earliest works were influenced by progressive rock, hard rock and heavy metal, but the band gradually ventured into more conventional and radio-friendly works by incorporating further styles, such as arena rock and pop rock, into their music. For more information, visit https://en.wikipedia.org/wiki/Queen_ (band).

4. Madonna Madonna Louise Ciccone is an American singer, songwriter, actress, and businesswoman. She achieved popularity by pushing the boundaries of lyrical content in mainstream popular music and imagery in her music videos, which became a fixture on MTV. Madonna is known for reinventing both her music and image, and for maintaining her autonomy within the recording industry. For more information, visit https://en.wikipedia.org/wiki/Madonna_(entertainer).

5. Britney Spears Britney Jean Spears (born December 2, 1981) is an American singer, dancer and actress. For more information, visit https://en.wikipedia.org/wiki/Britney_Spears.

6. Michael Jackson Michael Joseph Jackson (August 29, 1958-June 25, 2009) was an American singer, songwriter, record producer, dancer, actor, and philanthropist. Called the "King of Pop", his contributions to music, dance, and fashion along with his publicized personal life made him a global figure in popular culture for over four decades. For more information, visit https://en.wikipedia.org/wiki/Michael_Jackson.

7. Freddie Mercury Freddie Mercury (born Farrokh Bulsara; 5 September 1946 – 24 November 1991) was a British singer, songwriter and record producer, known as the lead vocalist and co-principal songwriter of the rock band Queen. He also became known for his flamboyant stage persona and four-octave vocal range. For more information, visit https://en.wikipedia.org/wiki/Freddie_Mercury.

8. Gwen Stefani Gwen Renée Stefani (born October 3, 1969) is an American singer, songwriter, and fashion designer. For more information, visit https://en.wikipedia.org/wiki/Gwen_Stefani.

9. Donatella Versace Donatella Francesca Versace (born 2 May 1955) is an Italian fashion designer and current vice president of the Versace Group, as well as its chief designer. For more information, visit https://en.wikipedia.org/wiki/Donatella_Versace.

10. MTV Video Music Awards An MTV Video Music Award (commonly abbreviated as a VMA) is an award presented by the cable channel MTV to honor the best in the music video medium. Originally conceived as an alternative to the Grammy Awards (in the video category), the annual MTV Video Music Awards ceremony has often been called the "Super Bowl for youth", an acknowledgment of the VMA ceremony's ability to draw millions of youth from teens to 20-somethings each year. For more information, visit https://en.wikipedia.org/wiki/MTV_Video_Music_Award.

11. Jersey Shore The Jersey Shore is the coastal region of the state of New Jersey. Famous for its many boardwalks with arcades, water parks, and amusement parks boasting hundreds of rides and attractions, the Jersey Shore is a popular vacation spot for New Jerseyans, New Yorkers, and Pennsylvanians, and various other states in the Northeastern United States. Certain communities are also popular with visitors from the nearby Canadian provinces of Québec and Ontario. For more information, visit https://en.wikipedia.org/wiki/Jersey_Shore.

12. Christina Aguilera Christina María Aguilera (born December 18, 1980) is an American singer, songwriter, actress and television personality. For more information, visit https://en.wikipedia.org/wiki/Christina_Aguilera.

Exercises

Comprehension of the Text

I Answer the following questions according to the passage.

1. What do you think of the role of fashion in pop music?

2. What is the controversy on Gaga's performance?

3. How do ordinary people evaluate an entertainer like Lady Gaga in an objective and unbiased manner?

Vocabulary

II. Fill in the blanks with the words given below. Change the form where necessary.

adore	echo	muse	bubbly	sturdy
booster	laud	revealing	trigger	debut
provocative	supplement	fabricate	philanthropist	unravel

1. Provide them with additional background or with ________ information.

2. The group's ______ album was immediately acclaimed a hip hop classic.

3. The thieves must have deliberately ________ the alarm and hidden inside the house.

4. The new law is expected to encourage more __________, by better-regulated charitable organizations, and establish more trusted methods of fund-raising for the public, especially online.

5. The destruction of the mosque has ______ anger throughout the Muslim world.

6. For example, social contact can ______ development of the brain and immune system, leading to better health and less chance of depression later in life.

7. Before the bridge opened, 20 volunteers were given the chance to swing sledgehammers at the glass bottom to test its ______. It withstood the pounding.

8. Once she was a nude model and ________ to French artist Henri Matisse.

9. When the development ________ burst, federal regulators started probing the balance sheets of the biggest banks.

10. Outsiders are not allowed to watch Blood Shehuo performers get ready and the inheritors of Blood Shehuo are not allowed to ______ the secrets of their preparation to others.

Translations

Ⅲ. Translate the following sentences into English.

1. 应美国的要求召开了这次会议。(in response to)

____

2. 一些餐厅修改菜谱为经典的英国菜注入新活力，而另一些餐厅使用更高质量的食材保持了英国菜的传统口味。(breathe…into…)

____

3. 飓风的后果是许多人的房屋被毁。(in the aftermath of…)

____

4. 与通常的看法相反，适度的运动事实上会降低食欲。(contrary to…)

____

5. 基于目前这种情况，我们不得不修改原来的计划。(in view of…)

____

Ⅳ. Translate the following passage into English.

1892 年，柴可夫斯基的《胡桃夹子》在圣彼得堡的第一场演出是个大失败。演出第二天，一位评论家这么写道：“要说舞蹈家，剧中根本没有什么舞蹈家；要说艺术，绝对没有；要说我们芭蕾艺术的命运呢，那是又下了一个台阶。”直到 20 年之后才有人尝试再把这部舞剧搬上舞台。一个世纪之后，《胡桃夹子》在美国成为高雅艺术中唯一一部最赚钱的作品，并被美国人看作是自己国家的产物。1996 年，美国有 2 万多名舞蹈演员参与了该舞剧约 2400 场的演出，票房总收入将近 5000 万美元。尽管这部舞剧广受欢迎，却没有多少美国人了解它的历史——或者说没有多少人知道它从原来的形式变成现在这样子的兴衰沉浮的命运。

TEXT B Guggenheim Museum, USA

(A) In 1932, New York's **Museum of Modern Art** assembled what was clearly meant to be a **definitive** exhibition of modern architecture. It presented the work of **Frank Lloyd Wright** along with that of **Le Corbusier**, **Ludwig Mies van der Rohe**, and **Walter Gropius**, two leaders of Germany's revolutionary design school, the **Bauhaus**. On that occasion, Wright commented, "I warn you that having made an excellent start, I fully intend not only to be the greatest architect that has ever been but also the greatest of all future architects."

(B) Wright's pride in his own work was understandable. When his three coexhibitors were still in grade school, he was already designing remarkably innovative houses, any one of which could have established him as first among **contemporary** architects. With the help of devoted assistants, Wright had created dozens of these houses, year after year. By 1932, Wright's work had become highly **individualistic**—often with hints of **expressionism** that would surface in his design for the **Guggenheim Museum**.

(C) Frank Lloyd Wright's childhood had been shaped by a **New England** heritage of liberal **Protestantism** and an acceptance of the "natural philosophy" that was expressed in the writings of **Walt Whitman** and **Henry David Thoreau**. These two American writers believed that much of modern human **anguish** was due to urban environments and loss of contact with nature. The human foot had been made to touch earth, not concrete, and human dwellings were meant to be **in harmony with** their natural surroundings. In the spirited and energetic atmosphere of the times, it is perhaps not surprising that Wright also developed that **insistence** upon absolute freedom of mind that marks the true pioneer as well as the **renowned** artist. This is why he so often seemed more concerned with finding the proper form for an idea than with pleasing his clients. To Wright, the artistic **integrity** of his work was far more important than its practical function. Once, when the owner of one of his houses called to say that rain was **dripping** on him from a crack in the ceiling, Wright is said to have suggested that the man move his chair.

(D) Both Wright's genius and **obstinacy** came to **play their role in** his design for the Guggenheim Museum in New York City. In the early 1940s, **Solomon R. Guggenheim**, who was committed to the development of modern painting, found himself in need of more space to house a growing collection of pictures. He decided that a museum of modern art ought to be the work of a leading modern architect. Ironically, he turned to Wright, a man known to **have little liking for** twentieth-century painting, and **commissioned** him to design the new museum. Wright's creation is one of the most original buildings in the world, a museum with its own place in the history of art. Yet as a picture gallery, it is a failure. Ultimately, the only thing it displays well is itself.

(E) Perhaps at the time that the plans for the Guggenheim were being drawn up, the administrators of the museum were unaware of Wright's growing **rejection** of **conventional** square and rectangular forms of city buildings and blocks. Wright was continually searching for natural forms appropriate to human needs, forms that he described as "organic architecture, opening onto the world rather than **insulating** people from it." So he had begun to explore the possibilities of the triangle, the **polygon** (recalling the form of mineral crystals), and even the circle. For some time, he had been ready to take the logical step from the circle to the **spiral**, the form of **conch** shells, "plastic and continuous." This form is more properly called a **helix**, and is really a circle carried to the third dimension. Wright **boldly** designed the new building in the shape of an inverted conical spiral, and convinced Solomon Guggenheim that this form would make a magnificent museum.

(F) The museum is essentially a long **ramp** that starts at ground level and spirals upward in five **concentric** turns, continually growing wider so that it opens out toward the top. Within the spiral is a vast central space, **illuminated** primarily by a huge skylight. At the first-floor level, the main spiral is joined with a smaller, round building, used for readings, lectures, and offices. A broad horizontal **rectilinear** base connects both elements and also relates the museum as a whole to its rectilinear environment of city blocks and conventional buildings.

(G) **In defense of** his **stunningly** original design, Wright declared that he was not merely playing a game with forms. He believed that the helix was really the best shape for a picture gallery. He claimed that the conventional manner of displaying paintings in one **dreary** room after another distracts the attention of visitors by making them concerned with the condition of their feet rather than the masterpieces on the walls. According to Wright, this museum **fatigue** was the result of bad architecture. At the Guggenheim, visitors would enter on the ground floor and be carried by elevator up to the top, where they would begin to slowly wind down along the spiral. Any **weariness** would be **counteracted** by the natural form of the shell, which would gently "spiral" visitors down to the first floor. As they descended, they would be able to study the paintings hung along the outward-leaning walls. In this way, each work of art would be viewed at an angle—as Wright believed the artist himself had seen it on the **easel**. But in reality, the museum is a challenge. Visitors must make their way down a ramp at an angle, studying paintings hung on a wall that both **curves** and **slopes**.

(H) As a building, however, the Guggenheim Museum defines a magnificent space and has become a **compulsory** stop on even the most basic tour of New York. The **startling** effect of the Guggenheim lies in its unusual form and **stark** simplicity. While it was under construction—and remaining upright in apparent **defiance** of gravity—Wright would **smirk** happily and say of his colleagues, "They'll spend years trying to work it out."

(Words: 1051)

New Words

definitive	*adj.* （书籍或表演）最佳的，最具权威的
contemporary	*adj.* 同时期的，同时代的
individualistic	*adj.* 强调个人独特性的，奉行个人主义的
expressionism	*n.* （艺术、文学或音乐的）表现主义
Protestantism	*n.* 新教；新教教义
anguish	*n.* 痛苦；苦恼
insistence	*n.* 坚持；坚决要求；坚称
renowned	*adj.* 有名的；有声望的
integrity	*n.* 完整；完全；完善
drip	*vi.* （液体）滴出，滴下
obstinacy	*n.* 顽固；顽强
commission	*vt.* 委任，授予
rejection	*n.* 拒绝；摒弃
conventional	*adj.* （行为、观念等）传统的，符合习俗的
insulate	*vt.* 将…隔离（以免受外界影响）
polygon	*n.* 多边形，多角形
spiral	*n.* 螺旋（形）
conch	*n.* 贝壳，海螺壳
helix	*n.* 螺旋形，螺旋体
boldly	*adv.* 大胆地，显眼地
ramp	*n.* 斜面；斜坡；坡面
concentric	*adj.* （圆等）同心的
illuminate	*vt.* 照亮，照明
rectilinear	*adj.* 直线的，形成直线的
stunningly	*adv.* 绝妙地，极好地；令人震惊地
dreary	*adj.* 沉闷的，枯燥无味的；令人沮丧的

续表

fatigue	*n.* 疲劳，疲乏
weariness	*n.* 疲倦；困乏；消沉；厌倦
counteract	*vt.* 抵消；阻碍；中和
easel	*n.* 画架
curve	*vi.* 弯曲；弯成曲线
slope	*vi.* 倾斜；有斜度
compulsory	*adj.* 强制性的，强迫的；义务的
startling	*adj.* 令人吃惊的
stark	*adj.* （对比）鲜明的；光秃的；简易的；荒凉的
defiance	*n.* 无视，不顾（规定、法律等）
smirk	*vi.* 傻笑；假笑着说

Phrases & Expressions

in harmony with…	与……相协调，与……相一致
play one's role in…	在……中发挥作用
have little liking for…	对……不太喜欢
in defense of…	为……辩护，为保护……

Proper Names

Museum of Modern Art	纽约现代艺术博物馆
Frank Lloyd Wright	弗朗克·洛德·莱特
Le Corbusier	勒·科尔比西埃
Ludwig Mies van der Rohe	德维希·密斯·凡德罗
Walter Gropius	格罗·皮乌斯
Bauhaus	包豪斯建筑学派
Guggenheim Museum	古根海姆博物馆
New England	新英格兰地区

续表

Walt Whitman	沃尔特·惠特曼
Henry David Thoreau	亨利·大卫·梭罗
Solomon R. Guggenheim	所罗门·R·古根汉姆

Cultural Notes

1. Museum of Modern Art The Museum of Modern Art (MoMA) is an art museum located in Midtown Manhattan in New York City, on 53rd Street between Fifth and Sixth Avenues. MoMA has been important in developing and collecting modernist art, and is often identified as one of the largest and most influential museums of modern art in the world. MoMA's collection offers an overview of modern and contemporary art, including works of architecture and design, drawing, painting, sculpture, photography, prints, illustrated books and artist's books, film, and electronic media. For more information, visit https://en.wikipedia.org/wiki/Museum_of_Modern_Art.

2. Frank Lloyd Wright Frank Lloyd Wright (born Frank Lincoln Wright, June 8, 1867-April 9, 1959) was an American architect, interior designer, writer, and educator, who designed more than 1,000 structures, 532 of which were completed. Wright believed in designing structures that were in harmony with humanity and its environment, a philosophy he called organic architecture. This philosophy was best exemplified by Fallingwater (1935), which has been called "the best all-time work of American architecture". Wright was a leader of the Prairie School movement of architecture and developed the concept of the Usonian home, his unique vision for urban planning in the United States. His creative period spanned more than 70 years. For more information, visit https://en.wikipedia.org/wiki/Frank_Lloyd_Wright.

3. Le Corbusier Charles-Édouard Jeanneret, known as Le Corbusier (October 6, 1887-August 27, 1965), was a Swiss-French architect, designer, painter, urban planner, writer, and one of the pioneers of what is now called modern architecture. For more information, visit https://en.wikipedia.org/wiki/Le_Corbusier.

4. Ludwig Mies van der Rohe Ludwig Mies van der Rohe (born Maria Ludwig Michael Mies; March 27, 1886-August 17, 1969) was a German-American architect. He is commonly referred to and was addressed as Mies, his surname. Along with Le Corbusier, Walter Gropius and Frank Lloyd Wright, he is widely regarded as one of the pioneers of modernist architecture. For more information, visit https://en.wikipedia.org/wiki/Ludwig_Mies_van_der_Rohe.

5. Walter Gropius Walter Adolph Georg Gropius (18 May 1883-5 July 1969) was a German architect and founder of the Bauhaus School, who, along with Ludwig Mies van der Rohe, Le Corbusier and Frank Lloyd Wright, is widely regarded as one of the pioneering masters of modernist architecture. For more information, visit https://en.wikipedia.org/wiki/Walter_Gropius.

6. Bauhaus Staatliches Bauhaus, commonly known simply as Bauhaus, was a German art school operational from 1919 to 1933 that combined crafts and the fine arts, and was famous for the approach to design that it publicized and taught. For more information, visit https://en.wikipedia.org/wiki/Bauhaus.

7. Guggenheim Museum The Solomon R. Guggenheim Museum, often referred to as The Guggenheim, is an art museum located at 1071 Fifth Avenue on the corner of East 89th Street in the Upper East Side neighborhood of Manhattan, New York City. It is the permanent home of a continuously expanding collection of Impressionist, Post-Impressionist, early Modern and contemporary art and also features special exhibitions throughout the year. For more information, visit https://en.wikipedia.org/wiki/Solomon_R._Guggenheim_Museum.

8. New England New England is a geographical region comprising six states of the northeast United States: Connecticut, Maine, Massachusetts, New Hampshire, Rhode Island, and Vermont. For more information, visit https://en.wikipedia.org/wiki/New_England.

9. Walt Whitman Walter "Walt" Whitman (May 31, 1819-March 26, 1892) was an American poet, essayist, and journalist. A humanist, he was a part of the transition between transcendentalism and realism, incorporating both views in his works. Whitman is among the most influential poets in the American canon, often called the father of free verse. His work was very controversial in its time, particularly his poetry collection *Leaves of Grass*, which was described as obscene for its overt sexuality. For more information, visit https://en.wikipedia.org/wiki/Walt_Whitman.

10. Henry David Thoreau Henry David Thoreau (July 12, 1817-May 6, 1862) was an American essayist, poet, philosopher, abolitionist, naturalist, tax resister, development critic, surveyor, and historian. A leading transcendentalist, Thoreau is best known for his book *Walden*, a reflection upon simple living in natural surroundings, and his essay "*Civil Disobedience*" (originally published as "*Resistance to Civil Government*"), an argument for disobedience to an unjust state. For more information, visit https://en.wikipedia.org/wiki/Henry_David_Thoreau.

11. Solomon R. Guggenheim Solomon Robert Guggenheim (February 2, 1861-November 3, 1949) was an American businessman, art collector and philanthropist. He is best known for establishing the Solomon R. Guggenheim Foundation and the Solomon R. Guggenheim Museum in New York City. For more information, visit https://en.wikipedia.org/wiki/Solomon_R._Guggenheim.

Exercises

Comprehension of the Text

I. The following 10 statements contain information given in the text. Identify the paragraph from which the information is derived. Some paragraphs may be used twice. Each paragraph is marked with a letter.

1. Wright found modernist paintings distasteful and unpleasant.

2. Within the museum, there is room designated for educational purposes such as readings and lectures on the first floor.

3. Wright was complacent with his design, which proved to be a challenging task for construction workers to complete.

4. Wright believed that ineffective building would lead to audience weariness by attracting their attention to the condition of their feet.

5. With the help from his assistants, Wright became a very innovative and productive architect.

6. Once, Wright displayed full confidence in becoming the greatest architect

history had ever produced.

7. Wright's architectural philosophy was significantly influenced by American transcendentalist writers.

8. The museum administrators did not know Wright had strong objection to traditional forms of city buildings.

9. Museum visitors saw it a difficult job to appreciate the paintings on the wall that both curves and slopes while walking down a ramp.

10. To Wright, the realistic purpose of the building was not as important as aesthetic integrity of his design.

Vocabulary

Ⅱ. Fill in the blanks with the words given below. Change the form where necessary.

definitive	individualistic	expressionism	heritage	anguish
insistence	integrity	obstinacy	commission	rejection
insulate	boldly	illuminate	fatigue	compulsory

1. High electricity bills point to a poor heating system or bad ________.

2. For instance, Robertson and colleagues found that males who were more traditionally masculine were more emotionally ________ in a structured exercise than when they were simply asked to talk about their emotions.

3. Besides these symptoms of altitude sickness, others such as headache and ________ may also occur.

4. The British government is expected to ________ the idea of state subsidy for a new high speed railway.

5. My ________ of a good hospice is one where some of the patients start feeling too good to die.

6. I believe no one Chinese language learner escaped being told the story about ________ Yugong who moved the mountains.

7. Five of the company's senior managers have been made ________ redundant.

8. She was in ________ until she knew that her husband's life had been

saved.

9. We ________ the enemy plane with searchlights in order to shoot at it.

10. He is now spearheading efforts to get leaf-blowing included on UNESCO's intangible cultural ________ list.

Further Reading

TEXT C Shirley Temple: Our Little Girl Forever

Shirley Temple, the enchanting singing and dancing child star with glowing corkscrew curls who saved a Hollywood studio and helped yank America from the throes of Great Depression, died, at the age of 85, on February 10, 2014. Temple died of natural causes at her Woodside, California, home surrounded by her family and caregivers.

Making \$1,250 a week at age 6, the incandescent Temple was a veteran of 46 features and one-reelers before she turned 13. A huge star in a pint-sized package, she received an average of 16,000 letters a month, and for one birthday, fans sent her 167,000 presents.

A bigger box-office draw than Clark Gable (another actor with famous dimples), Temple captivated moviegoers with her furrowed brow, perplexed pouts and unrelenting cheeriness in such films as Bright *Eyes* (1934), in which she belted out her signature song, "*On the Good Ship Lollipop.*"

"On the good ship Lollipop, it's a sweet trip to a candy shop. Where bonbons play, on the sunny beach of Peppermint Bay," she sang. The sheet music sold a half-million copies.

With the country still reeling from the Great Depression, President Franklin Roosevelt proclaimed, "As long as our country has Shirley Temple, we will be all right." Her influence extended to lands far away: even foreign dignitaries sent her such gifts as a miniature, drivable Rolls-Royce (from the Aga Khan in the Middle East) and a kid-size jade elephant (from Asia).

The Academy of Motion Picture Arts and Sciences presented Temple at age 6 with the first Juvenile Academy Award "in grateful recognition of her outstanding contribution to screen entertainment during the year 1934. "She is the youngest person ever to receive an Oscar statuette, miniature or otherwise.

Temple appeared in six other features that year, including the musical *Stand Up and Cheer*! She only had a small part in that movie—the plot sees the U. S. government creating a "Department of Amusement"to shake the nation from its Depression doldrums—but the movie quickly made Fox realize what a valuable asset it had on its hands.

On the verge of bankruptcy and tens of millions of dollars in debt, Fox merged with Twentieth Century Pictures in 1935, and studio chief Darryl F. Zanuck made the adorable tot his No. priority. He put the finest talents to work on her pictures, and the Shirley Temple Development Division at one time employed 19 writers.

Four of Temple's most memorable films were released in 1935, including *The Little Colonel*, a Civil War musical drama where she tap-danced with Bill Robinson on a staircase in one of the most enchanting cinematic sequences of all time.

She followed up that year with *Our Little Girl* and *Curly* Top—which introduced another of her songs that became a classic, " Animal Crackers in My Soup"—and *The Littlest Rebel*, in which she and Robinson appeal to President Lincoln for help in another Civil War saga.

A gold mine with glowing locks—her mother Gertrude did her hair for each movie, with 56 corkscrew curls each time—the plucky Temple was No. 1 at the box office for four straight years, from 1935 through 1938. During this stretch, Fox reworked her contract to pay her $50, 000 per film. The studio saw monstrous earnings from Temple's pictures, with the girl endorsing such products as dresses, cereal and soap. Her dolls sold at a rate of 1. 5 million a year. She lost her innocence, or at least her belief in Santa Claus, "when my mother took me to see him in a department store, and he asked for my autograph, "she once said.

In a 1998 interview with *People* magazine, she admitted she didn't realize how famous she was. "I really didn't know it, "she said. "When I asked my mother why crowds shouted my name and said 'We love you,' she would dust it off by saying, 'Your work makes them happy.' She never let it go to my head."

Shirley Jane Temple was born in Santa Monica on April 23, 1928. Her father, George, was a banker, and her mother was a homemaker. She had two older brothers. Her mom claimed that her baby's very first words were a lyric to a Ruby Vallee song, and she enrolled her incredibly bright daughter in dance school.

At age 5, Temple signed with Fox, meteorically ascending from contract player to full-fledged star after *Stand Up and Cheer*! played theaters.

The studio kept its biggest star sheltered in her own bungalow in an effort to preserve her natural childlike charm. "If I lost my innocence," she recalled a studio executive telling her, "it would show in my eyes." Her films were always filled with boundless optimism and an uncanny ability to melt the hardest of hearts.

From 1937 to 1940, she toplined such films as *Heidi, Rebecca of Sunnybrook Farm, Little Miss Broadway, The Little Princess, The Blue Bird and Young People*. Those last two films, though were flops. Soon, Mickey Rooney, another youngster, was king of the box office, and Fox and Temple ended their association in 1940. Her parents placed the 12 – year old Temple in a school for girls, and her last professional affiliation with show business was in the late 1950s and early '60s, when she hosted and sometimes starred in *Shirley Temple's Storybook* and *The Shirley Temple Show* on television.

In 1988, Temple published her best-selling autobiography, *Child Star*, and received Kennedy Center honors. She accepted the Screen Actors Guild's (SAG) Life Achievement Award in 2006 but stayed out of the public eye in her final years.

"When I was 3 years old, I was delighted to be told that I was an actress, even though I didn't know what an actress was," she said to much laughter at the SAG presentation. "I have one piece of advice for those of you who want to receive the Lifetime Achievement Award: Start early!"

(Words: 982)

Questions for discussions

1. Can you name some famous movies starred by Shirley Temple?

2. In your opinion, what made Shirley Temple a child star for American people?

3. Is it always a good thing to gain stardom in an early age?

More to Learn

The Oscar Statuette

The most recognized trophy in the world, the Oscar statuette has stood on the mantels of the greatest filmmakers in history since 1929.

Shortly after the formation of the Academy of Motion Picture Arts and Sciences in 1927, the fledgling organization held a dinner in the Crystal Ballroom of the Biltmore Hotel in downtown Los Angeles to set out its goals. Among the topics discussed that night was how best to honor outstanding moviemaking achievements and thereby encourage excellence in all facets of motion picture production.

Agreeing to institute an annual award, the group turned its attention to creating a suitably majestic trophy. MGM art director Cedric Gibbons designed a statuette of a knight standing on a reel of film gripping a crusader's sword. The Academy tapped Los Angeles sculptor George Stanley to realize the design in three dimensions—and the world renowned statuette was born.

A Knight Called Oscar

Since the initial awards banquet on May 16, 1929, in the Hollywood Roosevelt Hotel's Blossom Room, 2,809 statuettes have been presented. Each January, additional new golden statuettes are cast, molded, polished and buffed by R. S. Owens & Company, the Chicago-based awards manufacturer retained by the Academy since 1982.

Oscar stands 13. 5 inches tall and weighs in at a robust 8. 5 pounds. The film reel features five spokes, signifying the five original branches of the Academy: actors, directors, producers, technicians and writers. Although the statuette remains true to its original design, the size of the base varied until 1945, when the current standard was adopted.

Officially named the Academy Award of Merit, the statuette is better known by its nickname, Oscar. While the origins of the moniker aren't clear, a popular story has it that upon seeing the trophy for the first time, Academy librarian (and eventual executive director) Margaret Herrick remarked that it resembled her Uncle Oscar. The Academy didn't adopt the nickname officially until 1939, but it was widely known enough by 1934 that Hollywood columnist Sidney Skolsky used it in a piece referring to Katherine Hepburn's first Best Actress win.

The Stuff that Dreams Are Made Of

The statuettes presented at the initial ceremonies were gold-plated solid bronze. Within a few years the bronze was abandoned in favor of Britannia metal, a pewter-like alloy which is then plated in copper, nickel silver, and finally, 24 - karat gold. Due to a metal shortage during World War II, Oscars were made of painted plaster for three years. Following the war, the Academy invited recipients to redeem the plaster figures for gold-plated metal ones.

Achievements in up to 25 regular categories were honored on February 26, 2012, at the 84th Academy Awards presentation at the Kodak Theatre at Hollywood & Highland Center. However, the Academy won't know how many statuettes it will hand out until the envelopes are opened on Oscar Night. Although the number of categories is known in advance, the possibility of ties and of multiple recipients sharing the prize in some categories makes it possible to predict the exact number of statuettes to be awarded. As in previous years, any surplus awards will be housed in the Academy's vault until next year's event.

More than 80 years after that auspicious gathering in Hollywood, Oscar's success as a symbol of filmmaking achievement would probably amaze those who attended the dinner, as it would its designer, Cedric Gibbons.

MOVIES TO SEE (A) Mona Lisa Smile

I. Movie Introduction

Director: Mike Newell

Starring: Julia Roberts
Kirsten Dunst
Julia Stiles
Maggie Gyllenhaal
Ginnifer Goodwin

Running time: 117 mins

Released: 2003

Plot: Katherine Ann Watson has accepted a position teaching art history at the prestigious Wellesley College. Watson is a very modern woman, particularly for the 1950s, and has a passion not only for art but for her students. For the most part, the students all seem to be biding their time, waiting to find the right man to marry. The students are all very bright and Watson feels they are not reaching their potential. Although a strong bond is formed between teacher and student, Watson's views are incompatible with the dominant culture of the college. For more information, visit http://www.imdb.com/title/tt0304415/plotsummary.

Ⅱ. Classic Scenes

Task 1 Study the underlined sentences and expressions in the following classic scenes.

1. In Watson's first art history class.

Katherine Watson: This is History of Art 100. We'll be following Dr. Staunton's syllabus. Any questions so far?

Connie Baker: Your name?

Katherine Watson: Why don't you go first?

Connie Baker: Connie Baker.

Katherine Watson: Katherine Watson. Nice to meet you.

Giselle Levy: Dr. Watson, I presume. [the class laughs]

Katherine Watson: Not yet. And you are?

Giselle Levy: Giselle Levy.

Katherine Watson: Giselle. If someone could get the…

Susan Delacorte: Susan Delacorte.

Katherine Watson: Thank you, Susan Delacorte. From the beginning, man has always had the impulse to create art. Can anyone tell me what this?

Joan Brandwyn: "Wounded Bison", Altamira, Spain, about 1500 BC. Joan Brandwyn.

Katherine Watson: Very good, Joan. Despite the age of these paintings, they are technically very sophisticated because...

Joan Brandwyn: Because of the shading and the thickness of the lines moving over the hump of the bison. Is that right?

Katherine Watson: Yes, that's exactly right. Next slide. This one you are probably less familiar with. It was discovered by archaeologists in...

Betty Warren: [dryly] In 1879, Lascaux, France, dates back to 10,000 BC, singled out because of the flowing lines depicting the movement of the animal. [the class laughs]

Katherine Watson: Impressive. Name?

Betty Warren: "Herd of Horses."

Katherine Watson: I meant yours.

Giselle Levy: We call her Flicka.

Elizabeth Warren: Elizabeth Warren. They call me Betty.

Katherine Watson: Very good. Betty is also correct. Just because something is ancient doesn't mean that it is primitive. For example. Next slide, please.

Student A: Mycerinus and His Queen. 2470 B. C. It's a funerary statue of the pharaoh and queen, originally intended to preserve the pharaoh's ka, soul.

Katherine Watson: Have any of you taken Art History before? [the class says No.] Let's go on. Slide.

Student B: Seated Scribe. Egypt. 2400 B. C.

Betty Warren: Pleasant Couple Plowing. Sixteenth century B. C. Egypt.

Student C: Snake Goddess. Minoan. 1600 B. C.

Student D: Fresco. Minoan. 1600 B. C.

Student E: Funeral Mask. Mycenaean. 1200.

2. In Watson's second art history class. Katherine shows the class a painting of a rotting animal.

Betty Warren: What is that?

Katherine Watson: You tell me. "Carcass"by Soutine. 1925.

Susan Delacorte: It's not on the syllabus.

Katherine Watson: No, it's not. Is it any good? Hm? [the class turns over pages, looking confused.] Come on, ladies. There's no wrong answer. There's also no textbook telling you what to think. It's not that easy, is it?

Betty Warren: Alright. No. It's not good. In fact, I wouldn't even call it art. It's grotesque.

Connie Baker: Is there a rule against grotesque art?

Giselle Levy: I think there's something aggressive about it...and erotic.

Betty Warren: To you, everything is erotic.

Giselle Levy: Yeah, everything "is"erotic.

Katherine Watson: Girls.

Susan Delacorte: Aren't there standards?

Betty Warren: Of course there are. Otherwise, a tacky velvet painting could be equated to a Rembrandt!

Connie Baker: Hey, my uncle Ferdie has two tacky velvet paintings. He loves those clowns.

Betty Warren: There are standards, technique, composition, color, even subject. So, if you're suggesting that rotted side of meat is art, much less good art, then what are we going to learn?

Katherine Watson: Just that. You have outlined our new syllabus, Betty. Thank you. What is art? What makes it good or bad, and who decides? Next slide, please. Twenty-five years ago someone thought this was brilliant.

Connie Baker: I can see that. Who?

Katherine Watson: My mother. I painted it for her birthday. [the class laughs] Next slide. This is my mom. Is it art?

Susan Delacorte: It's a snapshot.

Katherine Watson: If I told you Ansel Adams had taken it, would that make a difference?

Betty Warren: Art isn't art until someone says it is.

Katherine Watson: It's art!

Betty Warren: The right people.

Katherine Watson: Who are they?

Giselle Levy: Betty Warren. We're lucky we have one right here.

Betty Warren: Screw you. [the class laughs]

Katherine Watson: Could you go back to the Soutine, please? Just look at it again. Look beyond the paint. Let us try to open our minds to a new idea. Alright, back to chapter three. Has anyone read it? [the class raises up hands] Okay.

3. In Watson's office. Joan Brandwyn comes to Watson, dissatisfied with a low mark.

Joan Brandwyn: Hello? Miss Watson?

Katherine Watson: Yes. I'm back here.

Joan Brandwyn: I've never been to this part of campus before. Where are we?

Katherine Watson: No man's land. So to speak. Come on in.

Joan Brandwyn: What's all this?

Katherine Watson: Different things different days. People who inspire me, artists I admire, editorials I don't. So you came to see me...

Joan Brandwyn: You gave me a C.

Katherine Watson: I'm kind.

Joan Brandwyn: The assignment was to write about Bruegel. That's what I did.

Katherine Watson: No, what you did was copy Strauss.

Joan Brandwyn: I was referencing an expert.

Katherine Watson: If I wanted to know what he thought, I'd buy his book.

Joan Brandwyn: Miss Watson, with all due respect...

Katherine Watson: Bruegel was a storyteller. Find the stories. Break them down into smaller pieces. You might actually enjoy it.

Joan Brandwyn: You're giving me another chance?

Katherine Watson: So it seems.

Joan Brandwyn: Is that my file? What does it say?

Katherine Watson: Well, let's see. Straight A's.

Joan Brandwyn: Until now?

Katherine Watson: President of the poetry society, captain of the debate team, co-captain of the tennis club, founder of the horticulture league.

Joan Brandwyn: I sound like a pompous ass.

Katherine Watson: Yes, you do, but a very busy one. And it says here that you're pre-law. What law school are you gonna go to?

Joan Brandwyn: I hadn't thought about that. After I graduate, I'm planning on getting married.

Katherine Watson: And then?

Joan Brandwyn: And then I'll be married.

Katherine Watson: You can do both. Just for fun, if you could go to any law school in the country, which would it be?

Joan Brandwyn: Yale. Yale. They keep five slots open for women, one unofficially for a Wellesley girl.

Katherine Watson: But you haven't really thought about it.

4. In a class about Vincent van Gogh.

Joan Brandwyn: "Sunflowers". Vincent van Gogh. 1888.

Katherine Watson: He painted what he felt, not what he saw. People didn't understand, to them it seemed childlike and crude. It took years for them to recognize his actual technique. To see the way his brush strokes seemed to make the night sky move. Yet, he never sold a painting in his lifetime. This is his self-portrait. There's no camouflage, no romance. Honesty. Now, sixty years later, where is he?

Giselle Levy: Famous.

Katherine Watson: So famous, in fact, that everybody has a reproduction. There are post cards...

Connie Baker: We have the calendar.

Katherine Watson: You go. With the ability to reproduce art, it is available to the masses. No one needs to own a van Gogh original...

Susan Delacorte: We do. In the Newport house. But it's small. Tiny.

Katherine Watson: They can paint their own. Van Gogh in a box, ladies! The newest form of mass-distributed art; paint by numbers.

Connie Baker: [reading from the box] "Now everyone can be van Gogh. It's so easy. Just follow the simple instructions and in minutes, you're on your way to being an artist."

Giselle Levy: Van Gogh by numbers?

Katherine Watson: Ironic, isn't it? Look at what we have done to the man who refused to conform his ideals to popular taste. Who refused to compromise his integrity. We have put him in a tiny box and asked you to copy him. So the choice is yours, ladies. You can conform to what other people expect or you can...

5. In one art history class after Betty Warren wrote her editorial.

Betty Warren: [Betty's Third Editorial Voice Over] Wellesley girls who are married have become quite adept at balancing their obligations. One hears such comments as, "I'm able to baste the chicken with one hand and outline the paper with the other." While our mothers were called to the workforce for lady liberty it is our duty, nay, obligation to reclaim our place in the home bearing the children that will carry our traditions into the future. One must pause to consider why, Ms. Katherine Watson, instructor in the art history department, has decided to declare war on the holy sacrament of marriage. Her subversive and political teachings encourage our Wellesley girls to reject the roles they were born to fill.

Katherine Watson: Slide-Contemporary art...

Connie Baker: No, that's just an advertisement...

Katherine Watson: Quiet. Today you just listen. What will future scholars see when they study us, a portrait of women today? There you are ladies: the perfect likeness of a Wellesley graduate, Magna Cum Laude, doing exactly what she was trained to do. Slide-A Rhodes Scholar, I wonder if she recites Chaucer while she presses her husband's shirts. Slide-hehe, now you physics majors can calculate the mass and volume of every meatloaf you make. Slide-A girdle to set you free. What does that mean? What does that mean? What does it mean? I give up, you win. The smartest women in the country, I didn't realize that by demanding excellence I would be challenging...what did it say?

[Walks over to a student and picks up her copy of the editorial]

Katherine Watson: What did it say? Um...the roles you were born to fill. Is that right?

[Looks up at Betty]

Katherine Watson: The roles you were born to fill? It's, uh, it's my mistake.

[Katerine drops the student's paper back onto her desk]

Katherine Watson: Class dismissed.

[Katherine walks out of the classroom]

Task 2 Work in pairs or groups and play the roles in one of your favorite scenes.

Ⅲ. Cultural Notes

1. Soutine: Chaïm Soutine (13 January 1893-9 August 1943) was a Russian painter of Belarusian Jewish origin. Soutine made a major contribution to the expressionist movement while living in Paris. For more information, visit https://en.wikipedia.org/wiki/Chaim_Soutine.

2. Rembrandt: Rembrandt Harmenszoon van Rijn (15 July 1606-4 October 1669) was a Dutch draughtsman, painter, and printmaker. A prolific and versatile master across three media, he is generally considered one of the greatest visual artists in the history of art and the most important in Dutch art history. For more information, visit https://en.wikipedia.org/wiki/Rembrandt.

3. Ansel Adams: Ansel Easton Adams (February 20, 1902-April 22, 1984) was an American photographer andenvironmentalist. His black-and-white landscape photographs of the American West, especially Yosemite National Park, have been widely reproduced on calendars, posters, books, and the internet. For more information, visit https://en.wikipedia.org/wiki/Ansel_Adams.

4. Vincent van Gogh: Vincent Willem van Gogh (30 March 1853-29 July 1890) was a Dutch Post-Impressionist painter who is among the most famous and influential figures in the history of Western art. In just over a decade he created about 2,100 artworks, including around 860 oil paintings, most of them in the last two years of his life in France, where he died. They include landscapes, still lifes, portraits and self-portraits, and are characterized by bold colors and dramatic, impulsive and expressive brushwork that contributed to the foundations of modern art. His suicide at 37 followed years of mental illness and poverty. For more infor-

mation, visit https://en.wikipedia.org/wiki/Vincent_van_Gogh.

5. Chaucer: Geoffrey Chaucer (c. 1343-25 October 1400), known as the Father of English literature, is widely considered the greatest English poet of the Middle Ages and was the first poet to be buried in Poets' Corner of Westminster Abbey. For more information, visit https://en.wikipedia.org/wiki/Geoffrey_Chaucer.

Ⅳ. Questions for discussion

1. Are there any objective standards in defining the quality of a piece of art work? If there are, what might those standards include?

2. What should be the role of women in modern society? Is it possible for women to strike a balance between career and family?

3. What should be the function of aesthetic education in general? Is it necessary for colleges and universities in China to offer courses on art history and appreciation?

Ⅴ. Movie Review

Task: Write a movie review on *Mona Lisa Smile.*

MOVIES TO SEE (B) Step Up Revolution

Movie Introduction

Director: Jon M. Chu

Starring: Ryan Guzman, Kathryn McCormick, Misha Gabriel Hamilton

Running time: 99 mins

Released: 2012

Plot: The Mob sets the dancing against the vibrant backdrop of Miami. Emily arrives in Miami with aspirations of becoming a professional dancer and soon falls in love with Sean, a young man who leads a dance crew in elaborate, cutting-edge flash mobs, called "The Mob". When a wealthy business man threatens to develop The Mob's historic neighborhood and displace thousands-of people, Emily must work together with Sean and The Mob to turn their performance art into protest art, and risk losing their dreams to fight for a greater cause.

To Recommend More Movies

❖ *The Words* (2012)

❖ *The Devil Wears Prada* (2006)

❖ *Georgia O'Keeffe* (2009)

❖ *American Splendor* (2003)

❖ *Exit Through the Gift Shop* (2010)

Unit Six　Religion

Pre-reading Activities

Answer the following questions before you read this text.

1. What is the most popular religion in the United States?
2. Do many Americans believe in God?
3. How has religion shaped American values?

TEXT A　The American Religious Heritage

Freedom of Religion in the United States

The fundamental American belief in individual freedom and the right of individuals to practice their own religion is at the center of religious experience in the United States. The great diversity of ethnic backgrounds has produced religious **pluralism**; almost all of the religions of the world are now practiced in the United States. Ninety-three percent of all Americans say that they believe in God. Only 7 percent say they have no religious preferences or beliefs. About 87 percent of Americans are **Christians**, 2 percent are **Jewish**, and the other 4 percent belong to other religious faiths such as **Moslem**, **Buddhist**, or **Hindu**. Of the 87 percent who are Christian, 59 percent are **Protestant**, 27 percent **Catholic**, and 1 percent **Eastern Orthodox**. This is a pattern that has persisted for decades.

Although **the overwhelming majority of** Americans are Christians, all religions make important contributions to the American culture. There are now almost as many Moslems living in the United States as there are Jews. People of **Hispanic** origin now make up nearly one-half of the Catholic church. The Asian immigrants have brought with them the traditional religions of East Asia— **Taoism**, **Confucianism**, and **Shintoism**, as well as **Buddhism**. And the Native American religions are still practiced and studied today, particularly for their teachings about **living in harmony with** nature.

From the beginning of its history, religion has played an important role in the United States. The Catholic faith was first brought to the North American continent by the Spanish in the 1500s. For the next 300 years, Catholic **missionaries** and settlers from Spain and then Latin America came to what is now California and the Southwest. Many of the cities were named by these missionaries and settlers—San Francisco, Sante Fe, and San Antonio, for example. French Canadian Catholic missionaries also came with the explorers and traders from Quebec, down the Mississippi River to New Orleans.

In the 1600s, the European settlers began establishing colonies along the east coast of North America. Although there were some Catholics, the vast majority of these settlers were Protestants. As the new nation formed, it was the Protestant branch of the Christian faith that had the strongest effect on the development of the religious climate in the United States. Today, almost two-thirds of all Americans are Protestants.

The Development of Protestantism

The Protestant branch of the Christian faith **broke away from** the Roman Catholic church in Europe in the 16th century because of important differences in religious beliefs. (The **Eastern Orthodox** branch of the Christian faith had separated from the Roman Catholic Church in 1054.) At the time of the Protestant Reformation, the Roman Catholic church was the center of religious life in Western European countries; the Catholic **Pope** and the **priests** played the role of parent to the people in spiritual matters. They told people what was right and wrong, and they granted them forgiveness for sins against God and the Christian faith.

The Protestants, on the other hand, insisted that all individuals must stand alone before God. If people sinned, they should seek their forgiveness directly from God rather than from a priest speaking in God's name. In place of the power and authority of priests, Protestants substituted what they called the "**priesthood** of all believers." This meant that every individual was solely responsible for his or her own relationship with God.

After the Protestants broke away from the Catholic church, they found that they could not agree among themselves about many things. Therefore, the Protestants began to form separate churches, called **denominations**. (The largest Protestant denominations in the United States now are the **Baptists**, **Methodists**, **Lutherans**, **Presbyterians**, **Episcopalians**, and the United Church of Christ.) In the 1600s, the Catholic church did not recognize the rights of such Protestant churches to exist. There was much bitterness among some of the religious groups, and many Protestant denominations experienced religious persecution. The result of this persecution was that many Protestants were ready to leave their native countries in order to have freedom to practice their particular religious beliefs. Consequently, among the early settlers who came to America in the 1600s, there were many Protestants seeking religious freedom.

In the previous chapter, we noted that this desire for religious freedom was one of the strongest reasons why many colonial settlers came to America. Generally speaking, the lack of any established national religion in America appealed strongly to European Protestants, whether or not they were being persecuted. A large number of Protestant denominations were established in America. At first, some denominations hoped to force their views and beliefs on others, but the colonies were simply too large for any one denomination to gain control over the others. The idea of separation of church and state became accepted. When the Constitution was adopted in 1789, the government was forbidden to establish a national church; no denomination was to be favored over the others. The government and the church had to remain separate. Under these conditions, a variety of different Protestant denominations developed and grew, with each denomination having a "**live and let live**" attitude toward the others. Diversity was accepted and strengthened.

Protestantism in the United States

To someone not familiar with the Protestant faith, the religious scene in the United States may be confusing. The various Protestant denominations have completely separate church organizations, and although there are many similarities, there are also significant differences in their religious teachings and beliefs. Some

Protestant denominations forbid dancing, playing cards, and drinking alcohol, for example, while others do not.

What causes this religious diversity? Perhaps the major cause is the Protestant belief that the individual, not the organized church, should be the center of religious life. This idea was brought to America and firmly established by European Protestants, and it is one reason why no single church has become the center of religious life in the nation. American religious tradition has encouraged not only the development of numerous denominations but also a tolerance and acceptance of all faiths that express the religious preferences of different individuals. This climate of religious freedom has, of course, strengthened the development of cultural pluralism in the United States.

The Protestant Heritage: Self-Improvement

Although many Protestant denominations exist in the United States today, all of them share a common heritage that has been a powerful force in shaping the values and beliefs of Americans. One of the most important values associated with American Protestantism is the value of self-improvement. Protestant Christianity, like Roman Catholic Christianity, often emphasizes the natural sinfulness of human nature. However, since Protestants do not go to priests for forgiveness of their sins, individuals are left alone before God to improve themselves or suffer eternal punishment by God for their sinful acts. In this way, Protestantism encourages a strong and restless desire for self-improvement.

The need for self-improvement, once established, reaches far beyond self-improvement in the purely moral or religious sense. It can be seen in countless books that explain how people can be happier and more successful in life by improving everything from their vocabulary to their tennis game, or even their whole personality Books of this type **are** often **referred to as** self-help books. They are the natural products of a culture in which people believe that "God helps those who help themselves."

One of the most popular self-help books ever written in the United States was written by a Protestant minister, Norman Vincent Peale. As its title states, it stresses The Power of Positive Thinking. According to Peale, the key to self-improvement and success is self-confidence. Reading the Bible is like doing regular daily exercises; it can improve one's self-confidence and ensure personal success in life.

Americans buy hundreds of millions of self-help books a year, and typically; half of the New York limes best-seller list of nonfiction books are related to self-help. In addition to that, Americans attend thousands of self-help **seminars** and support group meetings to help them stop smoking or drinking, lose weight, be better parents, have happier relationships, and, of course, develop self-confidence.

(Words: 1349)

New Words

Christian	*n.* 基督徒
Jewish	*adj.* 犹太人的；犹太族的
Moslem	*n.* 穆斯林；穆罕默德信徒；伊斯兰 *adj.* 穆斯林的；伊斯兰教的
Buddhist	*n.* 佛教徒 *adj.* 佛教的
Hindu	*n.* 印度人；印度教教徒 *adj.* 印度教的；印度的
Protestant	*n.* 新教；新教徒 *adj.* 新教的；新教徒的
Catholic	*n.* 天主教徒；罗马天主教 *adj.* 天主教的；宽宏大量的
Orthodox	*n.* 正统的人；正统的事物 *adj.* 正统的；传统的；惯常的
Hispanic	*adj.* 西班牙的
Taoism	*n.* 道家的学说；道教
Confucianism	*n.* 孔子学说；儒家思想
Shintoism	*n.* 日本之神道教
Buddhism	*n.* 佛教
missionary	*n.* 传教士 *adj.* 传教的；传教士的

续表

Pope	*n.* 罗马教皇
priest	*n.* 祭司；牧师；神父；教士
priesthood	*n.* 祭司职；神职；僧职
denomination	*n.* 教派；面额；名称
Baptist	*n.* 浸信会教友；施洗者约翰，施洗者
Methodist	*n.* 卫理公会派教徒 *adj.* 卫理公会教派的
Lutheran	*n.* 路德教会 *adj.* 路德教会的
Presbyterian	*n.* 长老教会员 *adj.* 长老会的
Episcopalian	*n.* 主教派的人；美国圣公会教徒 *adj.* 主教制度的；主教派的
seminar	*n.* 讨论会，研讨班

Phrases & Expressions

live in harmony with	和睦相处，和谐共处
break away from	与…脱离
the overwhelming majority of	绝大多数
be referred to as	被……称为
live and let live	待人宽容；和平共存

Proper Names

Eastern Orthodox	东正教

Cultural Notes

1. Protestantism is a form of Christianity which originated with the Reformation, a movement against what its followers considered to be errors in the Roman

Catholic Church. It is one of the three major divisions of Christendom, together with Roman Catholicism and Orthodoxy. The term derives from the letter of protestation from German Lutheran princes in 1529 against an edict condemning the teachings of Martin Luther as heretical. For more information, visit https://en.wikipedia.org/wiki/Protestantism.

2. Eastern Orthodox is the second largest Christian church and one of the oldest current religious institutions in the world. The Eastern Orthodox Church teaches that it is the One, Holy, Catholic and Apostolic Church established by Jesus Christ in his Great Commission to the apostles. It practices what it understands to be the original Christian faith and maintains the sacred tradition passed down from the apostles. For more information, visit https://en.wikipedia.org/wiki/Eastern_Orthodox_Church.

Exercises

Comprehension of the Text

Ⅰ Answer the following questions according to the passage.

1. What is the fundamental American belief?

2. What is one of the strongest reasons why many colonial settlers came to America?

3. What causes religious diversity in the United States?

Vocabulary

Ⅱ. Fill in the blanks with the words given below. Change the form where necessary.

pluralism	seminar	persecution	fundamental	ethnic
overwhelming	diversity	solely	tolerance	heritage
sinful	eternal	denomination	consequently	protestant

1. Our constitution embodies all the ______ principles of democracy.

2. Most ______ churches now have some women ministers.

3. The university ____ the educational program by introducing new subjects.

4. She is ______grateful to her family for their support.

5. Catholics go to confession to be purged of ______.

6. He always cleaves to his principle in spite of political ______.

7. Acceptance of women preachers varies greatly from ______to ______.

8. One bad ______of the Copenhagen accord was some people saw it as an undemocratic result.

9. In the end, our security and leadership does not come ______from the strength of our arms

10. Students are asked to prepare material in advance of each weekly ____.

Translations

Ⅲ. Translate the following sentences into English.

1. 我们的宗旨是致力于寻求人类与自然和谐共处的途径。(live in harmony with)

____

2. 旅途中我喜爱的一点就是我有机会可以打破常规生活，形成一些新的生活习惯。(break away from)

____

3. 事实上，绝大多数科学家都表示，假如我们现在不采取行动的话，地球将处于严重的困境之中。(the overwhelming majority of)

____

4. 这一情况可能是由多种原因造成的，这些原因可能是无意的，也可能是故意的。(a variety of)

____

5. 我们一直被认为是悲观厌世的，但我们喜欢被称作“现实主义者”。(be referred to as)

____

Ⅳ. Translate the following passage into English.

美国的基本信仰即个人自由和信仰自己宗教的权利在美国的宗教实践中处于中心位置。种族背景的多样性造就了宗教信仰的多重性；世界上大多数的宗教如今在美国都有人信仰。尽管并不是所有人都是传统宗教组织的一员，但还是有90%的美国人说他们信仰上帝。大约有80%的美国人是基督教徒，大约有2%的人是犹太教徒，还有4%的人信仰其他的教派，如伊斯兰教、佛教和印度教。

TEXT B Ten Facts about Religion in America

(A) It's a fascinating time for conversations about faith in the United States, with Pope Francis set to visit next month, a **presidential** election on the horizon and major trends reshaping the country's religious **landscape**.

(B) One of the most important and **well-documented** shifts taking place over the past decade is the steadily rising share of people who are religiously **unaffiliated**-from 16% in 2007 to 23% in 2014. As journalists and others gather in Philadelphia for the annual **Religion Newswriters Association** conference this week, here are 10 other things we've learned from our recent research:

(C) **1. Protestants no longer make up a majority of U. S. adults.** Closely tied to the rise of the religious "nones"is the decline of Christians, including Protestants. The U. S. has a long history as a majority Protestant nation, and, as recently as the 2007 **Pew Research Center** Religious Landscape Study, more than half of U. S. adults (51. 3%) identified as Protestants. But that figure has fallen, and our 2014 study found that 46. 5% of Americans are now Protestants.

(D) **2. Religious switching is a common occurrence in the U. S.** Depending on how "religious switching" is defined, as many as 42% of U. S. adults have switched religions. That definition counts switching between Protestant traditions, but even if Protestantism is regarded as a single group, about a third of Americans (34%) identify with a different religious group than the one in which they were raised.

(E) **3.** There is a wide range of racial and ethnic diversity among U. S. religious groups and denominations. **Seventh-day Adventists, Muslims and Jehovah's Witnesses are among the most racially and ethnically diverse U. S. religious groups.** The least diverse are the **National Baptist Convention, the Evangelical Lutheran Church** in America and the Lutheran Church-Missouri **Synod**.

(F) **4.** Before Pope Francis' **encyclical** on the environment was published in

June, U. S. Catholics' views of climate change mirrored those of Americans overall-including major partisan divisions. While six-in-ten Catholic Democrats say global warming is caused by humans and that it is a very serious problem, only about a quarter of Catholic Republicans feel the same way.

(G) **5. In a typical week, about one-in-five Americans share their faith online**. This is about the same as the number who tune in to religious talk radio, watch religious TV programs or listen to Christian rock music.

(H) **6. Americans have continued to become more supportive of same-sex marriage**. **Aggregated** data from 2015 polls show that fully 55% of U. S. adults favor same-sex marriage, which is now legal nationwide following a Supreme Court ruling in June. That represents a rise of 20 percentage points over the last decade or so. Among the major religious groups, White evangelical Protestants are the least supportive of gay marriage (24%), while those without any religious **affiliation** are the most likely to favor allowing gays and **lesbians** to wed (82%).

(I) **7.** Religious freedom or discrimination? A 2014 poll found **Americans are divided on the question of whether wedding-related businesses should be allowed to refuse service to same-sex couples** for religious reasons, with 47% saying businesses should be able to refuse service and 49% saying establishments should be required to serve same-sex couples.

(J) **8. On another hotly debated social issue-abortion-Americans' views in the last two decades have largely held steady**. A majority of U. S. adults (55%) continue to say abortion should be legal in all or most cases. At the same time, four-in-ten say it should be illegal in all or most cases.

(K) **9. Frequency of religious service attendance remains a strong predictor of how people will vote in elections**. In the 2014 midterm elections, **exit polls** showed that those who attend worship services at least weekly voted for **Republicans** over **Democrats** for **the House of Representatives** by a 58% - to - 40% margin. Meanwhile, those who never attend services leaned heavily toward Democrats (62% vs. 36%).

(L) **10.** Christians continue to make up an overwhelming majority of members of Congress (92%), compared with 71% of the general public (as of

2014). At the same time, **while 23% of U. S. adults are religiously unaffiliated, only one member of Congress (Rep. Kyrsten Sinema, D-Ariz.), or 0.2% of that body, claims no religious affiliation.**

(Words: 694)

New Words

presidential	*adj.* 总统的；首长的；统辖的
landscape	*n.* 风景；风景画；景色；山水画 *vt.* 对…做景观美化 *vi.* 美化（环境等）
well-documented	*adj.* 证据充分的
unaffiliated	*adj.* 独立的；未结合的；非附属的
occurrence	*n.* 发生；出现；事件；发现
ethnically	*adv.* 人种上；民族上
Baptist	*n.* 浸信会教友；施洗者约翰，施洗者
synod	*n.* 大会；宗教会议；教会法院
encyclical	*n.* 罗马教皇的通谕 *adj.* 通谕的；传阅的
partisan	*adj.* 党派的；效忠的；偏袒的；盲目推崇的 *n.* 游击队；虔诚信徒；党羽
aggregate	*adj.* 聚合的；集合的；合计的 *n.* 合计；集合体；总计 *vi.* / vt. 集合；聚集；合计
affiliation	*n.* 友好关系；加入；联盟；从属关系
lesbian	*n.* 女同性恋者 *adj.* ［心理］女同性恋的
predictor	*n.* ［气象］预报器；预言者
Republican	*n.* 共和党，共和党员
Democrat	*n.* 民主党；民主党人

Phrases & Expressions

a wide range of	大范围的，各种不同的

Proper Names

Religion Newswriters Association	宗教新闻写作协会
Pew Research Center	皮尤研究中心
Seventh-day Adventists	基督复临教派教友；星期六耶稣再生论者
Evangelical Lutheran Church	福音派路德教会
exit polls	投票后的民意调查

Cultural Notes

1. Religion Newswriters Association (RNA) is a non-profit professional association in the United States which seeks to promote better reporting on religion in the news media and to provide help and support to journalists who cover religion. It was founded in 1949 and in 2007 had 570 members and subscribers. Membership in the RNA is open to journalists who regularly report on religion in the secular print and broadcast media. For more information, visit https://en.wikipedia.org/wiki/Religion_Newswriters_Association.

2. Seventh-day Adventists is a Protestant Christian denomination distinguished by its observance of Saturday, the seventh day of the week in Christian and Jewish calendars, as Sabbath, and by its emphasis on the imminent Second Coming (advent) of Jesus Christ. For more information, visit https://en.wikipedia.org/wiki/Seventh-day_Adventist_Church.

3. Exit polls are surveys of a small percentage of voters taken after they leave their voting place. Pollsters use this data to project how all voters or segments of voters side on a particular race or ballot measure. For more information, visit http://edition.cnn.com/election/2014/results/exit-polls.

4. Pew Research Center is a nonpartisan fact tank that informs the public about the issues, attitudes and trends shaping America and the world. For more information, visit http://www.pewresearch.org/about/.

Exercises

Comprehension of the Text

Ⅰ. The following 10 statements contain information given in the text. Identify the paragraph from which the information is derived. You may choose a paragraph more than once. Each paragraph is marked with a letter.

1. Protestants no longer make up a majority of U. S. adults.

2. Less than half of U. S. adults have switched religions.

3. There is a wide range of racial and ethnic diversity among U. S. religious groups and denominations.

4. More than half of Catholic Democrats say global warming is caused by humans and that it is a very serious problem, and only a small number of Catholic Republicans hold the same view.

5. Most U. S. adults show their approval of same-sex marriage.

6. Americans hold the different view on the question of whether wedding-related businesses should be allowed to refuse service to same-sex couples for religious reasons.

7. A majority of U. S. adults think that abortion should be legal in all or most cases.

8. Those who never attend religious services leaned heavily toward Democrats.

9. Christians continue to make up an overwhelming majority of members of Congress.

10. Only a very small number of Congress are religiously unaffiliated.

Vocabulary

Ⅱ. Fill in the blanks with the words given below. Change the form where necessary.

presidential	landscape	well-documented	unaffiliated	occurrence
ethnically	partisan	aggregate	affiliation	predictor
discrimination	division	diversity	frequency	supportive

1. People have _____their capital, i. e. saved money, and started and expanded businesses since time immemorial.

2. The kidnappers had no _____with any militant group.

3. Complaints seemed to be an everyday _____.

4. It is already _____that baseball is losing the younger generation of fans.

5. She took early retirement and sued for illegal gender _____under the Civil Rights Act.

6. We expect the Russians to be _____of stability in the region.

7. The current _____of labour between workers and management will alter.

8. They help us grasp the _____of life on the planet

9. Opinion polls are an unreliable _____of election outcomes

10. The regime has _____cleansed several Sunni-majority villages on routes that lead to the coast.

Further Reading

TEXT C Religious Diversity in the United States: A Spiritual Kaleidoscope

The belief that the individual, not the organized church, should be the center of religious life has encouraged a tolerance and acceptance of all faiths. This climate of religious freedom has, of course, strengthened the development of cultural pluralism in the United States. Today there is growing religious diversity. The world Almanac now lists over 140 different religious groups that each have at least 5,000 members, and other estimates are that there are at least 2,000 distinct religious groups in the United States.

Wade Clark Roof, a professor of religion and society, cites four trends that are creating a spiritual kaleidoscope in the United States. First, there is the change from being a "Protestant-Catholic-Jewish nation" to one with multiple religions. The number of Protestants has declined to a little over 50 percent, and if trends continue, they will probably be in the minority in the next decade. The number of Catholics is increasing due to the large numbers of Latin American Catholic immigrants, who now make up about half the total Catholic community. The number of Jews has stayed the same in recent years, but the number of Americans who choose "Other or None" when asked their religious preference is growing. The number of Muslims, for example, has increased to the point that some estimates are that there are now as many Muslims as there are Jews in the United States.

Second, there is religious "expressive individualism", the switching of faiths—from one Protestant denomination to another, or even from one faith to another. Also, within the various faiths, Americans are now picking and choosing among the beliefs, particularly in the mainline faiths. Roof calls this "the privatizing of organized religion, "the search for a personal religious identity. For some, this results in a stronger faith; for others, it does not.

Third, there are many new religious organizational structures emerging in the United States. Some are ethnic denominations such as the Latvian Evangelical Lutheran Church in America, while others are "special purpose groups" — such as support groups or groups to help the homeless or clean up the environment. Some groups are "liberal, oriented to reforming society; others are conservative, aimed at reforming individual lives, " Roof says. He observes the same trend toward fragmentation that Michael J. Weiss noted in his description of American lifestyles. However, Roof says that these new special interest groups are energizing the American religious community.

The fourth trend is toward a new spirituality, especially among young Americans. Many young people prefer to identify themselves as being *spiritual*, rather than *religious*. The majority prefer also to explore the beliefs of several religions, rather than just one. In a survey that Roof conducted, he found that 22 percent of young Americans believe in reincarnation, and many are attracted to Eastern religious teachings. They are looking for a belief system that will help them grow and improve as individuals; they are not interested in participating in a religion out of duty.

Most Americans believe that religious freedom must be protected; that everyone has the right to practice his or her own religion without interference by the government or anyone else. While the majority of Americans follow the Judeo-Christian tradition, they also believe that freedom of religion should be a basic American right.

America's religious heritage seems to have encouraged certain basic values that members of many diverse faiths find easy to accept. This has helped to unite many different religious groups in the United States without requiring any to abandon their faiths. Cultural and religious pluralism has also created a context of tolerance that further strengthens the American reality of many different religions living peacefully within a single nation.

(Words: 620)

Questions for discussions

1. What is "cultural pluralism"?

2. What are the four trends that are creating a spiritual kaleidoscope in the United States?

3. Why do many young people prefer to identify themselves as being *spiritual*, rather than *religious*?

More to Learn

1. A Comparative Overview of the Three Main "Western" Religions

Religion	JUDAISM	CHRISTIANITY	ISLAM
Adherents	Jew (s)	Christian (s)	Muslim (s) (Moslems)
Corresponding Adjectives	Jewish; Judaic	Christian	Muslim; Islamic
Number of Adherents Today	ca. 15 Million (0. 25% of world)	ca. 2. 0-2. 2 Billion (33% of world)	ca. 1. 2-1. 5 Billion (20 – 25% of world)

续表

Religion	JUDAISM	CHRISTIANITY	ISLAM
Geographical Concentrations	USA, Israel, parts of Europe (esp. urban areas)	S&N America, Europe, Australia, parts of Africa & Asia	S. Asia (India, Pak., Bangl.), SE Asia (esp. Indonesia), Mid-East, N Africa
Major Branches Today	* Orthodox * Conservative * Reform/Liberal * Reconstructio-nist * [Secular/non-religious]	* (Eastern) Orthodox (12%): Greek; Russian; Armenian; etc. * (Roman) Catholic (50%): Latin, Byzantine, other "rites" * (Western) Protestant (25%): many "churches/denominations" * (Newer) Independent (18%): local & "non-denominational"	* Sunni (85%) * Shi'ite (15%)
Mystical Traditions	Kabbalah	Monasticism	Sufism
Core Scriptures	***Tanakh*** (Hebrew Bible; Mikra)	***Bible*** (OT & NT)	***Qur'an*** (Koran)
Structure of Scriptures (and main organizing principle)	Three Sections (in content/genre groups): Torah, Nevi'im, Khetuvim	Two Parts (mostly chronologically): Old Testament & New Testament	One Book: 114 Surahs (by decreasing length, except #1)
Scriptural Language (s)	Hebrew (and some Aramaic)	Greek (later Latin, etc.)	Arabic
Main "Prophet"	**Moses**	**Jesus** of Nazareth	**Muhammad** (Mohammed)

续表

Religion	JUDAISM	CHRISTIANITY	ISLAM
Foundational Event (s)	* Call and Migration of Abraham * Passover/Exodus out of Egypt	* Incarnation/Birth of Jesus * Death & Resurrection of Jesus	* Call of Muhammad as a prophet * Migration from Makka to Madinah
Major Annual Feasts	* **Yom Kippur** (Day of Atonement) * **Pesach** (Passover/Exodus)	* **Easter** (Resurrection of Jesus) * **Christmas** (Birth of Jesus)	* **Ramadan** (month of fasting/prayer) * **Hajj** (pilgrimage to Mecca)

MOVIES TO SEE (A) The Prince of Egypt

Ⅰ. Movie Introduction

Director: Brenda Chapman, Steve Hickner

Starring: Val Kilmer, Ralph Fiennes, Michelle Pfeiffer

Running time: 159 mins

Released: 1998

Plot: This is the extraordinary tale of two brothers named Moses and Ramses, one born of royal blood, and one an orphan with a secret past. Growing up the best of friends, they share a strong bond of free-spirited youth and good-natured rivalry. But the truth will ultimately set them at odds, as one becomes the ruler of the most powerful empire on earth, and the other the chosen leader of his people! Their final confrontation will forever change their lives and the world.

Ⅱ. Excerpts & Expressions

Task 1 Study the underlined sentences and expressions.

1. Miriam attempted to tell Moses about his secret past, but Moses refused to listen.

Miriam: Uh. Oh, I'm sorry. I'm so sorry. I—Oh, please forgive me. I—I didn't' expect to see...you...here, of all places, at—at—at our door. Mmm, at last!

Moses: (Chuckles) At last?

Miriam: Didn't I tell you, Aaron? I knew he would return to us when he was ready.

Aaron: Miriam, do you want us flogged?

Miriam: I knew you cared about our freedom.

Aaron: Miriam!

Moses: Freedoms? Why would I care about that?

Miriam: Because you're—well, you're our brother.

Moses: What?

Miriam: They— (Sighs) they never told you?

Moses: Who never told me what?

Miriam: But you're here. You must know. (She walks over and takes hold of Moses).

Moses: Be careful, slave!

Aaron: Oh, my good prince. Um, she's, he's exhausted from the day's work. Uh, not that it was too much. We—We quite enjoyed it. But—But she's confused and knows not to whom she speaks.

Miriam: I know to whom I speak, Aaron. I know who you are. You are not a prince of Egypt.

Aaron: Miriam.

Moses: What did you say?

Aaron: Your Highness, pay her no heed. C— Come, Miriam. May I discuss something with you

Miriam: No, Aaron. No! Please, Moses, you must believe!

Aaron: That's enough.

Miriam: You were born of my mother, Yocheved.

Aaron: Stop it.

Miriam: You are our brother!

Moses: Now you go too far. You shall be punished.

Aaron: No! Please, uh, Your Highness. She's ill. She's very ill. We beg your forgiveness. Please, Miriam, let us go.

Miriam: No, Aaron. Our mother set you adrift in a basket to save your life!

Moses: Save my life From whom?

Miriam: Ask the man that you call "Father."

Moses: How dare you!

Miriam: God saved you to be our deliverer.

Moses: Enough of this.

Miriam: And you are, Moses. You are the deliverer.

Moses: I said, enough! You will regret this night.

2. God told Moses to return to Egypt and guide the Hebrew slaves to freedom.

God: (Whispering Voice) Moses. Moses. Moses. Moses.

Moses: Here I am.

God: (Voicing) Take the sandals from your feet, for the place on which you stand is holy ground. (Rolling Sounds)

Moses: Who are you?

God: (Echoing) I am that I am.

Moses: I don't understand.

God: I am the God of your ancestors, Abraham, Isaac and Jacob. (Miriam's Voice) You were born of my mother, Yocheved. You are our brother.

Moses: What do you want with me?

God: I have seen the oppression of My people in Egypt... and have heard their cry. (Man Screams) (Moses) (Stop it! Leave that man alone!) So I have come down to deliver them out of slavery and bring them to a good land, a land flowing with milk and honey. And so, unto Pharaoh, I shall send...you.

Moses: Me? Wh—Who am I to lead these people They'll never believe me. They won't even listen.

God: I shall teach you what to say. (Moses's Voice) Let my people go!

Moses: But I was their enemy. I was the prince of Egypt, the son of the man who slaughtered their children. You' ve—You've chosen the wrong messenger H—How can I even speak to these people?

God: Who made man's mouth? Who made the deaf, the mute, the seeing or blind? Did not I? Now go! (Panting) Oh, Moses. I shall be with you when you go to the king of Egypt. But Pharaoh will not listen. So I will stretch out My hand and smite Egypt with all My wonders. Take the staff in your hand, Moses. With it, you shall do My wonders. I shall be with you, Moses. (Panting) Moses. (Whispering) Moses.

3. The origin of Passover

Moses: God has come to me again, saying, "Take a lamb, and with its blood mark the lintel and posts of every door for tonight I shall pass through the land of Egypt... and smite all the firstborn. But when I see the blood upon your door...I will pass over you, and the plague shall not enter."

Task 2 Work in pairs and play the roles in the expert above.

Ⅲ. Cultural Notes

1. Yocheved: She was the daughter of Yaakov (Jacob)'s son Levi. She was married to Levi's grandson Amram. The couple had two children, Miriam and Aharon (Aaron) when Pharaoh, the King of Egypt, decreed that all Jewish males born would be thrown into the Nile River. Yocheved found out she was pregnant and then gave birth to a boy, she knew that she had to do something to protect him, so she took the baby and put him in a basket made of river reeds and put tar on it to make it waterproof. One morning, while they watched, Pharaoh's daughter was washing in the river when she saw the baby in the basket. She reached out her hand to take him and decided to adopt him, naming him "Moshe" (Moses).

2. Scene III reveals the origin of the **Passover** (in Hebrew, **Pesach**). Passover commemorates the exodus of the Jews from slavery in Egypt. The holiday originated in the Torah, where the word **pesach** refers to the ancient Passover sacrifice (known as the Paschal Lamb); it is also said to refer to the idea that God "passed over" (**pesach**) the houses of the Jews during the 10th plague on the Egyptians, the slaying of the first born. The holiday is ultimately a celebration of freedom, and the story of the exodus from Egypt is a powerful metaphor that is appreciated not only by Jews, but by people of other faiths as well.

Ⅳ. Questions for discussion

1. What theme does this movie want to convey?
2. What do you know about Passover from the movie?

3. What is the unforgettable scene in this movie?

Ⅴ. Movie Review

Task: Write a movie review on *The Prince of Egypt*.

MOVIES TO SEE (B) The Passion of the Christ

Movie Introduction

Director: Mel Gibson

Starring: Jim Caviezel, Monica Bellucci, Maia Morgenstern

Running time: 127 mins

Released: 2004

Plot: The film focuses on the last twelve hours of Jesus of Nazareth's life. The film begins in the Garden of Gethsemane where Jesus has gone to pray after sitting the Last Supper. Jesus must resist the temptations of Satan. Betrayed by Judas Iscariot, Jesus is then arrested and taken within the city walls of Jerusalem where leaders of the Pharisees confront him with accusations of blasphemy and his trial results in a condemnation to death.

To Recommend More Movies

❖ *The Last Temptation of Christ* (1988)

❖ *Seven* (1995)

❖ *Kingdom of Heaven* (2005)

❖ *Ben-Hur* (2016)

Unit Seven American Values

Pre-reading Activities

Answer the following questions before you read this text.

1. How much do you know about American values?

2. What are the differences of attachment to family between American and Chinese?

3. Can you list some typical American values different from Chinese Values?

TEXT A Why Do Americans Act Like That

So you're going to visit the United States? Great! But be prepared: the values Americans live by may seem strange to you. As a result, you might find their actions confusing, even unbelievable. This is the kind of advice **Dr. L. Robert Kohls** gives first time visitors to the United States. Kohls, Director of **International Programs** at **San Francisco State University**, has developed a list of some commonly held values which help explain why Americans act as they do. He is careful and cautions visitors also, to avoid labeling these values positive or negative. His aim: "I simply want to help you understand the Americans with whom you will be relating-from their own value system rather than from yours". Whether one agrees with Kohls or not—or is willing to accept as **valid** any generalizations about Americans—his observations are **thought-provoking**.

1. PERSONAL CONTROL OVER THE ENVIRONMENT/RESPONSIBILITY

Americans do not believe in the power of fate, and they look at people who do as being backward, **primitive**, or **naive**. In the American context, to be "**fatalistic**" is to be **superstitious**, lazy, or unwilling to **take initiative**. Everyone should have control over whatever in the environment might potentially affect him or her. The problems of one's life are not seen as having **resulted from** bad luck as much as having come from one's laziness and unwillingness to take responsibility in pursuing a better life.

2. CHANGE SEEN AS NATURAL AND POSITIVE

In the American mind, change is seen as **indisputably** good, leading to development, improvement, progress. Many older, more traditional cultures consider change **disruptive** and **destructive**; they value stability, **continuity**, tradition, and ancient heritage—none of which are considered very important in the United States.

3. TIME AND ITS CONTROL

Time is of **utmost** importance to most Americans. It is something to be on, kept, filled, saved, used, spent, wasted, lost, gained, planned, given, even killed. Americans **are** more **concerned with** getting things accomplished on time than they are with developing interpersonal relations. Their lives seem controlled by the little machines they wear on their wrists, cutting their discussions off **abruptly** to make their next appointment on time. This philosophy has enabled Americans to be extremely productive, and productivity is highly valued in their country.

4. EQUALITY/FAIRNESS

Equality is so cherished in the U. S. that it is seen as having a religious basis. Americans believe that all people are created equal and that all should have an equal opportunity to succeed. This concept of equality is strange to seven-eighths of the world which views status and authority as desirable, even if they happen to be near the bottom of the social order. Since Americans like to treat foreigners "Just like anybody else", newcomers to the U. S. should realize that no insult or personal indignity is intended if they are treated in a less than—**deferential** manner by waiters in restaurants, clerks in stores and hotels, taxi drivers, and other **service personnel**.

5. INDIVIDUALISM/INDEPENDENCE

Americans **view** themselves **as** highly individualistic in their thoughts and actions. They resist being thought of as representatives of any **homogeneous** group. When they do join groups, they believe they are special. Just a little different from other members of the same group. In the U. S. you will find people freely expressing a variety of opinions anywhere and anytime. Yet, in spite of this independence, almost all Americans end up **voting for** one of their two major political parties. Individualism leads to privacy, which Americans see as desirable. The word privacy does not exist in many non-Western languages. If It does, it is likely to have a negative **connotation**, suggesting loneliness or forced isolation. It is not uncommon for Americans to say, and almost to believe: "If I don't have half an hour a day to myself, I go **stark raving** mad!"

6. SELF-HELP **INITIATIVE**

Americans take credit only for what they accomplish as individuals. They get no credit for having been born into a rich family but pride themselves in having climbed the ladder of success, to whatever level, all by themselves. In an English-language dictionary, there are more than 100 **composite words** that have the word "self" as a prefix: self-aware. self-confident, self-conscious, self-contented, self-control, self-criticism, **self-deception**, **self-defeating**, **self-denial**. **The equivalent of** these words cannot be found in most other languages. It is an **indicator** of how highly Americans regard the self-made man or woman.

7. COMPETITION

Americans believe that competition brings out the best in any individual and in any system. This value is reflected in the American economic system of free enterprise, and it is applied in the U. S. in all areas—medicine, the arts, education, sports.

8. FUTURE **ORIENTATION**

Americans value the culture and the improvements the future will surely bring. They **devalue** the past and are, **to a large extent**, **unconscious of** the present. Even a happy present goes largely unnoticed because Americans are hopeful that the future will bring even greater happiness. Since Americans believe that humans, not fate, can and should control the environment, they are good at planning short-term projects. This ability has caused Americans to be invited to all corners of the Earth to plan, and often achieve, the miracles which their

goalsetting methods can produce.

9. ACTION/WORK ORIENTATION

"Don't just stand there," says a typical bit of American advice "do something!" This expression, though normally used in a crisis situation, in a sense describes most Americans' waking life, where action—any action—is seen as **superior to** inaction. Americans routinely **schedule** an extremely active day. Any relaxation must be limited in time and aimed at "**recreating**" so that they can work harder once their "recreation" is over. Such a "**no-nonsense**" attitude toward life has created a class of people known as "workaholics" —people **addicted to**, and often wholly **identified with**, their job or profession. The first question people often ask when they meet each other in the U. S. is related to work: "What do you do?", "Where do you work?" or "Who (what company) are you with?" The United States may be one of the few countries in the world where people speak about the **dignity** of human labor—meaning hard physical labor. Even corporation presidents will engage in physical labor from time to time and, in doing so, gain rather than lose respect from others.

(Words: 1063)

New Words

valid	*adj.* 有效的；有根据的；合法的；正当的
thought-provoking	*adj.* 发人深省的；引起思考的
primitive	*adj.* 原始的，远古的；简单的，粗糙的 *n.* 原始人
naive	*adj.* 天真的，幼稚的
fatalistic	*adj.* 宿命论的
superstitious	*adj.* 迷信的；由迷信引起的
indisputably	*adv.* 无争论余地地
disruptive	*adj.* 破坏的；分裂性的；制造混乱的
destructive	*adj.* 破坏的；毁灭性的；有害的；消极的

续表

continuity	*n.* 连续性；一连串；分镜头剧本
utmost	*adj.* 极度的；最远的 *n.* 极限；最大可能
abruptly	*adv.* 突然地；唐突地
deferential	*adj.* 恭敬的；惯于顺从的
homogeneous	*adj.* 均匀的；[数] 齐次的；同种的
connotation	*n.* 内涵；含蓄；暗示，隐含意义；储蓄的东西（词、语等）
stark-raving	*adj.* 完全胡说的；完全胡言乱语的
initiative	*adj.* 主动的；自发的；起始的 *n.* 主动权；首创精神
self-deception	*n.* 自欺；自欺欺人的行为
self-defeating	*adj.* 弄巧成拙的；不利于自己的企图的
self-denial	*n.* 自我否定；克己；忘我
indicator	*n.* 指示器；[试剂] 指示剂；[计] 指示符；压力计
orientation	*n.* 方向；定向；适应；情况介绍；向东方
devalue	*vt.* 使贬值；降低…的价值 *vi.* 贬值
goalsetting	*adj.* 设定目标的
schedule	*n.* 时间表；计划表；一览表 *vt.* 安排，计划；编制目录；将…列入计划表
recreate	*vt.* 再创造；使得到娱乐/消遣 *vi.* 娱乐；消遣
no-nonsense	*adj.* 严肃的；实际的
dignity	*n.* 尊严；高贵

Phrases & Expressions

take initiative	积极主动
result from	起因于；由…造成
be concerned with	参与，干预；关心；相干；涉及

续表

service personnel	保修人员；服务行业人员
view…as…	把…看作…
vote for	投票选举；投票赞成
composite word	复合词；合成词
the equivalent of	相当于
to a large extent	在很大程度上
unconscious of	不知道；未发觉
superior to	优于；比…优越
addicted to	上瘾；沉迷于
identify with	认为…等同于，与…一致

Proper Names

Dr. L. Robert Kohls	罗伯特·科尔斯 博士
International Programs	国际项目部
San Francisco State University	美国旧金山州立大学

Cultural Notes

1. Dr. L. Robert Kohls Director of International Programs at San Francisco State University. For more information, visit http://cqvp. com.

2. San Francisco State University (commonly referred to as San Francisco State, SF State and SFSU) is a public comprehensive university located in San Francisco, California, United States. As part of the 23 – campus California State University system, the university offers 118 different Bachelor's degrees, 94 Master's degrees, 5 Doctoral degrees including two Doctor of Education, a Doctor of Physical Therapy, a Ph. D in Education and Doctor of Physical Therapy Science, along with 26 teaching credentials among six academic colleges. For more information, visit http://en. wikipedia. org/wiki/ San_ Francisco_ State_ University.

Exercises

Comprehension of the Text

Ⅰ Answer the following questions according to the passage.

1. What are the common American values held by Dr. L. Robert Kohls?
2. What is the American attitude towards time according to the text?
3. What should we learn from the American values?

Vocabulary

Ⅱ. Fill in the blanks with the words given below. Change the form where necessary.

thought-provoking	deferential	recreate	schedule	initiative
self-deception	self-defeating	valid	devalue	dignity
individualistic	destructive	superstitious	utmost	primitive

1. Meeting the man ________ is to try every means to avoid to suffer reprimand when his mood is bad.
2. We do this because we believe in the ______ and value of every person.
3. If the first date wasn't all that great, try ________ another more romantic occasion.
4. I cannot agree with this opinion, which seems too ________, and unduly indifferent to the importance of knowledge.
5. Your privacy on the Internet is of ________ importance to the World Health Organization (WHO).
6. One is a reasonable response to a challenging market. The other is a ____ trade-off.
7. We all know how ________ viruses on our computer can be and how important it is to have virus protection installed.
8. The picture is ________, and what it illustrates is a common phenomenon in our society today.
9. His mind was besotted with fear, ignorance and ________.

10. China, with the regions fastest-growing economy, had kept the crisis from growing even worse by refusing to ________ its currency.

Translations

Ⅲ. Translate the following sentences into English.

1. 我创作这部电影的原因在于，我相信如果我们这样的国家引起了如此大的混乱，那么我们也应该准备好去面对由此局面而产生的可怕的结果。(result from)

____

2. 他们参与培训课程，但是并不关心每一门课程的细节。（be concerned with)

____

3. 这些问题在很大程度上超出了卫生部门的直接控制。(to a large extent)

____

4. 动物既不逊于也不优于人类，只是种类不同。(superior to)

____

5. 我们可以从事园艺、写作、绘画、散步、烤面包，也可以纯粹花时间沉思。(engage in)

____

Ⅳ. Translate the following passage into English.

美国人的待客之道从家里开始——尤其是和食物有关。大多数美国人都同意，无论如何，好的家常菜胜过餐馆的菜。受邀吃饭时，你或许可以问："我可以带些什么吗？"除非是每人带一道菜的聚餐，否则主人很可能会回答："不用，你来就可以了。"大多数非正式的聚餐，你应该穿舒适、轻便的衣服。设法准时到，否则打电话告诉主人你会晚点到。用餐时，习惯上人们会称赞女主人烹调的美食。当然，最大的赞美是多吃！

TEXT B American Love and Marriage

(A) The American concept of love and romance begins with dating. Young people date in several ways. At first they might have group dates with several boys and girls together. Later, they start going on single dates—just one boy and one girl. Sometimes a boy and a girl will go to a movie. Maybe they will go to a party at a friend's house. Or they might go out to eat.

(B) Romantic love is very much a part of American culture. Movies, TV shows and books in America all picture people falling in love. Americans know that no romance is perfect, but still they try to find the ideal person. Actually, love is a part of every culture, not just American culture. People all over the world search for happiness in a loving relationship.

(C) Americans view dating differently from people in other cultures. American young people see a date as a time just to have fun. They don't always have a romantic interest in mind. Someone may go out with one person this week, and another person the next. After a while, a boy and a girl may decide they want to "go steady". This means they think of each other as "boyfriend and girlfriend". It also means they don't want to date anyone else. Romance is beginning to bloom.

(D) "I do". To Americans those two words carry great meaning. They can even change your life. Especially if you say them at your own wedding. Making **wedding vows** is like signing a **contract**. Now Americans don't really think marriage is a **business deal**. But marriage is serious business

(E) It all begins with **engagement**. Traditionally, a young man asks the father of his sweetheart for **permission** to marry her. If the father agrees, the man later proposes to her. Often he tries to surprise her by "**popping the question**" in a romantic way.

(F) Sometimes the couple just decides together that the time is right to get married. The man usually gives his **fiancee** a diamond ring as a symbol of their engagement. They may be engaged for weeks, months or even years. As the big day approaches, **bridal showers** and bachelor's parties provide many useful gifts. Today many couples also receive **counseling** during engagement. This prepares them for the challenges of married life.

(G) At last it's time for the wedding. Although most weddings follow long-held traditions, there's still room for American **individualism**. For example, the usual place for a wedding is in a church. But some people get married outdoors in a scenic spot. A few even have the ceremony while **skydiving** or riding on horseback! The couple may invite hundreds of people or just a few close friends. They choose their own style of colors, decorations and music during the ceremony. But some things rarely change. The bride usually wears a beautiful, long white wedding dress. She traditionally wears "something old, something new, something borrowed and something blue". The groom wears a formal suit or **tuxedo**. Several close friends participate in the ceremony as **attendants**, including the best man and the maid of honor

(H) As the ceremony begins, the **groom** and his attendants stand with the **minister**, facing the audience. Music signals the entrance of the bride's attendants, followed by the beautiful bride. Nervously, the young couple repeats their vows. Traditionally, they promise to love each other "for better, for worse, for richer, for poorer, in sickness and in health". But sometimes the couple has **composed** their own vows. They give each other a gold ring to symbolize their marriage **commitment**. Finally the minister announces the big moment: "I now pronounce you man and wife. You may kiss your **bride**!"

(I) At the **wedding reception**, the bride and groom greet their guests. Then they cut the wedding cake and feed each other a bite. Guests **mingle** while enjoying cake, **punch** and other treats. Later the bride throws her **bouquet** of flowers to a group of single girls. Tradition says that the one who catches the bouquet will be the next to marry. During the reception, playful friends "decorate" the couple's car with tissue paper, tin cans and a "Just Married" sign. When the reception is over, the **newlyweds** run to their "decorated" car and speed off. Many couples take a honeymoon, a one- to two-week vacation trip, to celebrate their new marriage.

(J) Almost every culture has **rituals** to signal a change in one's life. Marriage is one of the most basic life changes for people of all cultures. So it's no surprise to find many traditions about getting married ...even in America. Yet each couple follows the traditions in a way that is uniquely their own.

(Words: 777)

New Words

vow	*n.* 发誓；誓言；许愿 *vt.* 发誓；郑重宣告 *vi.* 发誓；郑重宣告
contract	*n.* 合同；婚约 *vt.* 感染；订约；使缩短 *vi.* 收缩；感染；订约
engagement	*n.* 婚约；约会；交战；诺言
permission	*n.* 允许；许可
fiancee	*n.* （法）未婚妻
counseling	*n.* 咨询服务
individualism	*n.* 个人主义；利己主义；个人特征
skydiving	*n.* 跳伞运动
tuxedo	*n.* 男士无尾半正式晚礼服；无尾礼服
attendant	*n.* 服务员，侍者；随员，陪从 *adj.* 伴随的；侍候的
minister	*n.* 部长；大臣；牧师 *vi.* 执行牧师职务；辅助或伺候某人
compose	*vt.* 构成；写作；使平静；排…版 *vi.* 组成；作曲；排字
commitment	*n.* 承诺，保证；委托；承担义务；献身
mingle	*vt.* 使混合；使相混 *vi.* 混合；交往
punch	*n.* 冲压机；打洞器；钻孔机 *vt.* 开洞；以拳重击 *vi.* 用拳猛击
bouquet	*n.* 花束；酒香
newlywed	*n.* 新婚夫妇 *adj.* 新婚的
ritual	*n.* 仪式；惯例；礼制 *adj.* 仪式的；例行的；礼节性的

Phrases & Expressions

business deal	交易；生意
bridal shower	新娘送礼会
pop the question	求婚
wedding reception	结婚宴会；婚宴

Proper Names

Wedding vows	结婚誓言
Groom	新郎
Bride	新娘

Cultural Notes

1. Wedding vows Traditional wedding vows remain the most popular choice for couples.

Traditional Wedding Vows 1:

I, (name), take you (name), to be my (wife/husband), to have and to hold from this day forward, for better or for worse, for richer, for poorer, in sickness and in health, to love and to cherish; from this day forward until death do us part.

Traditional Wedding Vows 2:

I, (name), take you, (name), to be my [opt: lawfully wedded] (husband/wife), my constant friend, my faithful partner and my love from this day forward. In the presence of God, our family and friends, I offer you my solemn vow to be your faithful partner in sickness and in health, in good times and in bad, and in joy as well as in sorrow. I promise to love you unconditionally, to support you in your goals, to honor and respect you, to laugh with you and cry with you, and to cherish you for as long as we both shall live.

Traditional Wedding Vows 3 (For a Civil Ceremony):

(Name), I take you to be my lawfully wedded (husband/wife). Before these witnesses I vow to love you and care for you as long as we both shall live. I take you with all your faults and your strengths as I offer myself to you with my faults and strengths. I will help you when you need help, and I will turn to you when I need help. I choose you as the person with whom I will spend my life.

Traditional Wedding Vows 4:

I, (name), take you, (name), to be my beloved (wife/husband), to have and to hold you, to honor you, to treasure you, to be at your side in sorrow and in joy, in the good times, and in the bad, and to love and cherish you always. I promise you this from my heart, for all the days of my life. For more information, visit http://weddings.about.com/od/weddingvows/a/traditionalvows.htm.

Exercises

Comprehension of the Text

Ⅰ. The following 10 statements contain information given in the text. Identify the paragraph from which the information is derived. You may choose a paragraph more than once. Each paragraph is marked with a letter.

1. Traditionally, if a young man wants to marry a girl, he must ask the father of his sweetheart for permission.

2. Except the traditional place for a wedding in a church, some American people get married outdoors in a scenic spot.

3. In America, many couples take a one-to two-week vacation trip for a honeymoon to celebrate their new marriage.

4. At the wedding, the bride and the groom's clothes rarely change. The bride usually wears a white wedding dress and the groom often wears a formal suit or tuxedo.

5. American young people begin their romantic love with dating.

6. Now Americans think marriage as a serious thing, not a business deal.

7. American young man usually gives his fiancee a diamond ring as a symbol of their engagement.

8. Love is not only American culture, but also a part of every culture in the world.

9. When the bride at the wedding reception throws her bouquet of flowers to a group of single girls, that means the one who catches the bouquet will be the next to marry in tradition.

10. When American young people decide to make their love "go steady", they only date one boy or one girl, not anyone else.

Vocabulary

Ⅱ. Fill in the blanks with the words given below. Change the form where necessary.

vow	contract	engagement	permission	fiancee
counseling	attendant	minister	compose	commitment
mingle	bouquet	punch	ritual	newlywed

1. Traditionally, a young man asks the father of his sweetheart for ______ to marry her. If the father agrees, the man later proposes to her.

2. We all know that nobody reads this stuff, but it is a binding ________.

3. England, Scotland and Wales __________ the island of Great Britain.

4. I have expressed my personal ___________ to finish the job.

5. Television, political slogans, advertising, and the people we __________ with-they shape us in ways we do not realize.

6. After he saw his dentist, he ___________ to do better this time, and he stayed on it for a few days.

7. In the first, 82 __________ couples were asked to report eight times over the course of four years on how satisfied they were with their marriage.

8. Besides the interview on the day of the __________, we have heard nothing from either him or from Kate.

9. We can't tell people what to do with their animals, but a veterinarian is going to __________ as to what's best for the animal.

10. When traveling, give your partner a _________ of roses; one rose for each day that you'll be away.

Further Reading

TEXT C Raising Children

The job of raising children is a tough one. Children don't come with an instruction manual. And each child is different. So parents sometimes pull their hair out in frustration, not knowing what to do. But in raising children—as in all of life—what we do is influenced by our culture. Naturally then, American parents teach their children basic American values.

To Americans, the goal of parents is to help children stand on their own two feet. From infancy, each child may get his or her own room. As children grow, they gain more freedom to make their own choices. Teenagers choose their own forms of entertainment, as well as the friends to share them with. When they reach young adulthood, they choose their own careers and marriage partners. Of course, many young adults still seek their parents' advice and approval for the choices they make. But once they "leave the nest"at around 18 to 21 years old, they want to be on their own, not "tied to their mother's apron strings".

The relationship between parents and children in America is very informal. American parents try to treat their children as individuals—not as extensions of themselves. They allow them to fulfill their own dreams. Americans praise and encourage their children to give them the confidence to succeed. When children become adults, their relationship with their parents becomes more like a friendship among equals. But contrary to popular belief, most adult Americans don't make their parents pay for room and board when they come to visit. Even as adults, they respect and honor their parents.

Most young couples with children struggle with the issue of childcare. Mothers have traditionally stayed home with their children. In recent years, though, a growing trend is to put preschoolers in a day care center so Mom can work. Many Americans have strong feelings about which type of arrangement is best. Some argue that attending a day care center can be a positive experience for children. Others insist that mothers are the best caregivers for children. A number of women are now leaving the work force to become full-time homemakers.

Disciplining children is another area that American parents have differing opinions about. Many parents feel that an old-fashioned spanking helps youngsters learn what "No!" means. Others prefer alternate forms of discipline. For example, "time outs" have become popular in recent years. Children in "time out" have to sit in a corner or by a wall. They can get up only when they are ready to act nicely. Older children and teenagers who break the rules may be grounded, or not allowed to go out with friends. Some of their privileges at home—like TV or telephone use—may also be taken away for a while. Although discipline isn't fun for parents or children, it's a necessary part of training.

Being a parent is a tall order. It takes patience, love, wisdom, courage and a good sense of humor to raise children (and not lose your sanity). Some people are just deciding not to have children at all, since they're not sure it's worth it. But raising children means training the next generation and preserving our culture. What could be worth more than that?

(Words: 535)

Questions for discussions

1. What are the distinctive features of raising Children about American family?
2. Why disciplining children is thought a differing opinion according to the text?
3. What enlightenment can you get from the text?

More to Learn

1. Appreciation

Friends Forever

A friend is a friend forever.

They'll ignite a flame of love
  and set your heart aglow.
And light up your life
  from your head down to your toe.
A faithful friend is always there
  to lend a helping hand.
They'll be there to defend your honor
  and take a firm of gentle stand.
When you least expect it,
  they may drop in to say,
  "Hello, how have you been?
I love you with all my heart,
  my true and special friend."
A friend will add beauty to your life,
  like a sweet scented flower.
A good conversation may last into the night
  or for many, many hours.
They will take time to stop and listen,
  when your life is in doubt.
That's what a good friend's love is all about.

MOVIES TO SEE (A) The Gua Sha Treatment

Ⅰ. Movie Introduction

Director: Zheng Xiaolong

Starring: Tony Lcung Ka Fai
Jiang Wenli
Hollis Huston
Tamara Tungate
Zhu Xu

Running time: 100mins

Released: 2001

Plot: *The Gua Sha Treatment is* a movie about the differences between American and Chinese culture. Xu datong is a video games designer in St. Louis. When his father visits from China, he performs Gua Sha (a Chinese traditional treatment) on his grandson, which leaves bright red marks on the skin and causes a lawsuit of child abuse. In the court, Datong loses his mind so that finally he loses custody of his son. This scene is shocking and thought-provoking to most of the Chinese audiences. But the most impressing scene to people is the ending. Datong wants to see his son on Christmas eve, he has to climb a pipe to the ninth floor which his son lives. The pipe is not only a pipe, but also a gap, a deep gap between American and 5000 - year Chinese culture. He wants to climb over the gap and he will never succeed, perhaps no Chinese people really could succeed.

Ⅱ. Classic Scenes

Task 1 Study the underlined sentences and expressions in the following classic scenes.

1. At the award ceremony

Xu Datong: Eight years ago, I was just a new immigrant, working so hard to earn my living by selling the art in the street. But I believe if I work hard enough, one day I will become one of you, a truly successful American. Today, this award proved that America is a true land of opportunity. I am the living prove of that: I have successful career, a loving wife, an adorable son. I especially like to say thanks to my boss Mr. Eric Qumran. Finally, I'd like to say thanks to all of you. I love you. I love America and this is my piece of American dream. Thank you.

2. At home to prepare the words for court

Xu Datong: Dennis was a premature birth, only 4 pounds, so small and treasure like a little monkey.

He's my son .

He's going to grow up as a man, to get marry, and continue the XU's family blood line in the circle of life.

As I think about his entire life still to have the pain, I feel the awesome responsibility of a father.

I'd like to take that responsibility in joyfully and gratefully.

I have to give him more hope.

All those matters are that he is in peace, true happiness, in good health.

Your honor, I am proud to be a father.

That's all I have to say .

3. Argument in court

Judge: If the prosecution also have a beautiful performance first.

Prosecution: There is a moving performance indeed. The CUVA has several witnesses to show US another side of Mr. Xu, the real Mr. Xu.

Your honor, this is the doorman of the royal apartment where Xu's living.

Judge: Mr Oberman, this is an informal hearing. so that Bible swear is not necessary. But I want you to tell the truth. Because if you do not, I will throw the book at you.

Oberman: Yes, sir.

Prosecution: Mr. O, were you on duty every night in the month?

Oberman: Yes!

Prosecution: Did Mr. Xu live the building at about 9:30 that night?

Oberman: Yes, and he was in an awful hurry.

Prosecution: Then, where was his son?

Oberman: Alone in the apartment. Ms. Xu does not come home from work yet, she does real estate business. And the boy's grandpa was in a police station, waiting to be picked up.

Marin: Your honor, we may see Mr. O know everything, we can call him god. This testimony is hearsay at best.

Judge: Mr Davis, not enough, strike one.

Prosecution: But, your honor, I intend to show……

Judge: What you intend is not important, but what your accomplishment is.

Prosecution: Yes, your honor. we are finished with this witness. I'd like to call a second witness, Ms. Kang.

Marin: Anything I need to know about her?

Xu Datong: I do not know, I do not ever remember her. Did you remember?

Ms. Xu: Yes, I do. Anything not good.

Prosecution: Your honor, this is K. R. She was an attending nurse. Ms. Rico, you were in attendance the day Dennis Xu was born?

Ms. Kang: Yes, I'll never forget that day as long as my life.

Prosecution: Please tell us what happened?

Ms. Kang: Gladly, that day, an oriental pregnant patient came in; her name is Jianning Xu. She was in bad shape. I was instructed by Dr Grand to call her husband, because, she may have to have an emergency cesarean production.

Ms. Kang: I have to call him, because apparently he had some meetings. That was my appointment. The meetings were more important than his child birth.

Xu Datong: That was crazy

Defense Attorney: Objection.

Judge: Let try to restrain yourself, they only the facts

Ms. Kang: That was what his wife said. Anyway, he finally returned my pager and after explaining everything that was happening, he had no regard for the child whatsoever. He said to save the wife, not the child.

Xu Datong: This is human nature.

I mean if my wife is alive, we can always have more children, but if she dies……

Ms. Kang: And you do not even give your child a chance to survive, your eastern are so barbaric.

Judge: Quiet, quiet! I wouldn't stand this chaos roars. I didn't display racism in my court room. Have questions, defendant lawyer?

Defense attorney: I have only one simple question . Since he said to save the wife not the child, you accuse him of child abuse , but if he said to save the child not the wife, would you now accuse him of wife abuse? None for the questions, your honor!

Judge: You can rest now.

Prosecution: You honor, five years ago, when Dennis was struggling for his life to live, his old father was coldly to give him death. Mr. Xu is an incompetent parent.

Xu Datong: No, you don't know me. You people know nothing about me. First, you come to take my boy away. Now you are coming here telling nothing but filling lies.

Marin: Sit down, keep quiet.

Xu Datong: What? not allow me to speak? not allow me to defend myself?

Judge: Put your client a night, can change his temper.

Marin: Good, but not necessary, your honor.

Prosecution: You honor, I want to call for a new witness, not on an original list.

Marin: Your honor, I don't like surprises.

Judge: This is from the beginning of surprises, so let me show the party to go on.

Prosecution: Thank you, you honor, summon Mr John Qumran.

All right, Mr. Qumran. Let's get to the point, shall we? Mr. Xu is an employee of you and also your best friend, right?

Mr. Qumran: Yes, I am proud to go on Mr. Xu, my friend.

Prosecution: I have had some game coincidence.

Mr. Qumran: What a coincidence.

Prosecution: "Death Crash", "Hell Racers", "Malcolm Massacre".

Mr. Qumran: We also create "Dream Seekers", "Salley Said Educational Series".

Prosecution: As far as I know, your company because the game content is too violent protests by citizens groups which are mostly Xu Datong designed, is not him?

Mr. Qumran: Yes...But...

Prosecution: And at the ceremony where Mr. Xu was being honored, your son and Dennis Xu got into a fight over one of your violent video game.

Mr. Qumran: How did you know about that?

Prosecution: That boy will be boy. But Mr. Xu struck Dennis fiercely on the head.

Mr. Qumran: Yes...

Marin: Your honor, it's not illegal for a father to discipline his son in public.

Prosecution: Hitting is not discipline.

Marin: Objection!

Judge: It supposed to me to determine.

Mr. Qumran: Yes, he did. But…

Prosecution: According to that, this is a man stick in a culture of violence.

Xu Datong: Culture violent?

Datong's Wife: Da tong—, no—

Xu Datong: I charactered my latest video according to agent Chinese hero. Sun Wukong is a good-heart, compassionate hero, he represents our traditional value and ethics.

Prosecution: I have read the English version of "Xi You Ji". The only moral Chinese monkeys to Taoyuan for himself, destroy all the peach trees and broke someone's workshop.

Xu Datong: Shit!

Who the hell you think you are? You know nothing about Chinese culture, YOYO cheeky liar, I love my son, and you know nothing.

Judge: Stop it! Stop it! I decide that Dennis Xu will be kept under the guardianship of CWVA.

Task 2 Work in pairs or groups and play the roles in one of your favorite scenes.

Ⅲ. Cultural Notes

1. *Xi You Ji*: here it refers to "Journey to the West". Journey to the West is a mythological novel based on many centuries of popular tradition. It was probably put into its present form in the 15708 by Wu Chengen (1500 – 82). This lively fantasy relates the amazing adventures of the priest San-zang as he travels west in search of Buddhist sutras with his three disciples, the irreverent and capable Monkey, greedy Pig, and friar Sand.

2. *Sun WuKong*: also known as Qi Tian Da Sheng, which title he appointed himself, an equivalent of emperor above. He was a spirit stone on the Hua Guo mountain many years ago, exposed naked in the alternative of sun and moon, ex-

perienced the bathing of sun and rains, he got some magic power and turned into a monkey, which had every character of human and was extremely clever. At an occasional chance, he met a Taoist whose name was Tai Yi Zhen Ren, who was a super natural being; Sun WuKong was attracted by his ability of turning himself into many animals, so he pleaded for being the Taoist; sap prentice, the Taoist agreed and taught him many skills, which helped Sun wukong to be in the high light of both in heaven and in the world.

Ⅳ. Questions for discussion

1. What are the themes involved in this movie?

2. Can you use your own words to describe the Chinese Gua Sha Treatment?

3. What is the difference between American values and Chinese values according to the *Gua Sha Treatment?*

Ⅴ. Movie Review

Task: Write a movie review on *The Gua Sha Treatment.*

MOVIES TO SEE (B) The Joy Luck Club

Ⅰ. Movie Introduction

Director: Wayne Wang

Starring: Ming-Na, Lauren Tom, Tamlyn Tomita, France Nuyen, Rosalind Chao, Kieu Chinh, Tsai Chin, Lisa Lu, Vivian Wu

Running time: 139 mins

Released: 1993

Plot: *The Joy Luck Club* is a best-selling novel written by Amy Tan. It focuses on four Chinese American immigrant families who start a club known as "the Joy Luck Club", playing the Chinese game of Mahjong for money while feasting on a variety of foods. As the novel opens Jing-Mei "June" Woo has just lost her mother, Suyuan, to an aneurysm. She is asked by her mother's three friends to take Suyuan's place in their Mah-Jong foursome and their "Joy Luck Club". The novel unfolds with interspersed chapters by each of the three remaining members of the Club and their American-born daughters. Lindo and Waverly Jong began their war over Waverly's childhood chess stardom and the effects it has on every aspect of

Waverly's adult life. An-Mei Hsu recounts the tragedy that gave her strength, and worries that her daughter, Rose, lacks the same determination. Lena St. Clair tries to care for her eccentric mother, while her mother recounts a secret history that has allowed her to see more deeply than her daughter imagines. Through it all, June Woo tries to piece together the stories that her own mother can no longer tell, and to be faithful to her mother's memory despite their sometimes rocky relationship. This story of the bonds between mothers and daughters has been popular with female readers.

To Recommend More Movies

❖ *Con Air* (1997)

❖ *Saving Private Ryan* (1997)

❖ *The Pursuit of Happiness* (2006)

❖ *Bathing Beauty* (1944)

❖ *One Flew Over the Cuckoo's Nest* (2007)

Unit Eight Education

Pre-reading Activities

Answer the following questions before you read this text.

1. What is a public university predominantly funded by as opposed to a private university?

2. How much do you know about Public Ivies?

3. Can you list the top 10 public colleges and universities in America?

TEXT A Public Universities in the United States

Public, or state, universities typically **enroll** tens of thousands of students and offer degrees in hundreds of subject areas. **Robert H. Bruininks** outlines the makeup and financing structure of large state universities and the opportunities for international students and scholars. He has been president of the **University of Minnesota** since 2002 and is a member of the **J. William Fulbright Foreign Scholarship Board**.

Large public universities in the United States, also referred to as state universities, are closely identified with and supported by the states in which they are located. They are exciting, **dynamic**, and highly regarded centers for higher education, with unique traditions and connections to their communities. They are also major **magnets** for talent from all over the country and the world.

Typically, universities of this type enroll tens of thousands of students. They produce the majority of graduate and professional degrees in the country, as well as a significant number of undergraduate degrees. Also common to large public universities are a wide range of **academic** programs. To use my own institution as an example, the University of Minnesota **Twin Cities campus** has 50, 000 students, offers hundreds of degrees, and is a leader in fields as varied as **neurology and transplant surgery**, economics and political science, material sciences and **nanotechnology**, and agriculture and natural resources.

Public universities play a critical role in regional economic, cultural, and civic development, and many, such as the University of Minnesota, are deeply involved in advancing knowledge and technology through research. These universities are among the major research universities in the United States and frequently have major involvement in international programs around the world. A series of federal actions in the second half of the 19th century provided resources to states to help establish and build universities. Public universities that arose from this **federal largesse** have a **mandate** to provide **outreach** and community engagement to the state in which they are located (e. g. technology transfer, support to agriculture, interaction with primary and secondary schools, and interaction with state and local policy makers).

The level of research **intensity** varies greatly among state universities. Competitive research grants and contracts awarded to the most **prestigious** public universities typically **amount to** hundreds of millions of dollars each year. There is also great variation in the level of support from the states. State universities with large research budgets typically receive 10 to 30 percent of their budgets from the state in which they are located. The remaining **portion** of their budget comes from tuition and fees, grants/contracts, and gifts.

As a result of the financing structure of large state universities, many graduate students receive financial aid through research **assistantships** associated with research grants and contracts received by the university. Although many public universities are seeking increased funding to support international exchanges and study, **access to** financial aid for international students is very limited outside of the **aforementioned** research/grant funding. Since undergraduates do not generally hold research assistantships, scholarship support for international students seeking undergraduate degrees is quite limited at these public universities.

Large state universities are located in **a variety of** communities, from **modest** towns to large **metropolitan** areas. Many universities also have **multiple** campuses at locations throughout their state, and many states also have more than one public university system.

Public universities are governed by boards of **trustees** or **regents**, with varying reporting responsibility to the state government. Unlike in many other countries, these U. S. universities don't report to a federal-level education minister, and higher education policy is largely **delegated** to the states, with the important exceptions of federal student financial aid and research funding through federal agencies such as the **National Science Foundation**, the **National Institutes of Health**, and many other federal agencies.

Some traditions of public universities in the United States are quite different from those in other countries. Even at these state-supported institutions, students have traditionally paid for part of their education through tuition and fees, and these costs to students are increasing. Today the average student takes out loans in order to help pay for his or her education. Private fundraising plays an increasingly important role in funding projects, scholarships, and positions at public universities. Finally, **intercollegiate athletics** attract intense interest from students, **alumni**, and members of the general public, and athletic events generate additional **revenue**.

Among all U. S. universities, large state universities often include the largest **percentage** of international students and scholars. At the University of Minnesota, our community includes more than 4, 500 international students and scholars from about 130 countries. The University of Minnesota provides support services such as counseling and advising on personal and academic issues, **orientation** to U. S. and university culture, **immigration** and **visa** advising, and English as a second language courses, as well as programs and workshops on a variety of topics including intercultural understanding and communication. Many state universities have similar programs in place to help students **navigate** what can sometimes be a confusing system of administration and academic **regulation**, although the scope of these services varies from institution to institution.

With growing competition from other countries, no major university in the United States can **afford to** take the interest of foreign students for granted. As a result, public universities are increasingly focused on attracting top students from around the world. If you are a motivated and **self-directed** student looking for **exposure to** the **cutting edge** of knowledge and creative work, I encourage you to investigate the rich opportunities available among large public universities in the United States.

(Words: 917)

New Words

enroll	*vt/vi.* . 登记；使加入；把…记入名册；使入伍
dynamic	*adj.* 有活力的；动态的；动力的；动力学的 *n.* 动态；动力
magnets	*n.* 磁性，［电磁］磁体（magnet 的复数形式）；［材］磁铁
academic	*adj.* 学术的；理论的；学院的
neurology	*n.* 神经病学；神经学
transplant	*vt/vi.* 移植；迁移；使移居 *n.* 移植；移植器官；被移植物；移居者
surgery	*n.* 外科；外科手术；手术室；诊疗室
nanotechnology	*n.* 纳米技术
federal	*adj.* 联邦的；同盟的
largesse	*n.* 慷慨的赠予；慷慨赠予物（等于 largess）
mandate	*n.* 授权；命令；委托管理；受命进行的工作 *vt.* 授权；托管
outreach	*n.* 延伸，拓广；adj. 扩大服务的 *vt. /vi.* 超越，伸出；超出…的范围
intensity	*n.* 强度；强烈；［电子］亮度；紧张
prestigious	*adj.* 有名望的；享有声望的
portion	*n.* 部分；一份；命运 *vt.* 分配；给…嫁妆
assistantship	*n.* 助教奖学金；助理职务

续表

aforementioned	*adj.* 上述的；前面提及的
modest	*adj.* 谦虚的，谦逊的；适度的；端庄的；羞怯的
multiple	*n.* 倍数；［电］并联 *adj.* 多重的；多样的；许多的
trustee	*n.* ［法］受托人，受托者（trustee 的复数形式）
regent	*n.* 摄政王；摄政者；州立大学董事会董事；统治者 *adj.* 摄政的；统治的
intercollegiate	*adj.* 学院间的；大学间的
athletics	n. 竞技；体育运动；田径运动
alumni	*n.* 男校友；男毕业生（alumnus 的复数）
percentage	*n.* 百分比；百分率，百分数
immigration	*n.* 外来移民；移居
visa	*n.* 签证 *vt.* 签发签证
navigate	*vi.* 航行，航空 *vt.* 驾驶，操纵；使通过；航行于
regulation	*n.* 管理；规则；校准 *adj.* 规定的；平常的
self-directed	*adj.* 自主的；自我指导的

Phrases & Expressions

amount to	相当于，总计为，总共达到
access to	接近；有权使用；通向…的入口
a variety of	种种；各种各样的…
afford to	（有条件）做；能承担；买得起某物；支付的起
vary from …to…	不同于…，与…各不相同
exposure to	曝光；显露
cutting edge	［机］切削刃；刀刃，刀口；先锋地位

Proper Names

Robert H. Bruininks	罗伯特·布鲁因克斯
University of Minnesota	明尼苏达大学（美国）
The J. William Fulbright Foreign Scholarship Board	美国J. 威廉·富布莱特外籍学术奖学金委员会
Twin Cities campus	明尼苏达大学双城分校（位于美国西部）
National Science Foundation	美国国家科学基金会
National Institutes of Health	美国国家卫生研究院

Cultural Notes

1. Robert H. Bruininks (born February 22, 1942) is the former President of the University of Minnesota. He was named president on November 8, 2002 after briefly serving as the interim president. He has been employed by the University of Minnesota since 1968. He was the 15th full-time president in the history of the University of Minnesota. For more information, visit http://en. wikipedia. org/wiki/Robert_ Bruininks.

2. University of Minnesota, Twin Cities is a public research university located in Minneapolis and St. Paul, Minnesota, United States. The Minneapolis and St. Paul campuses are approximately 5 miles (8.0 km) apart, and the Saint Paul campus is actually in neighboring Falcon Heights. It is the oldest and largest campus within the University of Minnesota system and has the sixth-largest main campus student body in the United States. The university is organized into 19 colleges and schools, and it has sister campuses in Crookston, Duluth, Morris, and Rochester. For more information, visit http://twin – cities. umn. edu. /.

3. The J. William Fulbright Foreign Scholarship Board was established by Congress for the purpose of supervising the Fulbright Program and certain programs authorized by the Fulbright-Hays Act and for the purpose of selecting students, scholars, teachers, trainees, and other persons to participate in the educational exchange programs. For more information, visit http://en. wikipedia. org/wiki/

J. _ William_ Fulbright_ Foreign_ Scholarship_ Board.

Exercises

Comprehension of the Text

Ⅰ Answer the following questions according to the passage.

1. What roles do public universities play in regional economic, cultural, and civic development?

2. In what way are some traditions of public universities in the United States quite different from those in other countries?

3. Why are public universities increasingly focused on attracting top students from around the world?

Vocabulary

Ⅱ. Fill in the blanks with the words given below. Change the form where necessary.

magnet	mandate	enroll	largesse	modest
academic	prestigious	dynamic	outreach	multiple
trustee	intercollegiate	orientation	navigate	regulation

1. The European Union has proposed new ______ to control the hours worked by its employees.

2. McNair consistently ranks as the top public high school in the state, and virtually all its students go on to college, including to some of the most ______ institutions in the United States.

3. The expedition was wrecked by bad planning and poor ______.

4. Prospect Park, with its vast lake, is a ______ for all health freaks.

5. The nation's balance of payments improved ______ last month.

6. The ______ of your pension fund decide which fund manager will invest some or all of your future income.

7. The president and his supporters are almost certain to read this vote as

a ______for continued economic reform.

8. He's one of the most ______imaginative jazz pianists of our time.

9. They give their freshman a three-day ______ course.

10. Student exchange programs, Chinese and Hindi language teaching and __ partnership are going on actively, producing positive result.

Translations

Ⅲ. Translate the following sentences into English.

1. 国籍核查过程中的成本，可以多达两或三个月的薪金，这数目对这些移民社区来说，是遥不可及的。(amount to)

____

2. 穷人忍饥挨饿和营养不良并不是因为世界上没有足够的粮食，而是因为他们买不起那些粮食。(afford to)

____

3. 关键就是选择适合孩子发展阶段的、他们喜欢的、可以达到各种目的的阅读和书写活动，并和他们一起参加。(a variety of)

____

4. 卫生官员认定，几乎在所有这些病例中，患者都是由于接触了病禽而受到感染的。(exposure to)

____

5. 艾里斯夫妇拥有一家玩具公司，研究尖端机器人技术已达30年。(cutting edge)

____

Ⅳ. Translate the following passage into English.

美国的教育机构反映了这个国家的基本价值体系，尤其是它机会均等的价值观。美国人坚信，从小学到大学，每个人在获得良好教育方面都应拥有同等的机会。美国的学校倾向于将注意力放在培养学生的判断性思维能力上，而不是放在培养学生学习既定事实上。美国教育鼓励学生提出问题、独立思考，以及在课堂上阐述自己的观点，这也反映了美国人个人自由和自力更生的价值观。美国教育系统的目标是教导学生如何学习和帮助他们发挥出自己的最大潜能。

TEXT B What is a Large, Private Research University?

(A) **James W. Wagner**, president of **Emory University** in Atlanta, Georgia, says that private research universities enjoy greater financial **flexibility** than their public **counterparts**. Thus, private institutions are more able to create **distinctive** programs.

(B) One of the strengths of the American system of higher education is its great variety. From small colleges with only several hundred students to large state-supported universities with tens of thousands of students, and from two-year community colleges with vocational programs to privately funded research universities, American higher education meets a wide variety of needs. For students, the right choice has much to do with possible career paths, financial **constraints**, and geography. In other words, it has to do with what they feel called to do and to study, how much they can afford, and whether or not they want to leave home. What matters most in the end is the **appropriateness** of the school to the **aspirations** of the student.

(C) In the United States, 92 of the 100 largest universities are public or "state-supported" (i. e. , supported by one of the 50 individual states, not the federal government) , and 77 percent of the nation's college students receive their education at public institutions. Still, the major private universities occupy all but three or four of the top 25 **slots** in most **rankings**. Thus, the private research university appears to **be held in especially high regard** in the United States and around the world.

(D) But what do we mean when we speak of a "private research university, "and what makes this type of institution so attractive?

(E) Private research universities offer professional training (for instance, in law, medicine, and engineering), as well as education leading to the Ph. D. degree. Besides teaching, the **faculty** members spend a great deal of their time in research. In fact, in these institutions, the quality of faculty, scholarship, and research is as important in determining **compensation** and promotion as is the quality of teaching. But public universities also offer professional training, Ph. D. education, and an emphasis on scholarship and research. So what makes private universities different?

(F) For one thing, private universities generally enjoy greater financial flexibility. They do not depend on state legislatures for funding, but draw their resources from alumni, **philanthropic** foundations, and scientific and other professional organizations, all of which support the universities by funding programs, scholarships, buildings, and professorships. These sources of funding, although increasing at public universities as well, now provide private universities with the ability to be more **nimble** and more able to step off in bold new directions of **inquiry**, creating specialized centers of study and distinctive programs. For students, this flexibility often translates into opportunity to stay in fields where they might otherwise expect to find little encouragement.

(G) Similarly, private universities' independence from public coffers has made them more able to establish "points of presence" in other countries. The citizens of Georgia, for instance, are unlikely to approve the use of their tax dollars to establish a study center in London. But they probably would welcome the establishment of such a center by privately controlled Emory University. In general, private universities can more easily open international **portals** for research, service, and teaching. Emory University, for example, has programs in global health throughout Africa, in the **Caucasus region**, and in Asia. It has business programs throughout Europe and Asia. Such activities provide opportunities for American students and professors to engage, whether in the United States or abroad, with the best minds and talent from other countries.

(H) Finally, most research universities are somewhat smaller than their public counterparts, offering a favorable mixture of rich resources and human scale. While the potential for learning and research is great at any of our nation's fine universities, public or private, the smaller scale of private campuses makes possible the easy interaction of scholars across disciplines, since the schools and departments generally are at most a short walk across campus. In a world where the most important discoveries are being made through **collaboration** across

boundaries, the capacity of the private university to **foster** and **intensify** collaborations both **within the confines of** the campus and beyond, to the far reaches of the globe, may be the private university's greatest attraction.

(Words: 703)

New Words

flexibility	*n.* 灵活性；弹性；适应性
counterparts	*n.* 相对物；相对应的人
distinctive	*adj.* 有特色的，与众不同的
constraint	*n.* 约束；局促，态度不自然；强制
appropriateness	*n.* 适当；适合；得体
aspiration	*n.* 愿望；志向
slot	*n.* 位置；狭槽；水沟；硬币投币口
ranking	*n.* 等级；地位；排名
faculty	*n.* 科，系；能力；全体教员
compensation	*n.* 补偿；报酬；赔偿金
philanthropic	*adj.* 博爱的；仁慈的
nimble	*adj.* 敏捷的；聪明的；敏感的
inquiry	*n.* 探究；调查；质询
portal	*n.* 大门，入口
collaboration	*n.* 合作；勾结；通敌
boundary	*n.* 边界；范围；分界线
foster	*vt.* 培养；养育，抚育；抱（希望等）
intensify	*vt.* /*vi.* 使加强，使强化；使变激烈

Phrases & Expressions

be held in high regard	受高度推崇
within the confines of	在…（范围）之内

Proper Names

James W. Wagner	詹姆斯·W. 瓦格纳（人名）
Emory University	埃默里大学（美国）
Caucasus region	高加索地区

Cultural Notes

1. **James W. Wagner** was born and reared in Silver Spring, Maryland. He earned his bachelor's degree in electrical engineering in 1975 from the University of Delaware and a master's degree in clinical engineering in 1978 from The Johns Hopkins University School of Medicine. In 1984, he completed his PhD degree in materials science and engineering from Johns Hopkins. He, an award-winning teacher and scientist, became the 19th president of Emory University on September 1, 2003. For more information, visit http://president.emory.edu/.

2. **Emory University** is a private research university in metropolitan Atlanta, located in the Druid Hills section of unincorporated DeKalb County, Georgia, United States. The university was founded as Emory College in 1836 in Oxford. Emory University, recognized internationally for its outstanding liberal arts colleges, graduate and professional schools. For more information, visit http://www.emory.edu/home/index.html.

Exercises

Comprehension of the Text

Ⅰ. The following 10 statements contain information given in the text. Identify the paragraph from which the information is derived. You may choose a paragraph more than once. Each paragraph is marked with a letter.

1. Compared to public universities, private universities generally enjoy greater financial flexibility.

2. Private universities can more easily open international portals for research, service, and teaching.

3. Most research universities are able to offer a favorable mixture of rich resources and human scale.

4. The smaller scale of private campuses makes possible the easy interaction of scholars across disciplines.

5. The private university's greatest attraction may be their capacity to foster and intensify collaborations both within the confines of the campus and beyond, to the far reaches of the globe.

6. What matters most is the appropriateness of the school to the aspirations of the student.

7. For students, the right choice has much to do with possible career paths, financial constraints, and geography.

8. The private research university seems to be highly regarded in the United States and around the world.

9. Private universities usually draw their resources from alumni, philanthropic foundations, and scientific and other professional organizations.

10. One of the advantages of the American system of higher education is its great diversity.

Vocabulary

II. Fill in the blanks with the words given below. Change the form where necessary.

intensify	appropriateness	constraint	aspiration	flexibility
foster	compensation	boundary	collaboration	nimble
ranking	faculty	legislature	distinctive	inquiry

1. The ______ of distance learning would be particularly suited to busy managers.

2. And these exchanges really offer the opportunity for people to connect and ______, and they remind us of how much we have in common.

3. Their sense of humour and ability to get along with people are two charac-

teristics that ______for their lack of experience.

4. WHO calls on all its Member States to ______action against cancer by developing and reinforcing cancer control programmes.

5. During the festival and celebration, you can appreciate the music and dance with ______features.

6. Soon after, I made confidential ______ as to how and when it all happened.

7. Journalists were given the freedom to visit, investigate, and report without ______.

8. A ______mind backed by a degree in economics gave him a firm grasp of financial matters.

9. He said that developed countries had a responsibility to ______global economic growth to help new democracies.

10. This is the modern city, not as a scene of fragmentation or despair, but rather a place of ascent and ______.

Further Reading

TEXT C U. S. Community Colleges: A Gateway to Higher Education for Many

Two-year colleges offer students an opportunity to begin their higher education in a small, community-based environment, often at lower cost than a four-year institution. George R. Boggs, president and chief executive officer of the American Association of Community Colleges, outlines the qualities that make community colleges an attractive alternative.

Community colleges are the gateway to higher education in the United States for a growing number of students. These colleges provide students with an opportunity to earn credits for the first two years of a four-year bachelor's degree at high-quality, accredited institutions. With their lower tuition costs, community colleges give students a way to save money while learning in a supportive environment. They also allow students to access training for associate-degree or nondegree careers, and they offer continuing education and personal development classes for the broad spectrum of adult learners.

Community colleges are the largest and fastest-growing sector of higher education in the United States. There are now nearly 1, 200 regionally accredited community colleges located throughout the country, serving more than 11 million students (approximately 46 percent of all U. S. undergraduates).

U. S. community colleges offer international students numerous benefits, including opportunities to improve English language skills and to build an understanding of American culture in a U. S. community.

Among the benefits of community colleges are: **Lower Cost**. Tuition costs are significantly lower than four-year colleges and universities (about \$5, 000 per year as compared to \$12,000 to \$20,000 or more for a four-year institution).

Easy Transfer to a University. A "2 + 2"system in the United States refers to an efficient system of "articulation"between a two-year college and a four-year college or university. Most community colleges have articulation agreements with four-year colleges and universities, ensuring that credits earned at the community college will count toward the four-year degree program.

Accredited Institutions. American community colleges, four-year colleges, and major universities are all accredited by the same agencies. That is why universities accept course credits obtained at community colleges.

Wide Variety of Programs. Community colleges have hundreds of majors from which to choose, including popular areas such as business management, computer science, engineering, and health sciences-related programs.

English as a Second Language. Most community colleges offer a wide range of English course offerings at multiple levels and an array of support services to ensure that students with different language proficiencies succeed.

A Supportive Learning Environment. Community colleges offer small class sizes, averaging fewer than 30 students, allowing personal attention and ongoing support from professors. The focus is on individual student success within an environment designed to support students' learning patterns and needs. Support services for students include tutoring, advising, writing labs, international student clubs, and international student service centers.

Diversity. U. S. community college students come from diverse cultural heritages and ethnicities. The colleges offer a wide spectrum of clubs and activities that celebrate and support the diversity that describes society in the United States.

Access to U. S. Culture. Because they are reflective of and responsive to their communities, community colleges tend to have strong local ties. This relationship provides international students with extensive opportunities to interact with Americans and to experience American culture.

Variety of Locations and Campus Sizes. Community colleges, like other educational institutions in the United States, differ widely. Some are large, multi-campus institutions located in big cities, while others are much smaller schools located in rural settings and serving small student populations. There is a community college conveniently located within commuting distance of 90 percent of the U. S. population.

Distinguished Alumni. Alumni of U. S. community colleges include California Governor Arnold Schwarzenegger and former Maryland Governor Parris Glendening, NASA space shuttle commander Eileen Collins, Star Wars movie series producer/director George Lucas, film actors Tom Hanks and Clint Eastwood, fashion designer Calvin Klein, human genome scientist Craig Venter, and U. S. Surgeon General Richard Carmona.

(Words: 641)

Questions for discussions

1. What are the distinctive features of community colleges, compared to public and private universities?

2. Why are community colleges the gateway to higher education in the United States for an increasing number of students?

3. What benefits can community colleges offer students?

More to Learn

1. U. S. News 2015 Best Colleges Rankings

U. S. News & World Report today released the 30th edition of its flagship Best Colleges rankings, which measure academic excellence. For the second year in a row, Princeton University claims sole possession of the No. 1 spot in the Best National Universities category. Williams College tops the list of Best National Liberal Arts Colleges, making it No. 1 for 12 years in a row. University of California—Berkeley holds onto its spot as the Top Public School among National Universities.

The 2015 edition of Best Colleges includes data on nearly 1,800 schools nationwide to help parents and students evaluate their options. Eligible schools are ranked on up to 16 measures of academic excellence. Outcome-related measures, such as graduation and retention rates, account for 30 percent of the rankings and are the most heavily weighted factors in the methodology. For the full list of rankings, visit *http://www.usnews.com/colleges.*

U. S. News 2015 Best Colleges Rankings

Best National Universities	Best National Liberal Arts Colleges
1. Princeton University (NJ)	1. Williams College (MA)
2. Harvard University (MA)	2. Amherst College (MA)
3. Yale University (CT)	3. Swarthmore College (PA)
4. Columbia University (NY)	4. Wellesley College (MA)
5. Stanford University (CA)	5. Bowdoin College (ME)
6. University of Chicago (IL)	6. Pomona College (CA)
7. Massachusetts Institute of Technology	7. Middlebury College (VT)
8. Duke University (NC)	8. Carleton College (MN)
9. University of Pennsylvania	9. Claremont McKenna College (CA)
10. California Institute of Technology	10. Haverford College (PA)

Best Public Schools

National Universities	Liberal Arts Colleges
1. University of California-Berkeley	1. United States Naval Academy (MD)
2. University of California-Los Angeles	2. United States Military Academy (NY)
3. University of Virginia	3. United States Air Force Academy (CO)
4. University of Michigan-Ann Arbor	4. Virginia Military Institute
5. University of North Carolina-Chapel Hill	5. New College of Florida

MOVIES TO SEE (A) Dead Poets Society

I. Movie Introduction

Director: Peter Weir

Starring: Robin Williams
Robert Sean Leonard
Ethan Hawke

Running time: 130mins

Released: 1989

Plot: *Dead Poets Society* is a 1989 film directed by Peter Weir. Set in 1959 at a conservative and aristocratic boys prep school, it tells the story of an English teacher who inspires his students to change their lives of conformity through his teaching of poetry and literature. The movie is a modern interpretation of the transcendentalist movement.

II. Classic Scenes

Task 1 Study the underlined sentences and expressions in the following classic scenes.

1. The opening ceremony of the school

Mr. Nolan (Principal): Ladies and gentlemen, boys, the light of knowledge. One hundred years ago, in 1859...41 boys sat in this room...and were asked the same question...that now greets you at the start of each semester. Gentlemen, what are the four pillars? Tradition, honor... discipline, excellence. In her first year...Welton Academy graduated five students. Last year, we graduated 51...and more than 75% of those...went on to the Ivy League. **This, this kind of accomplishment is the result of fervent dedication to the principles taught here**. This is why you parents have been sending us your sons. This is why we are the best preparatory school in the United States. As you know, our beloved Mr. Portius of the English Department retired last term. You will have the opportunity later to meet his replacement Mr. John Keating...himself an honor graduate of this school. And who, for the past several years has been teaching at the highly regarded Chester School in London.

2. Mr. Keating's first class

Keating: Well, come on! Let's go. - Let's go, guys. **O Captain! My captain!** Who knows where that comes from? Anybody. Not a clue? It's from a poem by Walt Whitman about Mr. Abraham Lincoln. Now, in this class, you can either call me Mr. Keating...or if you're slightly more daring O Captain, my Captain. Now let me dispel a few rumors, so they don't fester into facts. Yes, I, too, attended Hellton and have survived. And, no, at that time I was not the mental giant you see before you. I was the intellectual equivalent of a 98-pound weakling. I would go to the beach, and people would kick copies of Byron in my face. Now...Mr. Pitts. That's a rather unfortunate name. Mr. Pitts, where are you? Mr. Pitts, will you open your hymnal to page 542? Read the first stanza of the poem you find there.

Pitts: To The Virgins to Make Much of Time?

Keating: Yes. That's the one. Somewhat appropriate, isn't it? Gather ye rosebuds while ye may, old time is still a-flying...and this same flower that smiles today, tomorrow will be dying. Thank you, Mr. Pitts. Gather ye rosebuds while ye may. The Latin term for that sentiment is carpe diem. Now who knows what that means? Carpe diem. That's seize the day.

Keating: Very good, Mr. —Meeks. Meeks. Another unusual name. Seize the day. Gather ye rosebuds while ye may. Why does the writer use these lines?

Meeks: Because he's in a hurry.

Keating: No! Ding! Thank you for playing anyway. Because we are food for worms, lads. Because, believe it or not, each and every one of us in this room...is one day going to stop breathing...turn cold, and die. I would like you to step forward over here...and peruse some of the faces from the past. You've walked past them many times, but I don't think you've really looked at them. They're not that different from you, are they? Same haircuts ... full of hormones just like you. Invincible just like you feel. The world is their oyster. They believe they're destined for great things just like many of you. Their eyes are full of hope just like you. Did they wait until it was too late to make from their lives...even one iota of what they were capable? Because you see, gentlemen, these boys are now fertilizing daffodils. But if you listen real close...you can hear them whisper their legacy to you. Go on, lean in. Listen. Do you hear it? Carpe. Hear it? Carpe. Carpe diem. Seize the day, boys. Make your lives extraordinary.

3. Mr. Keating asks Anderson to read his poem

Keating: Now, who's next? Mr Anderson, I see you sitting there in agony. Anderson. Come on, Todd, step up. Todd. Let's put you out of your misery.

Anderson: I...I didn't do it. I didn't write a poem.

Keating: Mr Anderson thinks everything inside of him. Anderson is worthless and embarrassing. Isn't that right, Todd? Isn't that your worst fear? Todd. Well, I think you're wrong. I think you have something inside of you ... that is worth a great deal. "I sound my barbaric yawp over the rooftops of the world." Uncle Walt, again. Now, for those of you who don't know, a yawp is a loud cry or yell. Now, Todd, I would like you to give us a demonstration of a barbaric yawp. Come on, you can't yawp sitting down. Let's go. Come on, up. Got to get in yawping stance.

Anderson: A...A yawp?

Keating: Not just a yawp. A barbaric yawp. Right. Yawp. Come on. Louder.

Anderson: Yawp.

Keating: That's a mouse. Come on, louder!

Anderson: Yawp.

Keating: Oh, good God, boy, yell like a man!

Anderson: Yawp!

Keating: There it is. You see, you have a barbarian in you after all. You don't get away that easy. There's a picture of Uncle Walt up there. What does he remind you of? Don't think, answer. Go on.

Anderson: A m-m-m-madman.

Keating: What kind of madman? Don't think about it, just answer.

Anderson: A cr-crazy madman.

Keating: No, you can do better than that. Free up your mind. Use your imagination. Say the first thing that pops into your head, even if it's total gibberish.

Anderson: A-A-A sweaty-toothed madman.

Keating: Good God, boy, there's a poet in you after all! There. Close your eyes. Close your eyes. Close them. Now, describe what you see.

Anderson: Uh, I...I close my eyes...

Keating: Yes? uh, and his image floats beside me. A sweaty-toothed madman. A sweaty-toothed madman with a stare that pounds my brain.

Keating: Oh, that's excellent! Now, give him action, make him do something.

Anderson: H-His hands reach out and choke me.

Keating: That's it. Wonderful. Wonderful.

Anderson: And all the time he's mumbling.

Keating: What's he mumbling?

Anderson: Mumbling truth.

Keating: Yes.

Anderson: Truth is like a blanket that always leaves your feet cold.

Keating: Forget them. Forget them. Stay with the blanket. Tell me about that blanket.

Anderson: Y-Y-You push it, stretch it, it'll never be enough. You kick at it, beat it, it'll never cover any of us. From the moment we enter crying to the moment we leave dying, it'll just cover your face as you wail and cry and scream.

Keating: Don't you forget this.

Task 2 Work in pairs or groups and play the roles in one of your favorite scenes.

Ⅲ. Cultural Notes

1. Ivy League is a collegiate athletic conference comprising sports teams from eight private institutions of higher education in the Northeastern United

States, including Brown University, Columbia University, Cornell University, Dartmouth College, Harvard University, the University of Pennsylvania, Princeton University, and Yale University. The term "Ivy League" has connotations of academic excellence, selectivity in admissions, and social elitism. For more information, visit https://en.wikipedia.org/wiki/Ivy_League.

2. Preparatory school (also prep school) refers to a high school in America, either private or public, designed to prepare students aged 14-18 for higher education at a university or college

3. Walt Whitman (1819—1892) was a well-known American poet, essayist, and journalist. He was a part of the transition between transcendentalism and realism, incorporating both views in his works. Whitman is among the most influential poets in the American canon, often called "the father of free verse". His work was very controversial in its time, particularly his poetry collection Leaves of Grass, which was described as obscene for its overt sexuality. For more information, visit https://en.wikipedia.org/wiki/Walt_Whitman.

4. O Captain, my Captain is an extended metaphor poem written in 1865 by Walt Whitman in memory of American president Abraham Lincoln.

5. Carpe diem is a Latin aphorism, usually translated "seize the day", taken from the Roman poet Horace's work Odes (23 BC)

Ⅳ. Questions for discussion

1. What are the themes involved in this film?
2. Who should be responsible for Neil Perry's death?
3. What is an ideal teacher from your perspective?

Ⅴ. Movie Review

Task: Write a movie review on *Dead Poets Society*.

MOVIES TO SEE (B) Good Will Hunting

Ⅰ. Movie Introduction

Director: Gus Van Sant

Starring: Robin Williams, Matt Damon, Ben Affleck

Running time: 126 mins

Released: 1998

Plot: It is a touching tale of Will Hunting, a young janitor at MIT who struggles to find his identity, living in a world where he can solve any problem, except the one brewing deep within himself, until one day he meets his soul mate who opens his mind and his heart.

To Recommend More Movies

- *Cheers for Miss Bishop* (1941)
- *The Sound of Music* (1965)
- *Goodbye, Mr. Chips* (1969)
- *Mr. Holland's Opus* (1996)
- *Homeless to Harvard: The Liz Murray Story* (2003)
- *The Choir Boys* (2004)
- *The Great Debaters* (2007)

Unit Nine Literature

Pre-reading Activities

Answer the following questions before you read this text.

1. What are the distinctive voices and styles in American literature?
2. What characteristics of a literary work have made it influential over time?
3. How do social and political issues influence the American canon?

TEXT A A Survey of American Literature (I)

This outline of American literature intends to cover the whole range of the literary history of the United States of America from the early Colonial Period through the 1970s, and offer a brief account of the major authors and their **masterworks** and of the major literary trends and **currents** of thought which dominated the American literary scene at one time or another and became the **thematic** or formal concern of some major authors in their literary **endeavors**.

Before we begin our series of discussions on American literature, a simple statement about the plan of the course is in order. It is now a critical commonplace that American literature ***per se*** did not begin until the nineteenth century. Therefore we shall be brief about the **Colonial Period**, the period stretching roughly from the settlement of America in the early seventeenth century through the end of the eighteenth. The major topic here will be about **American Puritanism**, the one enduring influence in American literature, and the major figures to mention will be Jonathan Edwards and Benjamin Franklin who, between them, represent the heritage of American Puritanism.

The Romantic Period that follows covers the first half of the nineteenth century. A rising America with its ideals of democracy and equality, its industrialization, its westward expansion, and a variety of foreign influences such as Sir Walter Scott were among the important factors which made literary expansion and expression not only possible but also inevitable in the period immediately following the nation's political independence. Washington Irving (1783—1859) and James Fenimore Cooper (1789—1851) will be our first concern. The first important writer in American literature, Irving **deserves credit for** the part he played in inspiring the American romantic imagination. His fascinating *The sketch Book* with two of his most famous stories, "Rip Van Winkle" and "The Legend of Sleepy Hollow," will be placed at the top of any reading list for a course on American literature. We still be also reading James Fenimore Cooper and his *Leatherstocking* Tales which offers some fictional version of the American national experience of adventure into the wilderness of the American West. The importance of the frontier and the wilderness in American literature is for the first time well-illustrated in Cooper's *Leatherstocking* Tales and was to remain a major concern for many later authors. Quite a few **eminent** literary critics like Henry Nash Smith and Edwin S. Fussell have written on the subject for the simple reason that the history of the formation of the United States of America is, in a sense, a process in which the settlers moved continuously westward, pushing the frontier with them.

American Romanticism **culminated** around the 1840s in what has come to be known as "**New England Transcendentalism**" **or** "**American Renaissance**" (1836—1855). One of the major literary figures in this period is Ralph Waldo Emerson (1803—1882), the leading New England Transcendentalist, whose *Nature* (1836) has been called "the **Manifesto** of American Transcendentalism," and whose "The American Scholar" (1837) has been rightly regarded as America's "Declaration of Intellectual Independence." We are now entering the formative period of **indigenous** American literature. Calling for the creation of a native literature rather than always learning from other cultures, Emerson **exercised** a most **seminal influence on** the development of an independent American culture. Many of his **contemporaries** either drew from or reacted against his doctrine, thus either way benefiting from it. Henry David Thoreau

(1817—1862) was at first a faithful follower of Emerson, **but alienated** himself somewhat **from** the master later on. Thoreau built and went to live in a small cottage on **Walden Pond** for a little over years and then came back to write about his experience there in his famous book, *Walden.*

The Civil War (1861—65) brought the Romantic Period to an end. The Age of **Realism** came into existence. It came as a reaction against "the lie of romanticism and **sentimentalism**," as Everett Carter put it. It expresses the concern for the commonplace and the low, and offers an objective rather than an idealistic view of human nature and human experience. A fearless and enthusiastic champion of the new school was William Dean Howells (1837—1920) who, **by virtue of** his powerful critical writings and of his generous **patronage** as senior editor of the influential journal ***Atlantic Monthly***, made for the **triumph** of realism over romanticism and thus remained for over three decades the ***de facto*** dean of American literature, as his name **inadvertently** suggested. His reputation fell in the first years of this century, but has, in recent years, begun to rise.

Two other **staunch** fighters for realism were Mark Twain (1835—1910) and Henry James (1843—1916) with both of whom William Dean Howells sustained a personal friendship. Beginning as a local colorist, Mark Twain wrote works which have become part of the American cultural tradition. *The Adventures of Huckleberry Finn*, his masterwork, has, in the opinion of Ernest Hemingway, fathered modern American literature. Henry James, with his "international theme," and his psychological realism, is now considered as one of *the most*—if not the most—important literary figures coming out of the nineteenth century. For the moment, **suffice it to say that** his critical theory on the art of fiction, contributing as it does so much to the literary critical idiom, has made him exceptionally popular in the world of literary criticism.

In the last decade of the nineteenth century, with the development of industry and modern science, intelligent minds began to see that man was no longer a free ethical being in a cold, indifferent and essentially Godless universe. In this chance world he was both helpless and hopeless. European writers like Emile Zola had already developed this acute social consciousness. They saw man's life as governed by the two forces of **heredity** and environment, forces absolutely beyond man's control. **Literary naturalism** came into being. Three American writers who wrote in this tradition deserve special treatment: Stephen Crane (1871—1900), Frank Norris (1870—1902), and Theodore Dreiser (1871—1945). Crane's *Maggie: A Girl of the Streets* is the first American naturalistic work, Norris' McTeague the manifesto of American naturalism, and Dreiser's *Sister Carrie* the work in which naturalism attained maturity. Hamlin Garland (1864—1940) and Sherwood Anderson (1876—1941) are also names meriting notice in this connection. Of this period of a little later are O. Henry's short stories which brought him overwhelming success and made him a central figure in the peak period of the American magazine story, and Jack London's works which are a fine **specimen** of **scathing** social criticism.

(Words: 1086)

New Words

masterwork	*n.* 杰作；名著
current	*n.* 潮流；电流（current 的复数）；[流] 气流 *a.* 现在的，最近的
thematic	*adj.* 主题的，主旋律的；题目的；语干的
endeavor	*v./n.* 尽力；努力
per se	本身，自身
eminent	*adj.* 杰出的；有名的；明显的
culminate	*vi.* 到绝顶；达到高潮；达到顶点 *vt.* 使结束；使达到高潮
manifesto	*n.* 宣言；声明；告示 *vi.* 发表宣言
indigenous	4 本土的；土著的；国产的；固有的
seminal	*adj.* 有创造力的，对未来有影响的；重大的

续表

doctrine	*n.* 主义；学说；教义；信条
sentimentalism	*n.* 感伤主义，沉于情感
patronage	*n.* 赞助；光顾；任免权
triumph	*n.* 胜利，凯旋；欢欣 *vi.* 获得胜利，成功
de facto	（法）实际上的
inadvertently	*adv.* 非故意地，无心地
staunch	*adj.* 坚定的；忠诚的；坚固的 *vt.* 止住；止血
heredity	*n.* 遗传，遗传性
naturalism	*n.* 自然主义
specimen	*n.* 样品，样本；标本
scathing	*adj.* 严厉的；损伤的 *v.* 损伤；伤害（scathe 的 ing 形式）

Phrases & Expressions

deserve credit for	因…值得受到称赞
exercise influence on	对…产生影响
alienate…from	使疏远
by virtue of	由于，凭借
suffice it to say that	只要说…就够了

Proper Names

Colonial Period	殖民地时期，殖民时代
American Puritanism	美国清教主义
The Romantic Period	浪漫主义时期
New England Transcendentalism	新英格兰超验主义
American Renaissance	美国文艺复兴
Realism	现实主义

续表

Literary Naturalism	文学自然主义
Walden Pond	瓦尔登湖
Atlantic Monthly	大西洋月刊

Cultural Notes

1. American Puritanism is the practices and beliefs of the Puritans. The Puritans were originally members of a division of the Protestant Church. The first settlers who became the founding fathers of the American nation were quite a few of them. They were a group of serious, religious people, advocating highly religious and moral principles. As the word itself hints, Puritans wanted to purity their religious beliefs and practices. They accepted the doctrine of predestination, original sin and total depravity, and limited atonement through a special infusion of grace form God. As a culture heritage, Puritanism did have a profound influence on the early American mind. American Puritanism also had an enduring influence on American literature. For more information, visit http://wenku.baidu.com/link?url = X8xffUNxh8 - OfhDI - VqLP4FNR5ViaMrZqUsX - HwN7m - V7hZYcBUwPO6kXVvgQxNI - JGrPkBCfU1RCUp8QhfaH67LPSkgGxywMrLZJJF - v4RsKhGbDYa8ZdTe_ Hsg8f54.

2. The Romantic Period (also Romanticism) was an artistic, literary, musical and intellectual movement that originated in Europe toward the end of the 18th century and in most areas was at its peak in the approximate period from 1800 to 1850. Romanticism was characterized by its emphasis on emotion and individualism as well as glorification of all the past and nature, preferring the medieval rather than the classical. For more information, visit https://en.wikipedia.org/wiki/Romanticism.

3. Realism came into existence after the Civil War brought the Romantic Period to an end. It came as a reaction against the lie of romanticism and sentimentalism. Realism turned from an emphasis on the strange toward a faithful rendering of the ordinary, a slice of life as it is really lived. It expresses the concern for commonplace and the low, and it offers an objective rather than an idealistic view of human nature and human experience. For more information, visit http://wenku.baidu.com/link?url=X8xffUNxh8-OfhDI-VqLP4FNR5ViaMrZqUsX-HwN7m-V7hZYcBUwPO6kXVvgQxNI-JGrPkBCfU1RCUp8QhfaH67LPSkgGxywMrLZJJ F-v4RsKhGbDYa8ZdTe_ Hsg8f54.

4. Literary Naturalism is a literary trend prevailing in Europe, especially in France and Germany, in the second half of the 19th century. Its theory is that literature must be "true to life" and exactly reproduce real life, including all its details without any selection. American naturalism was a new and harsher realism, and like realism, it had come from Europe. Naturalism was an outgrowth of realism that responded to theories in science, psychology, human behavior and social thought current in the late nineteenth century. For more information, visit http://wenku.baidu.com/link?url=AFdGn3ueUXqtBvFt1MwEqZEaM09hALlgUucOlyxfrpQZKCfMAaDkt6sCigMSLYLkedA4HOp-AbXqT1RPkkVB9zqC27chB1gfgK_eGVwZmBu.

Exercises

Comprehension of the Text

Ⅰ Answer the following questions according to the passage.

1. In what aspects is Romanticism different from Realism?

2. What influence does American Puritanism have on American literature?

3. Why did Ernest Hemingway think Mark Twain's *The Adventures of Huckleberry Finn* fathered modern American literature?

Vocabulary

Ⅱ. Fill in the blanks with the words given below. Change the form where necessary.

eminent	endeavor	triumph	indigenous	inadvertently
culminate	current	thematic	staunch	masterwork
heredity	suffice	ethical	specimen	overwhelming

1. Indians were the ______inhabitants of America.

2. But he acknowledged he still has a long way to go to win over ______con-servatives

3. There are four distinct ______gardens named"Earth", "Wind", "Fire", and "Water", which represent the four elements.

4. A series of international meetings held over the last ten weeks will ______ in the Geneva meeting.

5. The trade association promotes ______business practices.

6. We go forward with complete confidence in the eventual ____of freedom.

7. We have provided _____information to you on this issue.

8. Sweden has failed in its ______ to rank among the world powers in table tennis.

9. Sometimes people find themselves ______ cultivating a desire for things that are out of harmony with their beliefs and values.

10. Such ______figures as Benjamin Franklin and Thomas Jefferson made clear their belief that we can only experience true success and happiness by making character the guideline of our lives.

Translations

Ⅲ. Translate the following sentences into English.

1. 由于她个人的努力和竞争力，她已经上升到网球运动联盟的最高点。(by virtue of)

____

2. 电视和互联网使人们与朋友疏远了，因为现在人们缺乏与朋友面对面的交流。(alienate…from)

____

3. 但现在我们可以说社交网络已经在经历这个变革了。(suffice it to say that)

____

4. 但是他们在促进和平进程中所做出的坚实努力也理应得到世界的认可。(deserve credit for)

____

5. 但如今，更多人认识到中国必须在国际事务中发挥正面影响。（exercise influence on）

Ⅳ. Translate the following passage into English.

莎士比亚，英国杰出的诗人、剧作家，于1564年出生于沃里克郡一个迷人的小山村。在约32年的写作生涯中，莎士比亚给观众带来了近40部戏剧，每一部都给观众带来不同的感觉或意象。莎剧情节取材于希腊传说、罗马历史、意大利故事和英国历史题材。但是，无论什么题材在他笔下总会散发独特的魅力，古老的传说也会变成戏剧艺术的杰作。虽然他创作的人物身着古老的异国服装，但他们的思维和情感却属于莎士比亚的时代，所以，莎士比亚戏剧生动再现了那个时代的生活，成为英国文艺复兴的里程碑。

TEXT B　A Survey of American Literature (Ⅱ)

(A) The First World War made America a different country, and its literature underwent a **substantial** change. The 1920s saw a vigorous literary activity in America. In poetry there appeared a strong reaction against **Victorian poetry**, the chief characteristics of which are its moralizing tendencies, its overpadding of extra-poetic matter, and its traditional **iambic pentameter**. The emphasis was now on the economy of expression and on the use of a dominant image. The movement which had these as its aims is known in literary history as **Imagism**. Its prime mover was Ezra Pound, and **expatriate** American poet who translated some of Li Po's poems and wrote his *Cantos*, quoting extensively from Chinese history and Confucius. Although short-lived, the Imagist movement had a tremendous influence on modern poetry. Most of the important twentieth-century American poets were related with it: William Carlos Williams, Wallace Stevens, E. E. Cummings, Carl Sandburg, and T. S. Eliot, to name just the important few.

(B) Ezra Pound (1885—1972) is regarded, and rightly, as the father of modern American poetry. Impatient with the **fetters** of English traditional poetics, he led the experiment in revolutionizing poetry. It was he who first discovered

T. S. Eliot and blue-penciled the latter's famous poem, *The Waste Land*. It was he who helped William Butler Yeats, James Joice, D. H. Lawrence, and William Carlos Williams in their literary careers. And he survived them all, writing continually right up to his death. Pound's contribution to the development of modern poetry cannot be exaggerated.

(C) By far the most important literary figure in this period is, of course, T. S. Eliot (1888—1965), author of the **epochal** poem, *The Waste Land*. A graphic illustration of the spiritual poverty of the West of the time, the poem has been recognized as representing a solid body of literary works, fiction, poetry, and other genres which came out of the decade of the 1920s and the years immediately after it.

(D) The poetry of William Carlos Williams (1883—1963) **is renowned for** its simplicity, directness and apparent formlessness. To discover a new art rooted in the local conditions of America was his lifelong **obsession**. His influence on contemporary American poetry, never negligible, has been on the increase ever since the 1950s.

(E) To Wallace Stevens (1879—1955), "the world we inhabit is one we half create; we make the order we perceive; and the world exists as meditation." Thus, art and poetry is the means by which we create order out of a world of chaos and confusion. Though never a "professional poet, "Stevens became a great influence on contemporary American poetry.

(F) The poetry of Robert Frost (1874—1963) is full of life, truth and wisdom. His view of man and his world is not always sunny and happy: the world as he depicts it can be frightening, too (the words are lionel Trilling's). Carl Sandburg (1878—1967) from the Chicago school of poets has been seen as **predominantly** optimistic, writing in the tradition of Walt Whitman. And Hart Crane (1899—1932) wrote his great work, The Bridge, a poem of epic stature, representing modern American experience.

(G) F. Scott Fitzgerald (1896—1940), Ernest Hemingway (1898—1961) and William Faulkner (1897—1962) were all writers painting the "Waste Land" landscape of the modern West. Fitzgerald's *The Great Gatsby* writes about the frustration and despair resulting from the failure of the American dream, great and beautiful as it had been held to be. Living **in the midst of** the "**roaring twenties**, "Fitzgerald was perceptive enough to foresee its doom and **embedded** his tragic vision in the best of his works. The works of Hemingway, portraying as they do the **dilemma** of modern man utterly thrown upon himself for survival in an indifferent world, reveal man's **impotence** and his despairing courage to assert himself against overwhelming odds. Taking his cue from mark Twain's masterpiece, Hemingway brought the **colloquial** style to near-perfection in American literature. Faulkner made the history of the Deep South the subject of the bulk of his work, and created a symbolic picture of the remote past, "to retell the **recurrent** story of human dreams, bravery, and defeat, to make a statement about the past and use that statement to talk about man's lot in his world. "His fictional Yoknapatawpha represents, **in a manner of speaking**, **a microcosm** of the whole **macrocosmic** nature of human experience.

(H) In the thirties the angry voice of a group of left or socialist-oriented writers was heard, crying out against the injustice of the capitalist system as best shown in the period of the *Great Depression*. John Dos Passos (1896—1970), John O'Hara (1905—1970), James T. Farrell (1904—1979) and Erskine Caldwell (1903—) came on the scene. There was a revival of naturalism, and there appeared the fashionable hard-boiled writings. Different in literary practice from both contemporary naturalism and the cult of the **hard-boiled**, were a few social realists, notably John Steinbeck (1902—1968) who managed to pick up a refreshing belief in human fellowship and courage.

(I) Here is, perhaps, as good a place as any to take a brief look at **Black American literature**. Unlike white American literature one recurrent theme of which relates to the biblical myth of the Garden of Eden. Black American literature is inspired in large measure by a different myth, that of **deliverance** from slavery. The Black spiritual of the nineteenth century, "Go Down, Moses, "is an illustration of the aspirations of the Black people for freedom. Although "all men are created equal, "the Black people in America were excluded, and during the nineteenth century it was against the law to teach them to read and write. Thus Black literature remained for a long time as oral traditions, folksongs and oratories. However, written Black literature appeared in the eighteenth and, especially, the nineteenth century when people like Frederick Douglass (1817—1895) appeared. A major voice for ht Blacks in the nineteenth century, Douglass wrote, among other things, My Bondage and My Freedom, in his **strenuous** fight against slavery and for equality.

(J) Turning from prose and poetry to the theatre, we notice the great American playwright of this century, Eugene O'Neill (1888—1953), carrying out his continual, vigorous, courageous experiments in the field of drama. O'Neill can be **nihilistic** in his outlook. Reading some of his plays can be a **nightmarish** experience. Along with T. S. Eliot, Ezra Pound, Faulkner and Hemingway, O'Neill has been regarded as one of the American authors writing in the Modernist tradition. In the thirties, playwrights such as Clifford Odets (1906—1963) continued experimentation in the theater. His Waiting for Lefty, a short play centering on a New York taxi-drivers' strike, with its famous **agitprop** ending and its influential use of European expressionist methods, proved to be a very brilliant and impressive performance on Broadway. In the forties, Tennessee Williams (1911—1983) and Arthur Miller (1915—2005) won international recognition. They were to be followed in the next decade or two by a younger generation of writers like Edward Albee (1928—2016).

(K) Then comes the forties and the post-war period, the period in which a new, post-Hemingway, generation of writers appeared as an impressive force on the literary scene. While older authors such as Hemingway and Faulkner sere still writing, young men and women began to publish. These include, in the field of the novel, Saul Bellow (1915—2005), Norman Mailer (1923—2007), Bernars Malamud (1914—1986), J. D. Salinger (1919—2010), Joseph Heller (1923—1999) Philip Roth (1933—), Kurt Vonnegut (1922—2007), John Updike (1932—2009), John Barth (1930—), Joyce Carol Oates (1938—) and many others. This is a very interesting phase in the literary history of the United States, one of robust energy and **bustling** activity. There were the war novel, the southern novel, the Jewish novel, the Beat novel, and the Black novel. Fantasy, **surrealism**, non-fiction, meta-fiction, science-fiction, parody and pop literature all came to the notice of critics and readers. The period is still in progress, in which reputations are still being made. Our survey can only include those authors who have won a measure of critical recognition and have shown signs of the likelihood to endure in the literary history of the country.

(L) This period has also witnessed the emergence of a new world of poets and poetry. The war produced no significant new body of verse, but a group of poets wrote and impressed the post-war readership. These include Randell Jarrell, Richard Eberhart, Karl Shapiro, John Berryman, Robert Penn Warren, Elizabeth Bishop, Richard Eilbur, Howard Nemerov, W. S. Merwin, and Robert Lowell. These poets constitute a new American "academy," so called partly because so many are connected with colleges and universities, and partly because they established themselves almost officially as the recognized poets of their generation. The next wave that came after the "academy" poets was a more violent one, containing poets who were all trying in some way "to find themselves outside traditional and institutional frameworks, or rather, to find more satisfying traditions and institutional possibilities." They all exhibited a stubborn posture of negation. The California Renascents like Allen Ginsberg and Lawrence Ferlinghetti (also known as the poets of the Beat generation), an ultimately more serious group of poets such as Charles Olson, Denise Levertov, Robert Duncan and Robert Bly (known as the "Black Mountain Poets"), and the New York poets like John Ashbery and Kenneth Koch who wrote under the influence of French surrealism and **impressionism**—all these poets have made their presence felt by their non-traditional poetry.

New Words

substantial	*adj.* 大量的；实质的；内容充实的
expatriate	*n.* 被流放者；移居国外者 *adj.* 移居国外的；被流放的 *vt.* 使移居国外；流放，放逐；使放弃国籍 *vi.* 移居国外；放弃原国籍
fetter	*n.* 束缚；羁绊；脚镣 *vt.* 束缚；加脚镣

续表

epochal	*adj.* 划时代的；新纪元的
obsession	*n.* 痴迷；困扰
predominantly	*adv.* 主要地；显著地
embed	*vt.* 使嵌入，使插入；使深留脑中
dilemma	*n.* 困境；进退两难
impotence	*n.* 虚弱；无效（等于 impotency）
colloquial	*adj.* 白话的；通俗的；口语体的
recurrent	*adj.* 复发的；周期性的，经常发生的
microcosm	*n.* 微观世界；小宇宙；作为宇宙缩影的人类；缩图
macrocosmic	*adj.* 宏观的
hard-boiled	*adj.* 强硬的，无情的
deliverance	*n.* 释放，解救；救助；判决
strenuous	*adj.* 紧张的；费力的；奋发的
nihilistic	*adj.* 虚无主义的；无政府主义的
nightmarish	*adj.* 可怕的；噩梦似的；不愉快的
agitprop	*n.* 宣传鼓动；宣传鼓动员；宣传鼓动部门 *adj.* 宣传鼓动的
bustling	*adj.* 熙熙攘攘的；忙乱的

Phrases & Expressions

be renowned for	因…而著名
in the midst of	在…之中
in a manner of speaking	说起来，在某个意义上说；不妨说

Proper Names

Victorian poetry	维多利亚诗歌
iambic pentameter	抑扬格五音步
Imagism	意象派
Surrealism	超现实主义
Impressionism	印象派，印象主义

Cultural Notes

1. **Iambic pentameter** is a commonly used type of metrical line in traditional English poetry and verse drama. The term describes the rhythm that the words establish in that line, which is measured in small groups of syllables called "feet". The word "iambic" refers to the type of foot that is used, known as the iamb, which in English is an unstressed syllable followed by a stressed syllable. The word "pentameter" indicates that a line has five of these "feet". For more information, visit https://en.wikipedia.org/wiki/Iambic_pentameter.

2. **Imagism** was a literary movement launched by British and American poets early in the 20th century in reaction against Victorian sentimentalism that advocated the use of free verse, common speech patterns, and clear concrete images. For more information, visit http://baike.sogou.com/v7716895.htm?fromTitle=imagism.

3. **Surrealism** is a cultural movement that began in the early 1920s, and is best known for its visual artworks and writings. The aim was to "resolve the previously contradictory conditions of dream and reality". Surrealist works feature the element of surprise, unexpected juxtapositions and non sequitur; however, many Surrealist artists and writers regard their work as an expression of the philosophical movement first and foremost, with the works being an artifact. For more information, visit https://en.wikipedia.org/wiki/Surrealism.

4. **Impressionism** is a 19th-century art movement characterized by relatively small, thin, yet visible brush strokes, open composition, emphasis on accurate depiction of light in its changing qualities (often accentuating the effects of the passage of time), ordinary subject matter, inclusion of movement as a crucial element of human perception and experience, and unusual visual angles. Impressionism originated with a group of Paris-based artists whose independent exhibitions brought them to prominence during the 1870s and 1880s. For more information, visit https://en.wikipedia.org/wiki/Impressionism.

5. **Roaring Twenties** is a term for Western society and culture in the 1920s. It was a period of sustained economic prosperity with a distinctive cultural

edge in the United States, Canada and Western Europe. This era saw the large-scale use of automobiles, telephones, motion pictures, radio, and electricity; commercial, passenger, and freight aviation; as well as unprecedented industrial growth, accelerated consumer demand, plus significant changes in lifestyle and culture. The spirit of the Roaring Twenties was marked by a general feeling of novelty associated with modernity and a break with traditions. Everything seemed to be feasible through modern technology. For more information, visit https://en.wikipedia.org/wiki/Roaring_Twenties.

Exercises

Comprehension of the Text

Ⅰ. The following 8 statements contain information given in the text. Identify the paragraph from which the information is derived. You may choose a paragraph more than once. Each paragraph is marked with a letter.

1. Ezra Pound is the prime mover of the Imagist movement that had a tremendous influence on modern poetry.

2. T. S. Eliot is regarded as the father of modern American poetry.

3. Carl Sandburg from the Chicago school of Poets has been seen as predominantly optimistic, writing in the tradition of Walt Whitman.

4. F. Scott Fitzgerald, Ernest Hemingway and William Faulkner were all writers painting the "Waste Land" landscape of the modern West.

5. Black American literature is inspired in large measure by a different myth, that of freedom from slavery.

6. Written Black literature appeared in the eighteenth and, especially, the nineteenth century when people like Frederick Douglass appeared.

7. The poetry of William Carlos Williams **is renowned for** its simplicity and directness.

8. Eugene O'Neill carried out his continual, vigorous, courageous experiments in the field of drama.

Vocabulary

Ⅱ. Fill in the blanks with the words given below. Change the form where necessary.

substantial	strenuous	bustling	dilemma	fetter
epochal	recurrent	obsession	impotence	predominantly
embed	deliverance	expatriate	nightmarish	colloquial

1. Power controls human activity, but it cannot ______human soul, where literature originates.

2. Race is a ______theme in the literary work.

3. Why should Chinese film critics be ______with box-office revenue?

4. He was faced with the _____of whether or not to return to his country.

5. But, recalling those _____reforms of 30 years ago, it is worth remembering that they too tended to come in baby steps rather than great leaps, and often were formulated retrospectively

6. Greece, Spain and Italy all made ______efforts to qualify for the euro.

7. Hong Kong is a _____coastal city that offers a full-on assault of sounds, sights and smells

8. I think that hatred of the other is deeply ______in our society

9. No matter who you are, if you have a problem with sin, look to Jesus for ______.

10. The thesis may at first strike one as extreme, but ______evidence exists to support it.

Further Reading

TEXT C The Road Not Taken

Robert Frost

Two roads diverged in a yellow wood,

And sorry I could not travel both
And be one traveler, long I stood
And looked down one as far as I could
To where it bent in the undergrowth;

Then took the other, as just as fair,
And having perhaps the better claim,
Because it was grassy and wanted wear;
Though as for that the passing there
Had worn them really about the same,

And both that morning equally lay
In leaves no step had trodden black.
Oh, I kept the first for another day!
Yet knowing how way leads on to way,
I doubted if I should ever come back.

I shall be telling this with a sigh
Somewhere ages and ages hence:
Two roads diverged in a wood, and I—
I took the one less traveled by,
And that has made all the difference.

(Words: 148)

Questions for discussions

1. What is the main theme of this poem by Robert Frost?

2. Why is the poem entitled "The Road Not Taken", instead of "The Road Taken"? What do the two roads stand for?

3. How do you understand the word "sigh"? Is it a kind of nostalgic relief or regret?

4. Why does Frost himself claim that this is a tricky poem? What does he

want to convey in this poem?

More to Learn

1. The Outline of American Literature

Ⅰ. Literature of the Colonial Period (1607—1776)

Historical Background:

- Settlement
- Puritanism: predestination, original sin
- Puritan values: hard work, thrift, and piety
- Individualism and American Dream

Features of Literature:

- The first American literature was neither American nor real literature.
- Types of Writing: Diary, history, journal, letter, narrative...

Writers: John Smith, Anne Bradstreet and Edward Taylor

Ⅱ. Literature of Reason and Revolution (1776—1820)

Historical Background:

- The Age of Revolution (1776—1783): Britain's suppression on America in economy and politics; Revolt against Britain
- The Age of Reason: Enlightenment (Intellectual movement in Europe, Humanism, Rationalism)

Features of Literature:

- Utilitarian tendency (Nothing is good or beautiful but in the measure that is useful.)
- Clear, concise and powerful expression
- Essay as a prominent part

Writers: Thomas Paine (Common Sense); Thomas Jefferson (Declaration of Independence); Benjamin Franklin (Autobiography)

Ⅲ. Romanticism (1820—1860)

Historical Background: Development of politics, economy and culture

- Expansion of the West

- Rise of industrialism
- Transmission of literature
- Progressive and developing society

Features of Literature:

- American puritanism as a cultural heritage
- American romanticism was both imitative and independent
- It presented a new experience, the exotic landscape, the frontier life and the westward expansion

Writers: Washington. Irving, James Fenimore Cooper, Ralph Waldo Emerson, Henry David Thoreau, Edgar Allan Poe, Nathaniel Hawthorne, Walt Whitman, Emily Dickinson.

Ⅳ. Rise of Realism (1860—1914)

Historical Background:

- Civil War (1861—1865)
- Capitalism—freedom and democracy
- Development of society before 1880
- Financial crisis—unrest society after 1880

Features of Literature: Two literary streams

- Realism (1860—1880): Truthful description of life; Objective rather than idealized; hopeful and optimistic.
- Naturalism (1880—1914): Theory of Darwinism; Focus on environment and human; hopeless and gloomy.

Writers: Mark Twain, Henry James, W. D. Howells, Jack London, Stephen Crane, Theodore Dreiser.

Ⅴ. Modern Period (1914—)

Historical Background:

- The first world war: Economically (great wealth, economic boom, highly-consuming society); Spiritually (fragmentation)
- Freud's theory (psychology)
- Emigration (to Asia): the influence of Japanese and Chinese culture and literature

Features of Literature:

- Imagism
- Lost Generation
- Southern Literature

Writers: Ezra Pound, T. S. Eliot, Robert Frost, Ernest Hemingway, F. Scott. Fitzgerald, W. Faulkner, Eugene O'Neill

2. Nobel Prize in Literature winners (American authors)

♣ 1930: Sinclair Lewis (novelist) 辛克莱·刘易斯

♣ 1936: Eugene O'Neill (playwright) 尤金·奥尼尔

♣ 1938: Pearl S. Buck (biographer and novelist) 赛珍珠 (珀尔·塞登斯特里克·布克)

♣ 1948: T. S. Eliot (poet and playwright) T·S. 艾略特

♣ 1949: William Faulkner (novelist) 威廉·福克纳

♣ 1954: Ernest Hemingway (novelist) 欧内斯特·海明威

♣ 1962: John Steinbeck (novelist) 约翰·斯坦贝克

♣ 1976: Saul Bellow (novelist) 索尔·贝娄

♣ 1978: Isaac Bashevis Singer (novelist, wrote in Yiddish) 艾萨克·巴什维斯·辛格

♣ 1993: Toni Morrison (novelist) 托尼·莫里森

3. Major American literary awards

♣ American Academy of Arts and Letters 美国艺术与文学学院奖

♣ Pulitzer Prize 普利策奖 (Fiction, Drama and Poetry, as well as various non-fiction and journalist categories)

♣ American National Book Award 美国国家图书奖 (Fiction, Non-Fiction, Poetry and Young-Adult Fiction)

♣ PEN literary awards 美国笔会文学奖 (multiple awards)

♣ United States Poet Laureate 美国桂冠诗人

♣ Bollingen Prize 博林根奖

♣ Pushcart Prize 手推车奖

♣ O. Henry Award 欧·亨利短篇小说奖

MOVIES TO SEE (A) Pride & Prejudice

Ⅰ. Movie Introduction

Director: Joe Wright

Starring: Keira Knightley, Matthew Macfadyen, Brenda Blethyn

Running time: 129 mins

Released: 2005

Plot: *Pride & Prejudice* is a 2005 British-American romantic drama directed by Joe Wright and based on Jane Austen's 1813 novel of the same name. This tale of love and values unfolds in the class-conscious England of the late 18th century. The five Bennet sisters-including strong-willed Elizabeth and young Lydia-have been raised by their mother with one purpose in life: finding a husband. When a wealthy bachelor takes up residence in a nearby mansion, the Bennets are abuzz. Amongst the man's sophisticated circle of friends, surely there will be no shortage of suitors for the Bennet sisters. But when Elizabeth meets up with the handsome and-it would seem-snobbish Mr. Darcy, the battle of the sexes is joined.

Ⅱ. Excerpts & Expressions

Task 1 Study the underlined sentences and expressions.

1. At the ball

Mrs. Bennet: How well you dance, Mr. Bingley. My daughter Jane is a splendid dancer, is she not?

Bingley: She is indeed. (To Elizabeth) Your friend Miss Lucas is a most amusing young woman.

Elizabeth: Oh, yes, I adore her.

Mrs. Bennet: It is a pity she's not more handsome.

Elizabeth: Mama!

Mrs. Bennet: Oh, but Lizzie would never admit that she's plain. Of course it's my Jane who's considered the beauty of the county.

Elizabeth & Jane: No, Mama, please!

Mrs. Bennet: When she was 15, a gentleman was so much in love with her, that I was sure he would <u>make her an offer</u>. However, he did write her some very pretty verses.

Elizabeth: And that put paid to it. I wonder who discovered the power of poetry in driving away love.

Darcy: I thought poetry was the food of love.

Elizabeth: Of a fine, stout love, it may. But if it is only a vague inclination one poor sonnet will kill it.

Darcy: So what do you recommend to encourage affection?

Elizabeth: Dancing. Even if one's partner is barely tolerable.

Jane: Mr. Bingley is just what a young man ought to be. Sensible, good-humoured...

Elizabeth: Handsome, conveniently rich...

Jane: You know perfectly well I do not believe marriage should be driven by thoughts of money.

Elizabeth: I agree entirely. Only the deepest love will persuade me into matrimony, which is why I'll end up an old maid.

Jane: Do you really believe he liked me, Lizzie?

Elizabeth: Jane, he danced with you most of the night, and stared at you for the rest of it. But I give you leave to like him. You've liked many a stupider person. You're a great deal too apt to like people in general, you know. All the world is good and agreeable in your eyes.

Jane: Not his friend. I still can't believe what he said about you.

Elizabeth: Mr. Darcy? I could more easily forgive his vanity had he not wounded mine. But no matter, I doubt we shall ever speak again.

2. In the rain, Mr. Darcy expressed his love for Elizabeth, but rejected by her.

Darcy: Miss Elizabeth. I have struggled in vain and can bear it no longer. These past months have been a torment. I came to **Rosings** with the single object of seeing you. I had to see you. I have fought against my better judgment, my family's expectation, the inferiority of your birth, my rank, all these things, and I'm willing to put them aside and ask you to end my agony.

Elizabeth: I don't understand.

Darcy: I love you. Most ardently. Please do me the honor of accepting my hand.

Elizabeth: Sir, I appreciate the struggle you have been through, and I am very sorry to have caused you pain. Believe me, it was unconsciously done.

Darcy: Is this your reply?

Elizabeth: Yes, sir.

Darcy: Are you...are you laughing at me?

Elizabeth: No.

Darcy: Are you rejecting me?

Elizabeth: I'm sure the feelings which, as you've told me have hindered your regard will help you in overcoming it.

Darcy: Might I ask why with so little endeavor at civility I am thus repulsed?

Elizabeth: And I might as well enquire with so evident a design of insulting me you chose to tell me that you liked me against your better judgment?

Darcy: No, believe me...

Elizabeth: If I was uncivil, then that is some excuse! But I have other reasons. You know I have.

Darcy: What reasons?

Elizabeth: Do you think anything might tempt me to accept the man who has ruined perhaps forever the happiness of a most beloved sister? Do you deny it Mr. Darcy, that you separated a young couple who loved each other, exposing your friend to center of the world for caprice and my sister to its derision for disappointed hopes and involving them both in misery of the acutest kind?

Darcy: I do not deny it.

Elizabeth: How could you do it?

Darcy: Because I believed your sister's indifferent to him.

Elizabeth: Indifferent?

Darcy: I watched them most carefully and realized his attachment was deeper than hers.

Elizabeth: That's because she's shy!

Darcy: Bingley, too, is modest and was persuaded she didn't feel strongly for him.

Elizabeth: Because you suggested it.

Darcy: I did it for his own good.

Elizabeth: My sister hardly shows her true feelings to me. I suppose you suspect that his fortune had some bearing?

Darcy: No! I wouldn't do your sister the dishonor, though it was suggested...

Elizabeth: What was?

Darcy: It was made perfectly clear that an advantageous marriage...

Elizabeth: Did my sister give that impression?

Darcy: No! No. No. There was, however, I have to admit, the matter of your family...

Elizabeth: Our want of connection? Mr. Bingley didn't seem to vex himself about that.

Darcy: No, it was more than that.

Elizabeth: How, sir?

Darcy: It was the lack of propriety shown by your mother, your three younger sisters and even, on occasion, your father. Forgive me. You and your sister I must exclude from this.

Elizabeth: And what about Mr. Wickham?

Darcy: Mr. Wickham?

Elizabeth: What excuse can you give for your behavior towards him?

Darcy: You take an eager interest in that gentleman's concerns.

Elizabeth: He told me of his misfortunes.

Darcy: Oh, yes, his misfortunes have been very great indeed.

Elizabeth: You ruin his chances and yet you treat him with sarcasm.

Darcy: So this is your opinion of me? Thank you for explaining so fully. Perhaps these offences might have been overlooked had not your pride been hurt by my honesty...

Elizabeth: My pride?

Darcy: ...in admitting scruples about our relationship. Could you expect me to rejoice in the inferiority of your circumstances?

Elizabeth: And those are the words of a gentleman. From the first moment I met you, your arrogance and conceit, your selfish disdain for the feelings of others made me realize that you were the last man in the world I could ever be prevailed upon to marry.

Darcy: Forgive me, madam, for taking up so much of your time.

3. The ending of the movie:

Darcy: How are you this evening, my dear?

Elizabeth: Very well. Only I wish you would not call me "my dear".

Darcy: Why?

Elizabeth: It's what my father calls my mother when he's cross.

Darcy: What endearments am I allowed?

Elizabeth: Well, let me think. Lizzie for every day. My pearl for Sundays. And...Goddess Divine, but only on very special occasions.

Darcy: And what shall I call you when I'm cross? Mrs. Darcy?

Elizabeth: No, No. You may only call me Mrs. Darcy when you completely and perfectly and incandescently happy.

Darcy: And how are you this evening...Mrs. Darcy? Mrs. Darcy...Mrs. Darcy Mrs. Darcy...

Task 2 Work in pairs and play the roles in the expert above.

Ⅲ. Cultural Notes

1. make her an offer: to propose to her (向她求婚).

2. put paid to sth: If an unexpected event puts paid to someone's hopes, chances, or plans, it completely ends or destroys them (了结……, 结束……)

3. have some bearing: If something has a bearing on a situation or event, it is relevant to it. (与……有一定关系)

4. Rosings: Lady Catherine De Bourgh (Darcy's aunt)'s estate in Kent, 25 miles south of London. (罗新斯庄园)

Ⅳ. Questions for discussion

1. Why did Elizabeth refuse to take Darcy in his first proposal?

2. What should be the rational relationship between money and marriage?

3. What will happen when pride encounters prejudice?

V. Movie Review

Task: Write a movie review on ***Pride & Prejudice***

MOVIES TO SEE (B) Hamlet

Movie Introduction

Director: Kenneth Branagh

Starring: Kenneth Branagh, Julie Christie, Derek Jacobi

Running time: 242 mins

Released: 1996

Plot: Hamlet, son of the king of Denmark, is summoned home for his father's funeral and his mother's wedding to his uncle. In a supernatural episode, he discovers that his uncle, whom he hates anyway, murdered his father. In an incredibly convoluted plot—the most complicated and most interesting in all literature—he manages to (impossible to put this in exact order) feign (or perhaps not to feign) madness, murder the "prime minister", love and then unlove an innocent whom he drives to madness, plot and then unplot against the uncle, direct a play within a play, successfully conspire against the lives of two well-meaning friends, and finally take his revenge on the uncle, but only at the cost of almost every life on stage, including his own and his mother's.

To Recommend More Movies

- ❖ *The Old Man and the Sea* (1958)
- ❖ *Romeo + Juliet* (1996)
- ❖ *Tess Of The D'Urbervilles* (1998)
- ❖ *David Copperfield* (1999)
- ❖ *The Merchant of Venice* (2004)
- ❖ *The Great Gatsby* (2013)

Unit Ten Sports

Pre-reading Activities

Answer the following questions before you read this text.

1. What do you know about the Summer Olympic Games and the Winter Olympic Games?

2. How much do you know about American sports?

3. Can you list popular sports in America?

TEXT A American Sports

Sport is all forms of usually **competitive** physical activity which, through casual or organized participation, **aim to** use, maintain or improve physical ability and skills while providing entertainment to participants, and in some cases, spectators. Hundreds of sports exist, from those requiring only two participants, through to those with hundreds of **simultaneous** participants, either in teams or competing as individuals.

Sport is generally recognized as activities which are based in physical **athleticism** or physical **dexterity**, with the largest major competitions such as the Olympic Games admitting only sports meeting this definition, and other organizations such as the **Council of Europe** using definitions precluding activities without a physical element from **classification** as sports. However, a number of competitive, but non-physical, activities claim recognition as mind sports. **The International Olympic Committee** (through ARISF) recognizes both chess and bridge as bona fide sports, and **Sport Accord**, the international sports federation association, recognizes five non-physical sports, although limits the amount of mind games which can be admitted as sports.

Sports are an important part of the culture of the United States. The four major professional sports leagues in the United States are **Major League Baseball (MLB), the National Basketball Association (NBA), the National Football League (NFL), the National Hockey League (NHL)**; all four enjoy massive US media exposure and are considered the **preeminent** competitions in their **respective** sports in the world, although only basketball and baseball (and **to a lesser extent** hockey) have substantial followings in other nations. Three of those leagues have teams that represent Canadian cities, and all four are among the most financially **lucrative** sports leagues in the world. The top professional soccer league in the United States, **Major League Soccer**, has yet to reach the popularity levels of the top four US sports leagues or of its international **counterparts**, although its popularity and average attendances have been increasing in recent years.

Professional teams in all major sports in the US operate as **franchises** within a league, meaning that a team may decide to move to a different city if it feels it is of financial benefit, a concept which **is regarded as anathema** in Europe, where teams have a historic and traditional connection to their hometown community. All major sports leagues use the same type of schedule with a **playoff tournament** after the regular season ends. **In addition to** the major league-level organizations, several sports also have professional minor leagues, active in smaller cities across the country.

Sports **are** particularly **associated with** education in the United States, with most high schools and universities having organized sports. College sports competitions play an important role in the American sporting culture, and certain college sports—particularly college football and college basketball—are at least as popular as professional sports. The major **sanctioning** body for college sports is the NCAA.

The United States has sent athletes to every celebration of the modern Olympic Games, except the 1980 Summer Olympics in Moscow, USSR, which it **boycotted due to** the Soviet war in Afghanistan. **The United States Olympic Committee (USOC)** is the National Olympic Committee for the United States.

American athletes have won a total of 2570 medals at the Summer Olympic

Games and another 253 at the Winter Olympic Games. More medals have been won in athletics (track and field) (738, 29%) and swimming (489, 19%) than any others. Thomas Burke was the first athlete to represent the United States at the Olympics. He **took first place** in both the 100 meters and the 400 meters of the 1896 Summer Olympics in Athens, Greece. American swimmer Michael Phelps is the most decorated Olympic athlete of all time, with 22 Olympic medals, 18 of them gold.

United States has won more gold and overall medals than any other country in the Summer Games and overall. The US also has the second-most overall medals at the Winter games, **trailing** only Norway. Earlier United States mainly **conceded to** Soviet Union at summer Games and to Soviet Union, Norway, East Germany at winter Games only and now strongly fights with China only at summer Games. The United States is the only country to have won at least one gold medal at every Winter Olympics, and has won the total medal count at Lake Placid in the 1932 Winter Olympics and at Vancouver in the 2010 Winter Olympics. During the Vancouver 2010 Winter Olympics, the United States **set a record** for most total medals of any country at a single Winter Olympics.

The United States has hosted both Summer and Winter Games in 1932 and most occasions of the Games among other countries—eight times, four times each for the Summer and Winter Games: 1904 Summer Olympics in St. Louis, 1932 Summer Olympics and 1984 Summer Olympics in Los Angeles, 1996 Summer Olympics in Atlanta, 1932 Winter Olympics and 1980 Winter Olympics in Lake Placid, 1960 Winter Olympics in Squaw Valley, 2002 Winter Olympics in Salt Lake City.

(Words: 819)

New Words

competitive	*adj.* 竞争的；比赛的
spectator	*n.* 观众；旁观者

续表

simultaneous	*adj.* 同时的，同时发生的；联立的 *n.* 同时译员
athleticism	*n.* 崇尚运动，竞技热；运动竞赛
dexterity	*n.* 灵巧；敏捷；机敏
classification	*n.* 分类；类别；等级
preeminent	*adj.* 卓越的；超群的
respective	*adj.* 分别的；各自的
lucrative	*adj.* 有利可图的，赚钱的；合算的
counterpart	*n.* 副本；配对物；极相似的人或物
franchise	*n.* 特权；公民权；经销权；管辖权 *vt.* 给…以特许（或特权）；赋予公民权
anathema	*n.* 诅咒；革出教门；被诅咒者；令人厌恶的人
playoff	*n.* 双方得分相等时的最后决赛；复赛；季后赛
tournament	*n.* 锦标赛，联赛；比赛
sanction	*n.* 制裁，处罚；认可；支持 *vt.* 制裁，处罚；批准；鼓励
boycott	*n.* 联合抵制 *vt.* 联合抵制；拒绝参加
overall	*adj.* 全部的；整体的；一切在内的 *n.* 工装裤；罩衫 *adv.* 全部地；总的来说
trail	*vt.* 追踪；拖；蔓延；落后于 *vi.* 飘出；蔓生；垂下；拖曳 *n.* 小径；痕迹；尾部；踪迹

Phrases & Expressions

aim to	计划，打算；目标在于…；以…为目标
in some cases	在某些情况下；有时候
bona fide	善意的；真实的；真诚的

续表

to a lesser extent	在较小程度上
be regarded as	被认为是；被当做是
in addition to	除…之外
be associated with	与…有联系；与…相联系
due to	由于；应归于
take first place	居首位；得第一
conceded to	让步
set a record	创造纪录

Proper Names

Council of Europe	欧洲理事会；欧洲委员会
The International Olympic Committee	国际奥林匹克委员会
Sport Accord	国际体育大会
Major League Baseball (MLB)	(美) 职业棒球大联盟
the National Basketball Association (NBA)	国家篮球协会；国家篮球联盟
the National Football League (NFL)	全国橄榄球联赛
the National Hockey League (NHL)	国家冰球联盟
Major League Soccer	职业体协；职业性运动联盟
The United States Olympic Committee (USOC)	美国奥林匹克运动委员会

Cultural Notes

1. Sport Accord is the umbrella organization for all (Olympic and non-Olympic) international sports federations as well as organizers of multi-sports games and sport-related international associations. For more information, visit http://en.wikipedia.org/wiki/SportAccord.

2. Major League Baseball (MLB) is a professional baseball organization that is the oldest of the four major professional sports leagues in the United States and Canada. For more information, visit. http://en.wikipedia.org/wiki/Major_

League_ Basketball.

3. the National Basketball Association (NBA) is the preeminent man's professional basketball league in North America, and is widely considered to be the premier man's professional basketball league in the world. It has 30 franchised member clubs (29 in the United States and 1 in Canada), and is an active member of USA Basketball (USAB), which is recognized by FIBA (also known as the International Basketball Federation) as the national governing body for basketball in the United States. For more information, visit http://en.wikipedia.org/wiki/The_ National_ Basketball_ Association.

Exercises

Comprehension of the Text

Ⅰ Answer the following questions according to the passage.

1. Which two mind bona fide sports are mentioned by the International Olympic Committee?

2. What kind of teams in all major sports in the US operates as franchises within a league if it feels it is of financial benefit?

3. How many Summer and Winter Games has been hosted in the United States?

Vocabulary

Ⅱ. Fill in the blanks with the words given below. Change the form where necessary.

competitive	simultaneous	classification	preclude	preeminent
respective	substantial	lucrative	franchise	boycott
trail	overall	playoff	tournament	sanction

1. Two detectives were ______ him when he was on his way to the theater.

2. Steve and I were at very different stages in our ______ careers.

3. I present an alternate ______ of recommendation systems in my book.

4. But villagers warned that they would ______ the vote, if the secretary in

the village was not democratic.

5. They dropped two games in the basketball and were eliminated from the ______.

6. Only by keeping down costs will America maintain its ______ advantage over other countries.

7. Russia, Australia, and Canada have ______ deposits as well.

8. Indeed, if you could ______ hardware failures and Mother Nature, a UNIX system might run perpetually.

9. This event was almost ______ with that one.

10. The process would not be pretty but ______, investors should be relieved by the result.

Translations

Ⅲ. Translate the following sentences into English.

1. 在这个阶段，你的目标是通过改变环境或者自身行为来减少你和企业氛围的差别。(aim to)

____

2. 新闻媒介只有这样进行报道，才会被视为对社会的负责。(be regarded as)

____

3. 因此许多年来，蛋白质总是与动物性食物联系在一起的。(be associated with)

____

4. 从某种程度上来说，这是由于世界局势所决定的。(due to)

____

5. 经我们劝说，他最终同意不再捐钱，只写了一封感谢信表达他的谢意。(conceded to)

____

Ⅳ. Translate the following passage into English.

那些强调高尚体育精神的成年人，却把获胜看作是希望于自己孩子完成的众多目标之一。在比赛中取得成就的自豪感，使孩子们视自己为赢家，即使他们的比分并不尽如人意。好的教练和家长鼓励孩子们在体育场上公平竞争，感受快乐，注重对团队的贡献。还记得“事实胜于雄辩”这句老话吗？这句话在教育孩子们健康的体育精神时格外受用。成年人在孩子训练和比赛时，如果能够以身作则，其效果要比任何鼓舞士气的讲话和说教都好得多。

TEXT B Michael Jordan

(A) **Michael Jeffrey Jordan** (born February 17, 1963), also known by his **initials**, MJ, is an American former professional basketball player, **entrepreneur**, and principal owner and chairman of **the Charlotte Hornets**. He played 15 seasons in the National Basketball Association (NBA) for **the Chicago Bulls** and **Washington Wizards**. His biography on the NBA website states: "**By acclamation**, Michael Jordan is the greatest basketball player of all time." Jordan was one of the most **effectively** marketed athletes of his generation and was considered instrumental in popularizing the NBA around the world in the 1980s and 1990s.

(B) After a three-year performance at the University of North Carolina, where he was a member of the Tar Heels' national championship team in 1982, Jordan joined the NBA's Chicago Bulls in 1984. He quickly **emerged** as a league star, entertaining crowds with his **prolific** scoring. His leaping ability, illustrated by performing **slam dunks** from the **free throw line** in slam dunk contests, earned him the nicknames "**Air Jordan**" and "His Airiness". He also gained a **reputation for** being one of the best **defensive players** in basketball. In 1991, he won his first NBA championship with the Bulls, and followed that achievement with titles in 1992 and 1993, securing a "**three-peat**". Although Jordan **abruptly** retired from basketball before the beginning of the 1993—94 NBA season to pursue a career in baseball, he rejoined the Bulls in 1995 and led them to three additional championships in 1996, 1997, and 1998, as well as an NBA-record 72 regular-season wins in the 1995—1996 NBA season. Jordan retired for a second time in 1999, but returned for two more NBA seasons from 2001 to 2003 as a member of the Wizards.

(C) Jordan's individual **accolades** and accomplishments include five **Most**

Valuable Player (MVP) Awards, ten All-NBA **First Team** designations, nine All-Defensive First Team honors, fourteen NBA All-Star Game appearances, three All-Star Game MVP Awards, ten scoring titles, three steals titles, six NBA Finals MVP Awards, and the 1988 NBA **Defensive Player of the Year Award**. Among his numerous accomplishments, Jordan holds the NBA records for highest career regular season scoring average (30.12 points per game) and highest career playoff scoring average (33.45 points per game). In 1999, he was named the greatest North American athlete of the 20th century by ESPN, and was second to Babe Ruth on the **Associated Press's** list of athletes of the century. He is a two-time **inductee** into the Basketball Hall of Fame-in 2009 for his individual career, and in 2010 as a member of the 1992 United States men's Olympic basketball team ("**The Dream Team**").

(D) Jordan is also known for his product **endorsements**. He **fueled** the success of Nike's Air Jordan **sneakers**, which were introduced in 1985 and remain popular today. Jordan also **starred in** the 1996 **feature film** Space Jam as himself. In 2006, he became **part-owner** and head of basketball operations for the then-**Charlotte Bobcats**, buying controlling interest in 2010. In 2015, Jordan became the first athlete in history to become a billionaire, according to **Forbes**.

(E) Jordan was born in Brooklyn, New York, the son of Deloris (née Peoples), who worked in banking, and James R. Jordan, Sr., an **equipment supervisor**. His family moved to Wilmington, North Carolina, when he was a **toddler**. Jordan is the fourth of five children. He has two older brothers, Larry Jordan and James R. Jordan, Jr., one older sister, Deloris, and a younger sister, Roslyn. Jordan's brother James retired in 2006 as the Command Sergeant Major of the 35th Signal Brigade of the XVIII Airborne Corps in the U. S. Army.

(F) Jordan attended Ensley A. Laney High School in Wilmington, where he **anchored** his athletic career by playing baseball, football, and basketball. He **tried out for** the **varsity** basketball team during his **sophomore year**, but at 5' 11" (1.80m), he was **deemed** too short to play at that level. His taller friend, Harvest Leroy Smith, was the only sophomore to make the team.

(G) Motivated to prove his worth, Jordan became the star of Laney's junior

varsity squad, and **tallied** several 40-point games. The following summer, he grew four inches (10 cm) and trained **rigorously**. Upon earning a spot on the varsity **roster**, Jordan averaged about 20 points per game over his final two seasons of high school play. As a senior, he was selected to the McDonald's All-American Team after averaging a **triple-double**: 29.2 points, 11.6 rebounds, and 10.1 **assists**.

(H) Jordan was **recruited** by numerous college basketball programs, including Duke, North Carolina, South Carolina, Syracuse, and Virginia. In 1981, Jordan accepted a basketball scholarship to North Carolina, where he **majored in** cultural geography.

(I) As a freshman in coach Dean Smith's **team-oriented** system, he was named ACC Freshman of the Year after he averaged 13.4 points per game (ppg) on 53.4% **shooting (field goal percentage)**. He made the game-winning jump shot in the 1982 **NCAA** Championship game against Georgetown, which was led by future NBA rival Patrick Ewing. Jordan later described this shot as the major turning point in his basketball career. During his three seasons at North Carolina, he averaged 17.7 ppg on 54.0% shooting, and added 5.0 rebounds per game (rpg). He was selected by **consensus** to the NCAA All-American First Team in both his sophomore (1983) and junior (1984) seasons. After winning the Naismith and the Wooden College Player of the Year awards in 1984, Jordan left North Carolina one year before his scheduled graduation to enter the 1984 NBA Draft. The Chicago Bulls selected Jordan with the third overall pick, after Hakeem Olajuwon (Houston Rockets) and Sam Bowie (Portland Trail Blazers). One of the primary reasons why Jordan was not **drafted** sooner was because the first two teams were **in need of** a center. However, the Trail Blazers general manager Stu Inman contested that it was not **a matter of** drafting a center, but more a matter of taking Sam Bowie over Jordan, in part because Portland already had a guard with similar skills to Jordan, Clyde Drexler. In 2005 ESPN, citing Bowie's injury-laden college career, named the Blazers' choice of Bowie as the worst draft pick in North American professional sports history. Jordan returned to North Carolina to complete his degree in 1986.

(Words: 1030)

New Words

initial	*n.* 词首大写字母 *adj.* 最初的；字首的 *vt.* 用姓名的首字母签名
entrepreneur	*n.* 企业家；承包人；主办者
effectively	4 有效地，生效地；有力地，实际上
emerge	*vi.* 浮现，显现
prolific	*adj.* 多产的，丰富的
three-peat	*n.* 三连冠 *vi.* 赢得
abruptly	*adv.* 突然地；唐突地
accolade	*n.* 荣誉；称赞
inductee	*n.* 应召入伍的士兵；就任者
endorsement	*n.* 认可，支持；背书；签注（文件）
fuel	*n.* 燃料；刺激因素 *vt.* 供以燃料，加燃料 *vi.* 得到燃料
sneaker	*n.* 运动鞋；胶底运动鞋
part-owner	*n.* 共有者；共有人
toddler	*n.* 学步的小孩
anchor	*vt.* 抛锚；使固定；主持节目 *vi.* 抛锚 *n.* 锚；靠山
varsity	*n.* 大学运动代表队 *adj.* 大学运动代表队的
deem	*vt.* 认为，视作；相信 *vi.* 认为，持某种看法；作某种评价
squad	*n.* 班；小队；五人组（篮球队的非正式说法） *vt.* 把…编成班；把…编入班

续表

tally	*vt.* 使符合；计算；记录 *vi.* 一致；记分 *n.* 计数器；标签；记账
rigorously	*adv.* 严厉地；残酷地
roster	*n.* 花名册；执勤人员表；逐项登记表
triple-double	*n.* 三双（即三项技术统计指标超过两位数）
assist	*n.* 助攻；帮助 *vt.* 帮助；促进 *vi.* 参加；出席
recruit	*n.* 招聘；新兵；新成员 *vt.* 补充；聘用；使…恢复健康 *vi.* 复原；征募新兵；恢复健康
team-oriented	*adj.* 具有团队精神的
shooting	*n.* 射门；射击
consensus	*n.* 一致；舆论；合意
draft	*n.* 汇票；草稿；选派 *vt.* 起草；制定；征募 *vi.* 拟稿；绘样；作草图

Phrases & Expressions

by acclamation	通过口头表决方式
slam dunk	扣篮；灌篮高手
free throw line	罚球线
reputation for	名声；名气；以…闻名
defensive players	防守型运动员
star in	主演
feature film	正片，故事片；长片
equipment supervisor	设备总监
try out for	竞争；参加选拔

续表

sophomore year	大学二年级
major in	主修；专攻
field goal percentage	投篮命中率；投球命中率
in need of	需要
a matter of	大约；需要…的问题

Proper Names

Michael Jeffrey Jordan	迈克尔 J. 乔丹
the Charlotte Hornets	夏洛特黄蜂队
the Chicago Bulls	芝加哥公牛队
the Washington Wizards	华盛顿奇才队
Air Jordan	空中飞人；飞人乔丹
Most Valuable Player (MVP) Awards	最有价值球员奖
First Team	首发阵容；第一阵容
Defensive Player of the Year Award	年度最佳防守球员
Associated Press	美国联合通讯社；美联社
the Dream Team	梦之队
the Charlotte Bobcats	夏洛特山猫队
Forbes	福布斯（美国出版及媒体集团）；福布斯（美国著名财经杂志）
NCAA	（美国）全国大学生体育学会（National Collegiate Athletic Association）

Cultural Notes

1. Associated Press (AP) is an American multinational nonprofit news agency headquartered in New York City. The AP is owned by its contributing newspapers, radio, and television stations in the United States, all of which contribute stories to the AP and use material written by its staff journalists. For more information, visit https: //en. wikipedia. org/wiki/Associated_ Press.

2. Forbes is an American business magazine owned by Forbes, Inc. Published biweekly, it features original articles on finance, industry, investing, and marketing topics. Forbes also reports on related subjects such as technology, communications, science, and law. Its headquarters is located in Jersey City, New Jersey. For more information, visit https: //en. wikipedia. org/wiki/Forbes.

Exercises

Comprehension of the Text

Ⅰ. The following 10 statements contain information given in the text. Identify the paragraph from which the information is derived. You may choose a paragraph more than once. Each paragraph is marked with a letter.

1. Michael Jordan won a "three-peat"with the Bulls in NBA contest.

2. During his sophomore year, Michael Jordan tried out for the varsity basketball team, but he was considered too short to play because of his height.

3. In 1982, Michael Jordan made the game-winning jump shot in the NCAA Championship game against Georgetown.

4. On earning a spot on the varsity roster, Michael Jordan won about 20 points per game on average over his final two seasons of high school play.

5. During the 1980s and 1990s Michael Jordan was thought helpful in popularizing the NBA around the world.

6. Michael Jordan returned to North Carolina to finish his degree in 1986.

7. In 1981, Michael Jordan majored in cultural geography in North Carolina and accepted a basketball scholarship there.

8. According to Forbes, Michael Jordan became the first athlete billionaire in history in 2015.

9. Michael Jordan was named the greatest North American athlete of the 20th century by ESPN In 1999.

10. By the performance of slam dunks from the free throw line in slam dunk

contests, his leaping ability was illustrated and earned him the nicknames "Air Jordan" and "His Airiness"

Vocabulary

Ⅱ. Fill in the blanks with the words given below. Change the form where necessary.

effectively	emerge	prolific	abruptly	accolade
endorsement	fuel	anchor	varsity	deem
rigorously	assist	recruit	rival	consensus

1. We planned to work together, but he is too ______ and I cannot keep up with him.
2. He says he would support the use of force if the UN ______ it necessary.
3. If science would ______ me, the contemporary human says, I could live as a brain without a body.
4. Our football fan club began to ______ new members last week.
5. If you can use a word correctly and ______, you comprehend it.
6. Yet in doing so, I could believe that I am ________ working.
7. Take a straw poll of your friends and we guarantee that you will find no ______.
8. You are to be given one method of communication with your ______, albeit indirect communication.
9. ______, she looked up at him, and he saw in her eyes that his determination and anxiety and readiness were flowing into her through the thing he held, and that they had become her own.
10. She then ______ from the courthouse to thank her supporters.

Further Reading

TEXT C American Football

American football, known within the U. S. simply as football, has the most participants of any sport at both high school and college levels.

The history of American football can be traced to early versions of rugby football and association football. Both games have their origin in varieties of football played in Britain in the mid-19th century, in which a football is kicked at a goal or run over a line.

American football resulted from several major divergences from rugby, most notably the rule changes instituted by Walter Camp, a Yale and Hopkins School graduate considered to be the "Father of American Football". Among these important changes were the introduction of the line of scrimmage and of down-and-distance rules. In the late 19th and early 20th centuries, game play developments by college coaches such as Eddie Cochems, Amos Alonzo Stagg, Knute Rockne, and Glenn "Pop" Warner helped take advantage of the newly introduced forward pass. The popularity of college football grew as it became the dominant version of the sport in the United States for the first half of the 20th century. Bowl games, a college football tradition, attracted a national audience for college teams. Boosted by fierce rivalries, college football still holds widespread appeal in the US.

The origin of professional football can be traced back to 1892, with William "Pudge"Heffelfinger's $500 contract to play in a game for the Allegheny Athletic Association against the Pittsburgh Athletic Club. In 1920 the American Professional Football Association was formed. This league changed its name to the National Football League (NFL) two years later, and eventually became the major league of American football. Primarily a sport of Midwestern industrial towns in the United States, professional football eventually became a national phenomenon. Football's increasing popularity is usually traced to the 1958 NFL Championship Game, a contest that has been dubbed the "Greatest Game Ever Played". A rival league to the NFL, the American Football League (AFL), began play in 1960; the pressure it put on the senior league led to a merger between the two leagues and the creation of the Super Bowl, which has become the most watched television event in the United States on an annual basis.

Millions watch college football throughout the fall months, and some communities, particularly in rural areas, place great emphasis on their local high school football teams. The popularity of college and high school football in areas such as the Southern United States (Southeastern Conference) and the Great Plains (Big 12 Conference and Big Ten Conference) stems largely from the fact that these areas historically generally did not possess markets large enough for a professional team. Nonetheless, college football has a rich history in the United States, predating the NFL by decades, and fans and alumni are generally very passionate about their teams.

During football season in the fall, fans have the opportunity to watch high school games on Fridays and Saturdays, college football on Saturdays, and NFL games on Sundays, the usual playing day of the professional teams. However, some colleges play games on Tuesday (the Mid-American Conference in particular played a national game Tuesday nights through the 2013 season) and Wednesday nights, while the NFL offers weekly games on Monday (since 1970) and Thursday (since 2006). As recently as 2013, one could find a nationally televised professional or college game on television any night between Labor Day and Thanksgiving weekend (as of 2014, the MAC's Tuesday night games now only occur in November, to accommodate baseball season).

Super Bowl Sunday is the biggest annual sporting event held in the United States. The Super Bowl itself is always among the highest-rated programs off all-time in the Nielsen ratings.

Notable NFL players include Jim Kelly, Joe Montana, Roger Staubach, Dick Butkus, Joe Greene, Bart Starr, Johnny Unitas, Walter Payton, Steve Young, Jerry Rice, Brett Favre, Emmitt Smith, and Ray Lewis. Notable current NFL players include Peyton Manning, Tom Brady, and Adrian Peterson.

Nationwide, the NFL obtains the highest television ratings among major sports. This situation began in the late 1960s and early 1970s with the establishment of the Super Bowl and merger of the existing professional leagues, the old NFL and the American Football League, into one NFL league. Since then, watching NFL games on television on Sunday afternoons has become a common routine for many Americans during the football season. Among the NFL teams which have become practically identified with their host cities are the Pittsburgh Steelers, the

Dallas Cowboys, the Green Bay Packers and the Washington Redskins.

College football is popular in the southeast, where there are fewer major professional sports teams. In many of these areas, college football is the most avidly followed sport, with the Saturday college games being the biggest event of the week.

Indoor American football, a form of football played in indoor arenas, has several professional and semi-professional leagues. The Arena Football League, which plays by the formerly proprietary code of arena football, was active from 1987 to 2008 and folded in 2009, but several teams from the AFL and its former minor league, af2, relaunched the league in 2010. Most other extant indoor leagues date to the mid – 2000s(decade) and are regional in nature.

(Words: 865)

Questions for discussions

1. What can the history of American football be traced to?

2. Which places are the popularity of college and high school football according to the text?

3. Why does the NFL obtain the highest television ratings among major sports in the United States?

More to Learn

1. Some words about sports

manager 经纪人

instructor 教练，技术指导

guide 领队

coach 教练

trainer 助理教练

team, side 队

referee, umpire (网球或棒球)裁判

linesman, touch judge (橄榄球)裁判

contestant, competitor, player 运动员

professional 职业运动员

amateur 业余运动员，爱好者

enthusiast, fan 迷，爱好者

favourite 可望取胜者（美作: favorite）
championship 冠军赛，锦标赛
record 纪录
ace 网球赛中的一分
Olympic Games, Olympics 奥林匹克运动会
Winter Olympics 冬季奥林匹克运动会
ground, field 场地
court 网球场
race 跑
long-distance runner 长跑运动员
the 400 meter hurdles 400 米栏
decathlon 十项
jump 跳跃
high jump 跳高
triple jump, hop step and jump 三级跳
throw 投掷
putting the shot, shot put 推铅球
throwing the hammer 掷链锤
walk 竞走
gymnastic apparatus 体操器械
parallel bars 双杠
rings 吊环
trapeze 秋千
side horse 鞍马
weights 重量级
Greece-Roman wrestling 古典式摔跤
judo 柔道
winter sports 冬季运动
ski 滑雪板

outsider 无取胜希望者
champion, gold medalist 冠军
record holder 纪录创造者
stadium 运动场
track 跑道
ring 圈
pitch（足球、橄榄球）场地
relay race; relay 接力
middle-distance race 中长跑
sprint 短跑（美作: dash）
marathon 马拉松
cross-country race 越野跑
jumping 跳跃运动
long jump 跳远（美作: broad jump）
pole vault 撑竿跳
throwing 投掷运动
throwing the discus 掷铁饼
throwing the javelin 掷标枪
gymnastics 体操
horizontal bar 单杠
uneven bars; high-low bars 高低杠
pommel horse 鞍马
wall bars 肋木
weight-lifting 举重
boxing 拳击
hold, lock 揪钮
fencing 击剑
skiing 滑雪
downhill race 速降滑雪赛，滑降

slalom 障碍滑雪
ski jumping competition 跳高滑雪比赛
figure skating 花样滑冰
bobsleigh, bobsled 雪橇
rugby 橄榄球
volleyball 排球
baseball 垒球
hockey 曲棍球
cricket 板球
goalkeeper 球门员
goal kick 球门发球
to score a goal 射门得分
to convert a try 对方球门线后触地得分
men's singles 单打运动员
swimming pool 游泳池
medley relay 混合泳
breaststroke 蛙式
freestyle 自由式
sidestroke 侧泳
diving competition 跳水
water skiing 水橇
canoe 划艇
yacht 游艇
sailing 帆船运动
outboard boat 船外马达
riding 骑马
polo 马球
racecourse, racetrack 跑马场, 赛马场
show jumping competition 跳跃赛
fence 障碍
tug-of-war 拔河
baseball (soft ball) field/ground 棒/垒球场
ski jump 跳高滑雪
ice skating 滑冰
roller skating 滑旱冰
football 足球
basketball 篮球
tennis 网球
handball 手球
golf 高尔夫球
ice hockey 冰球
center kick 中线发球
throw in, line-out 边线发球
batsman 板球运动员
batter 击球运动员
in the mixed doubles 混合双打
swimming 游泳
crawl 爬泳
backstroke 仰式
butterfly (stroke) 蝶泳
dolphin stroke/kick 海豚式
water polo 水球
rowing 划船
boat race 赛艇
kayak 皮船
yachting; sailing 帆船运动
water-skiing 滑水
jockey 骑师
rider 马球运动员
trotter 快跑的马
steeplechase 障碍赛
surfing 冲浪
shooting range 靶场
baseball 棒球

to produce an unexpected winner 爆冷门

to outscore 比分领先

competition gymnasiums and stadiums 比赛场馆

spectator 比赛观众

competition/sports venue (s) 比赛地点

javelin throw 标枪

skating rink; ice rink 冰场

puck; rubber 冰球

rink 冰球场

ice hockey 冰球运动

ice sports 冰上运动

chief referee 裁判长

referee, umpire 裁判员

the handicapped/disabled 残疾人

playground; sports ground; drill ground 操场

setting-up exercises to music 广播操

label 称号, 绰号

pole jump 撑竿跳高

to undertake obligation 承担义务

make one's mark 出名

to draw/to tie/to play even/to level the score 打成平局

up to one's best level in skill and style of play 打出水平, 打出风格

individual event 单项

third; bronze medalist 第三名

mountaineering; mountain-climbing 登山运动

mat exercises 垫上运动

host country/nation 东道国

contingent 队伍, 代表团

accuracy jump; precision landing 定点跳伞

alpine skiing 高山滑雪

Build up a good physique to defend the country 锻炼身体, 保卫祖国

Promote physical culture and build up the people's health 发展体育运动, 增强人民体质

International Olympic Committee 国际奥林匹克委员会

international tournament 国际比赛

national team 国家队

(international) chess 国际象棋

dark horse 黑马

marine modeling; model ship 航海模型

aeromodel; model aeroplane 航空模型

canoeing 划艇，皮艇
sports acrobatics 技巧
jianqiu; shuttlecock playing 毽球
championship 锦标赛
in good form 竞技状态好
gliding 滑翔运动
acrobatic gymnastics 技巧运动
shuttlecock 毽子
competitive sport 竞技性运动
track events 竞赛

MOVIES TO SEE (A) Facing the Giants

Ⅰ. Movie Introduction

Director: Alex Kendrick

Starring: Erin Bethea
James Blackwell
Bailey Cave
Shannen Fields
Tracy Goode

Running time: 111 mins

Released: 2006

Plot: *Facing the Giants* is a 2006 American Christian drama film directed by and starring Alex Kendrick. Grant Taylor (Alex Kendrick) is the head coach at Shiloh Christian Academy, and has yet to post a winning record in his six-year tenure. After his seventh season begins with a three-game losing streak, the players' fathers start making noises about replacing him with defensive coordinator Brady Owens. This is not the only problem Grant is facing. His car is breaking down, and he discovers that he is the reason that his wife Brooke cannot become pregnant.

Grant Taylor creates a new coaching philosophy and decides to praise God, no matter what the result. At the same time he guides and urges each one of his players to give the maximum effort, and motivates them to believe they can win under God's provision. From that point on, the Eagles lose only one more game for the rest of the season and advance all the way to the state championship game against the three-time defending champion Richland Giants. Even though the Eagles have only a third as many players as the Giants, the Eagles hold their own and ultimately win the game on a 51-yard field goal from a backup kicker who had never kicked more than a 35-yarder before. Grant's prayers for children are also answered as Brooke conceives after four years.

Ⅱ. Classic Scenes

Task 1 Study the underlined sentences and expressions in the following classic scenes.

1. Words from the Commentator

The Eagles will go for it on fourth down with 42 seconds left in the football game and no timeouts. Coach Taylor can get his first winning season for the Shiloh Christian Academy if they can pull this play off. Avery will take the snap. He pitches back to Jacob Hall. Jacob's gonna try to pass it. He's got Jeremy Johnson going down the field. Jacob's gonna try to tuck and run. And he's taken down at the 40 yard line and stopped there by Lewis Slaughter. Jeremy Johnson was wide open down the field. If he'd only had a few seconds more to throw this game might have had a different outcome. As it is, the Tigers will take over now, and will no doubt run out the clock ending Coach Grant Taylor's bid for his first winning season in six years. Now he'll have to wait until next season for that all-elusive winning record. That's if they let him come back next year.

2. In Taylor's Home

Wife: Why'd you park all the way out there?

Taylor: Had to. It died again.

Wife: Why don't we get a new battery?

Taylor: I'll get Brady to help me tomorrow. I don't wanna think about it now.

Wife: Do you want me to take a look at it?

Taylor: Stop it.

Wife: Oh, Sweetheart. Grant, I don't know what that smell is. I've scrubbed everything I can.

Taylor: It's terrible.

Wife: I know it is, but what else can I do? I don't even know where it's coming from.

Taylor: Well, this day stunk. Why shouldn't my house?

Wife: What do you mean?

Taylor: Darren transferred to Tucker.

Wife: What? He did not.

Taylor: Yep. Came by and got his papers, didn't even say goodbye.

Wife: Why?

Taylor: Why do you think? Didn't see a chance of winning at Shiloh. But it ain't like Tucker's gonna guarantee him a scholarship.

Wife: Oh, I bet the boys are frustrated.

Taylor: More than you know.

Wife: I meant to throw that away.

Taylor: Did you think you were pregnant?

Wife: I don't know. I just wanna be pregnant so bad that my mind plays tricks on me. You know, it's been four years since we started trying. Would you be opposed to me going to see a specialist?

Taylor: No.

Wife: I'd just like to know what she says.

Taylor: Okay. I thought we were having Spaghetti tonight.

Wife: Stove's not working.

Taylor: You are kidding me. So we got a leak in the back room, the dryer only works half the time, the car's dying on us and now the stove's broken. That's about right. No wonder I'm losing my hair.

Wife: I love you.

3. Georgia Sports Break

Alice: And now your Georgia Sports Break with Alicia Houston. The Richland Giants started practice as the school year gets under way. The team will be defending a three-year state Championship run. Now they prepare to fight for a fourth. I'm here with head coach Bobby Lee Duke of the Giants. Coach Duke, how does this year look for the team?

Bobby Lee Duke: Alice, we've grown real fond of the state title. And we don't see any reason to give it up this year. I've got most of my starters coming back and I've got a strong bench. So I've only got one thing to say: Get off the tracks, because the freight train's coming.

Task 2 Work in pairs or groups and play the roles in one of your favorite scenes.

Ⅲ. Questions for discussion

1. What are the themes involved in this film?
2. How do you think of Darren transferred to Tucker?
3. What can you learn the spirit from Grant Taylor?

Ⅳ. Movie Review

Task: Write a movie review on *Facing the Giants*.

MOVIES TO SEE (B) Rudy

Ⅰ. Movie Introduction

Director: David Anspaugh

Starring: Sean Astin, Jon Favreau, Ned Beatty, | Charles S. Dutton

Running time: 114 mins

Released: 1993

Plot: *Rudy* is a 1993 American sports film directed by David Anspaugh. It is an account of the life of Daniel "Rudy" Ruettiger, who harbored dreams of playing football at the University of Notre Dame despite significant obstacles. It was the first movie that the Notre Dame administration allowed to be shot on campus since Knute Rockne, All American in 1940.

To Recommend More Movies

❖ *Ice Princess* (2005)
❖ *Money Ball* (2011)
❖ *Raging Bull* (1980)
❖ *Space Jam* (1996)

Unit Eleven Travel

Pre-reading Activities

Answer the following questions before you read this text.

1. Can you name some world famous places of interest in the U. S?

2. What are the pros and cons of traveling on your own? What kind of trip best caters to your personality?

3. What things should you do before your trip to prepare for safe travel in the U. S. ? What should you do during your trip to stay safe?

TEXT A Best Places to Visit in the USA (Excerpt)

Thousands of travelers **weighed in on** which vacation spots can be considered the best in the USA. Based on those user votes and expert analysis of factors like the variety of attractions, **accommodations** and dining options in a destination, U. S. News came up with the top places to visit in the USA. These stateside **getaways** range from beaches to national parks to big cities. Use this list for your vacation planning, and cast your vote below to help us determine next year's list.

Grand Canyon

"Grand" doesn't begin to **do** this canyon **justice**. Measuring approximately 277 miles in length, up to 18 miles in width and a mile deep, this massive **chasm** in northern Arizona is truly a natural wonder. For six million years, the **Grand Canyon** has expanded with the help of the **mighty Colorado River**, and for centuries, people from all over the globe have traveled to **gaze out over** its red and orange **grandeur**. Managed by the National Park Service and officially designated as a **UNESCO World Heritage site**, the Grand Canyon leaves its approximately 4. 5 million visitors per year **awestruck**.

But if you're seeking a **secluded** escape to Mother Nature, you should be prepared: The Grand Canyon can be very crowded.

Yellowstone

With dramatic peaks and **pristine** lakes, **Yellowstone** is an outdoor enthusiast's paradise. Multicolored pools **swirl** around hot springs; **verdant** forests weave past expansive **meadows**; and **volatile geysers** launch streams of steaming water toward the sky. With so much **unspoiled** natural beauty, it's no wonder everyone suspected **John Colter** (a **scout** for explorers Lewis and Clark) was **embellishing** when he first described Yellowstone's **geothermal** curiosities in 1807. Nowadays, there's no doubt that the park is indeed extraordinary. While you **traverse** the park's 3, 000-plus square miles of mountains, canyons, geysers and waterfalls, be prepared to share the trails with permanent residents like **buffalo**, **elk** and sometimes even **grizzlies**.

San Francisco

A **jumbled collage** of colorful neighborhoods and beautiful views, San Francisco draws those free-spirited types who have an eye for **edgy** art, a taste for imaginative **cuisine** and a **zeal** for adventure. It's really not surprising that songwriter **Tony Bennett** left his heart here: The city boasts **jaw-dropping** sights, world-class cuisine, cozy cafes and plenty of booming nightlife **venues**—there's no shortage of ways to stay busy here. Spend an hour or two sunning yourself alongside sea lions on the bay, admiring the views of the city from **Twin Peaks**, or **strolling** along the **Marina**. And for the **quintessential** San Franciscan experience, enjoy a ride on a cable car.

New York City

Cool, **cosmopolitan**, crowded, constantly evolving... the **Big Apple** blends big-city splendor with small-town charm. Amid **Gotham's** iconic landmarks and towering skyscrapers, you'll experience a **vibrant** culture **permeating** each of the city's distinctive neighborhoods and **boroughs**. Follow trendsetters to the **East Village** and **Brooklyn** to check out **indie boutiques**, iconic bakeries and trendy coffee shops. Afterward, **peruse** the **racks** of the **sleek** shops lining **Fifth Avenue**, admire the **cutting-edge** art collections at **the MoMa** and **the Met**, catch a memorable show on Broadway or sit down for a meal at the latest "it" restaurant.

As the most populous city in the U. S. — set at the **forefront** of food, fashion and the arts—NYC requires **stamina**. But don't let the Big Apple's **frenetic** sights and sounds intimidate you from **soaking up** its grandeur. Wander through the concrete jungle and you'll discover roaring taxicabs **pouring down bustling** blocks, fast-paced **pedestrians** whizzing past on their way to **marquee** galleries and innovative cocktail bars and **Times Square's** neon lights **flickering** at all hours. And yet, the city's **twinkling** lights and **chaotic** corners also invite you to embrace every New York minute, explore every flourishing **enclave** and create your own urban adventure. There are virtually endless ways to occupy your time in the city that never sleeps, but before you leave, stop and look around—what's here today will be transformed into something bigger and better tomorrow.

Honolulu—Oahu

Oahu blends cosmopolitan luxury and breathtaking scenery more than any other Hawaiian island. The state's capital city, **Honolulu, showcases** the island's urban appeal. Nearby you'll find a host of cultural and historical sites, from the **austere USS Arizona Memorial** to ornate ' **Iolani Palace**. In the nearby **Waikiki** neighborhood, a skyline of high-rises and resort hotels contrasts with **sprawling** white-sand beaches. For a taste of rural Hawaii, visit the **North Shore**. Here, you'll find the most brilliant blue waters and meandering hikes. But those three spots aren't all Oahu offers. Its high-class restaurants, vibrant cultural events, and wild nightlife further showcase this island as a "Gathering Place" of Hawaiian culture.

Las Vegas

Sin City, America's Playground, the Entertainment Capital of the World ...all worthy names for this Nevada hotspot. Think of Vegas as a theme park rather than a city—it can awe as much as it can overwhelm, and that's part of the appeal. This is a city where **inhibitions** are not welcome: Every night, Las Vegas draws pleasure **mongers** to the brightly lit Striplike **moths** to a flame. While you may not want to go as far as to re-enact "**The Hangover**," you certainly don't want to leave without experiencing a bit of "Viva Las Vegas." Just remember: What happens here, stays here.

Chicago

"It is hopeless for the occasional visitor to try to keep up with Chicago. She outgrows his **prophecies** faster than he can make them." Although he made up his mind about the **Windy City** before it even reached its 50th year, **Mark Twain's** impression of Chicago has proven long-lasting. America's third-largest city has been described in a **myriad** of ways throughout its lifetime. When **Thomas Edison** and **Nikola Tesla** were competing for the right to use their forms of electricity to illuminate the **1893 World's Columbian Exposition** (also known as the Chicago World's Fair), Chicago was known as a city of industry. When **Prohibition set in**, **notorious mobsters** like **Al Capone** transformed Chicagoland into their own dangerous playground. And intense immigration surges throughout the 20th century brought a host of new identities to the Windy City, including Greek, Polish, Italian, Irish and Jewish.

Today, Chicago remains just as diverse, **boasting** a thriving arts scene, various shopping districts and a **cornucopia** of eateries.

(Words: 1038)

New Words

accommodation	*n.* 住处，住所
getaway	*n.* 短假
chasm	*n.* 峡谷；裂缝
mighty	*adj.* 巨大的，浩瀚的
grandeur	*n.* 伟大，宏伟，壮观
awestruck	*adj.* 敬畏的，肃然起敬的
secluded	*adj.* 僻静的，隐蔽的
pristine	*adj.* 一尘不染的，纯洁的
swirl	*vt.* （使）打旋，（使）旋动，（使）起漩涡

续表

verdant	*adj.* （草、田地等）翠绿的，嫩绿的
meadow	*n.* 草地，牧场
volatile	*adj.* 易变的，不稳定的；快活的，轻快的
geyser	*n.* 间歇喷泉
unspoiled	*adj.* （地方）未经开发的，有自然美的
scout	*n.* 侦察员，侦察机，侦察舰
embellish	*vt.* 装饰；润色；修饰
geothermal	*adj.* 地热的，地温的
traverse	*vt.* 横穿；横越；穿过
buffalo	*n.* （南非或北美的）野牛
elk	*n.* 麋鹿
grizzly	*n.* 北美洲灰熊
jumbled	*adj.* 混乱的，乱七八糟的
collage	*n.* 拼贴画；大杂烩
edgy	*adj.* 前卫的，时尚的
cuisine	*n.* 烹饪，烹调法；菜肴
zeal	*n.* 热情；激情；热忱
jaw-dropping	*adj.* 令人目瞪口呆的；印象深刻的；令人震惊的
cozy	*adj.* 舒适的，安逸的
venue	*n.* （事件或活动的）发生地，举办地点；场地
stroll	*vt.* 散步；溜达；闲逛
quintessential	*adj.* 精髓的；典型的
cosmopolitan	*adj.* 世界性的，国际化的；受各国文化影响的
vibrant	*adj.* 充满生气的；精力充沛的；活跃的
permeate	*vt.* 渗透；弥漫；扩散
borough	*n.* 纽约市五个行政区之一
indie	*adj.* 独立的

续表

boutique	*n.* （女士）时装店，精品店
peruse	*vt.* 研读；（尤指）细阅
rack	*n.* 挂物架；搁物架
sleek	*adj.* 时髦的
cutting-edge	*adj.* 前沿的，最尖端的
forefront	*n.* 最前部；活动中心
stamina	*n.* 持久力；耐力；毅力
frenetic	*adj.* 发狂似的；狂热的
bustling	*adj.* 繁忙的，熙熙攘攘的
marquee	*n.* （饭店、剧院等入口处的）遮篷，遮檐
flicker	*vi.* （灯光等）闪烁，摇曳
twinkle	*vi.* 闪烁；闪耀
chaotic	*adj.* 混乱的；乱糟糟的
enclave	*n.* （国家或城市中隶属另一民族或文化的）飞地，孤立地区
showcase	*vt.* 展示（优点）
austere	*adj.* 简朴的；朴素的
sprawl	*vi.* 扩展；延伸
inhibition	*n.* 顾虑；禁忌
monger	*n.* 商人，贩子
moth	*n.* 飞蛾，蛾子
prophecy	*n.* 预言
myriad	*n.* 无数；大量；各种各样
notorious	*adj.* 声名狼藉的；臭名昭著的
mobster	*n.* 犯罪集团分子；黑社会成员
boast	*vt.* 有，拥有（值得骄傲的成就或财产）
cornucopia	4 丰盛；丰富；丰饶

Phrases & Expressions

weigh in on	对……权衡
do…justice	对……公正
gaze out over…	凝视……，眺望……
soak up	沉浸于……；充分体验……
pour down	倾泻而下；奔泻
set in	（不好的事情）产生，开始，到来

Proper Names

Grand Canyon	大峡谷（美国亚利桑那州）
Colorado River	科罗拉多河
UNESCO World Heritage site	联合国教科文组织世界遗产
Yellowstone	黄石国家公园
John Colter	约翰·科尔特
Tony Bennett	托尼·班尼特
Twin Peaks	旧金山双子峰
Marina	旧金山马里纳街区
Big Apple	大苹果城（纽约市的别名）
Gotham	哥谭镇（纽约市的别名）
East Village	纽约东村（在美国纽约市曼哈顿）
Brooklyn	布鲁克林（美国纽约市西南部的一区）
Fifth Avenue	纽约市第五大道
the MoMa	纽约现代艺术博物馆
the Met	纽约大都会艺术博物馆
Times Square	时代广场
Honolulu	火奴鲁鲁（即“檀香山”，美国夏威夷州的首府和港市）
Oahu	欧胡岛（夏威夷群岛的主岛）
USS Arizona Memorial	美国海军亚利桑那号战列舰纪念馆

续表

'Iolani Palace	伊欧拉尼皇宫
Waikiki	怀基基海滩（美国夏威夷州）
North Shore	欧胡岛北岸
Las Vegas	拉斯维加斯
The Hangover	《宿醉》（美国电影）
Windy City	风城（美国芝加哥市的别称）
Mark Twain	马克·吐温
Thomas Edison	托马斯·爱迪生
Nikola Tesla	尼古拉·特斯拉
1893 World's Columbian Exposition	1893 年世界哥伦比亚博览会
Prohibition	（美国 1919 年至 1933 年间的）禁酒令；禁酒令时期
Al Capone	艾尔·卡彭（芝加哥黑社会大亨）

Cultural Notes

1. Grand Canyon Grand Canyon is a steep-sided canyon carved by the Colorado River in the U. S. state of Arizona in North America. It is contained within and managed by Grand Canyon National Park, the Kaibab National Forest, Grand Canyon-Parashant National Monument, the Hualapai Tribal Nation, the Havasupai people and the Navajo Nation. President Theodore Roosevelt was a major proponent of preservation of the Grand Canyon area, and visited it on numerous occasions to hunt and enjoy the scenery. For more information, visit https://en. wikipedia. org/wiki/Grand_ Canyon.

2. Yellowstone Yellowstone National Park is a national park located in the U. S. states of Wyoming, Montana and Idaho. It was established by the U. S. Congress and signed into law by President Ulysses S. Grant on March 1, 1872. Yellowstone was the first National Park in the U. S. and is also widely held to be the first national park in the world. The park is known for its wildlife and its many geothermal features, especially Old Faithful Geyser, one of its most popular features. It has many types of ecosystems, but the subalpine forest is the most abundant. It is part of the South Central Rockies forests ecoregion. For more information, visit https://en.wikipedia.org/wiki/Yellowstone_National_Park.

3. San Francisco San Francisco, officially the City and County of San Francisco, is the cultural, commercial, and financial center of Northern California. It is the birthplace of the United Nations. For more information, visit https://en.wikipedia.org/wiki/San_Francisco.

4. New York City The City of New York, often called New York City or simply New York, is the most populous city in the United States. With an estimated 2015 population of 8,550,405 distributed over a land area of about 302.6 square miles (784 km^2), New York City is also the most densely populated major city in the United States. For more information, visit https://en.wikipedia.org/wiki/New_York_City.

5. Honolulu Honolulu is the capital and largest city of the U. S. state of Hawaii. It is an unincorporated part of and the county seat of the City and County of Honolulu on the island of Oahu. For more information, visit https://en.wikipedia.org/wiki/Honolulu.

6. Las Vegas Las Vegas, officially the City of Las Vegas and often known simply as Vegas, is the 28th-most populated city in the United States, the most populated city in the state of Nevada, and the county seat of Clark County. For more information, visit https://en.wikipedia.org/wiki/Las_Vegas.

7. Chicago Chicago, officially the City of Chicago, is the third-most populous city in the United States. With over 2.7 million residents, it is also the most populous city in both the state of Illinois and the Midwestern United States. For more information, visit https://en.wikipedia.org/wiki/Chicago.

Exercises

Comprehension of the Text

Ⅰ Answer the following questions according to the passage.

1. What influence do you think national parks exert on average Americans'

character?

2. Do you agree that New York city is the embodiment of diverse cultures in the U. S. ?Why?

3. What role does immigration play in the formation of big metropolitan cities in the U. S. ?

Vocabulary

Ⅱ. Fill in the blanks with the words given below. Change the form where necessary.

grandeur	secluded	verdant	boast	unspoiled
embellish	venue	cuisine	zeal	permeate
cutting-edge	chaotic	flourish	austere	notorious

1. Wuxi is the cradle of modern national industry in China and ________ many famous industrialists such as Rong Zongjing and Rong Desheng. .

2. Famous for its panda reserves, spicy ________ and laid-back lifestyle, Chengdu welcomed 2. 2 million visitors in 2015, an 82 percent increase on 2011.

3. Some ________ developments in today's world are challenging the red line of the international order and the moral bottom line of mankind, and our blue planet is, from time to time, smeared by the bloody stains of the law of the jungle.

4. The railway major's ________ technology and product development have been fueled by the country's Made in China 2025 strategy, which was designed to promote high-end manufacturing.

5. Hutong and the houses (siheyuan, or "courtyards distributed evenly") ________ people from the hustle and bustle of the streets outside, from where you can see the sedimentation of hundreds of years of history.

6. This growing feeling of mistrust that has ________ every segment of society is widely seen to have greatly impeded the development of Hong Kong despite repeated warnings that it is falling behind other fast growing cities in the region.

7. Besides over-________ parents, the central government has also played a part in the current craze for traditional Chinese culture.

8. In violation of the CPC's eight-point rules on ____________, Li used public funds to pay for expensive dinners and frequented private clubs.

9. Once a _____________ village during the Soviet times, Naumovka lost most of its younger generation, who left in search of better life in the city.

10. Lindeberg-Bernhardsson began to use fruits, vegetables, plants and everything at hand to ____________ her dining table instead of expensive vases and tablecloth a decade ago, which she says changed the Swedish idea that setting a dining table was expensive.

Translations

Ⅲ. Translate the following sentences into English.

1. 约翰和其他老师都认为，在这个重要的决定上发表意见是很愚蠢的。(weigh in on)

____

2. 没有哪一篇文章能把欺诈这一话题讲得恰到好处。(do…justice)

____

3. 基顿每年到这里来一两次，为的是尽情感受这里的气氛。(soak up)

____

4. 度假者不断涌至海边冲浪和享受阳光。(pour down)

____

5. 当他们发现魔力已失的时候，失望的情绪开始蔓延。(set in)

____

Ⅳ. Translate the following passage into English.

去年十一月四日，我到了纽约，这是世界上最大的城市之一。傍晚，我住进了曼哈顿区的一家旅馆，地处纽约最繁华的市区。夜晚，我漫步在银行、公司、商店、事务所密聚的街头。高楼耸立夜空，像陡峻的山峰；墙壁是透明的玻璃，好像水晶宫。五颜六色的街灯闪闪烁烁，远远近近，高高低低，时隐时现。走在路上，就像浮游在布满繁星的天空。汽车如风如龙，飞驰而过，车上的尾灯，似无数条红色丝带不断地向远方延伸。这边，明亮的橱窗里，陈列着锃锃发亮的金银餐具、红的玛瑙、青翠的碧玉，金刚钻在耀眼，古铜器也在诱人。那边，是巍峨的宫殿，门口站着穿制服的巡警，美丽的花帘在窗后掩映。人行道上，走着不同肤色的人群，服装形形色色，打扮五花八门，都那样来去匆匆……我徜徉在这热闹的街头，四顾灿烂似锦似花，但我却看不出它的美丽……我在这里只是一个偶然的、匆忙的过客。

TEXT B The Best USA Guided Tour for Every Personality

(A) You may have heard the **buzzword** phrase "experiential travel," which basically means trips that focus more on connecting with a place or with the locals, or on a personalized and **immersive** journey aimed at teaching you something new. Experiential travel is **on the rise**, according to a special report by the travel company Peak DMC. Moreover, 72 percent of **millennials** prefer to spend their hard-earned cash on experiences rather than on material things.

(B) No matter what your favorite things are (think: food, nature, animals, or wine), read on for tour ideas that will match your interests and personality.

For the Budding Photographer: Fall Foliage Trip

(C) "Travel Vision Journeys" offers a unique way to see fall **foliage** like you've never seen it before in Maine. Professional photo guides known for their beautiful images of the area will lead you to their favorite hard-to-find spots to take in the autumn scenery. You'll find beautiful sights throughout the trail as you make your way to an incredible view of **the Bigelow Mountains**; get a guided **canoe** trip, meals with fresh local food, and photography lessons and tips from experts.

(D) The trip lasts six days and five nights and starts at $1,195 per person. All meals are included in addition to lodging and activities and, of course, the amazing tour guides.

For the Fitness Fanatic: Cycling Hawaii Trip

(E) Hawaii is famous for unbelievable beaches, stunning views, and perfect weather. Cycling through it is the perfect trip for the fitness **fanatic** who is looking to see paradise on two wheels.

(F) "Ride and Seek" offers an eight-day tour of **the Big Island** led by ex-pro cyclist Alex Candelario. You'll ride through volcanoes and the Volcanic national parks, along stunning beaches, and on the roads of the famous **Hawaiian Ironman**.

(G) In 2017, the bike tour begins on November 4th and ends on November 11th. It costs $3900 per person and includes all hotels, four dinners, all breakfasts and lunches, and biking supplies.

For the Nature Lover: An Alaskan Bear Tour and the Northern Lights

(H) Dreaming of nights in the wilderness seeing animals in their natural habitats? "Gondwana Ecotours" has you covered. In this trip to Alaska, you'll see bears hunt salmon in stunning waterfalls. You might get lucky and spot whales, sea otters, **puffins**, and sea lions in **Kenai Fjords National Park**.

(I) Activities include bear-viewing in Katmailand, a boat tour through Kenai Fjords National Park, **kayaking**, hiking, and a tour of **Exit Glacier**.

(J) Tours are guided by knowledgeable locals. This is a unique trip that offers an opportunity to safely see bears hunt in the wilderness!

(K) The tour includes seven nights with accommodations, all transportation in the Kenai Peninsula, tour guides, and four lunches. Prices start at $4,325.

(L) If you're wanting a natural **excursion** that focuses less on wildlife spotting and more on star gazing, Alaska's **Northern Lights** are truly magical. Gondwana Ecotours offers a six-night tour of Alaska outside of Fairbanks, and the trip includes a wake-up service when the **Aurora Borealis** is active so you'll never have to risk missing the lights. You'll get to experience a dog-sledding excursion, the **Chena Hot Springs**, two Alaskan museums, **Running Reindeer Ranch**, and tours of the area from Alaskan guides—all in addition to viewing the unforgettable Northern Lights.

(M) This trip includes a hotel stay, **gourmet** Alaskan breakfasts and the fun activities listed above and more. There are dates available from September until March every year.

(N) Packages start at $2,345 per person.

For the Foodie: Cajun and Creole Cultural Road Trip

(O) If you're looking for the perfect way to enjoy Louisiana food and culture, a tour from "Cox & King USA" offers "a customized driving adventure" through southern Louisiana. It includes an **antebellum** plantation excursion and time in New Orleans. On this tour, you'll dine with local families, visit the **Tabas-**

co factory, take a cooking course with a local celebrity chef, and dance to **zydeco** (a kind of dance music that usually showcases a guitar and **accordion**).

(P) In New Orleans, you'll get to take a **culinary** and cocktail tour, go inside **French Quarter** homes, and learn all about New Orleans food, culture, and music.

(Q) This tour includes seven days and six nights, hotels in each destination, some meals, sightseeing, and sedan rental. Starting rates may be about $7,970.

For the Wine Aficionado: Sonoma & Napa Valley Wine Tour

(R) If you're a wine lover, a trip to the Northern California vineyards is a must do. "Classic Journeys" offers a trip through the area where you'll sample some of the regions best wines, as well as see the sights of Northern California, like the Golden **Gate Bridge** and the Redwood forests. In addition to tasting the wine at the vineyards, you'll get to see the sights in one of the most beautiful areas of the USA.

(S) This tour is six days and five nights, and boasts full-time experienced guides with you throughout the entire trip. This trip also includes admissions to tastings and historic sites. All breakfasts and three lunches and dinners are also included. Prices start at $3,795.

For the Spiritual Seeker: Recharge in Tucson

(T) For those wanting to reconnect to their spiritual side as well as get a healthy dose of relaxation, a spa in the luxurious Southwest is a perfect **antidote**. The travel and tour company "Butterfield & Robinson" offers an inclusive spa trip and spiritual journey hosted at the well-known and luxurious **Canyon Ranch** with mindfulness tips you can use when you return home. The trip includes Spirit Walks, **yoga** and **pilates** classes, and calming bike rides.

(U) It allows you as much time as you need to **unwind** with beautiful natural scenery surrounding you.

(V) The trip includes five days and four nights and is priced at $5,495 for four people.

(Words: 955)

New Words

buzzword	*n.* (媒体上的)时髦术语, 流行行话
immersive	*adj.* 沉浸式的
millennial	*n.* 新千年一代人
budding	*adj.* 崭露头角的, 刚起步的; 新出现的
foliage	*n.* (植物的)叶, 枝叶
canoe	*n.* 独木舟
fanatic	*adj.* 狂热的, 入迷的
puffin	*n.* 角嘴海雀
kayak	*n.* (因纽特人使用的或独木舟运动中所用的)独木舟, 单人划子
excursion	*n.* 短途旅行; 远足
gourmet	*n.* 美食家
antebellum	*adj.* (美国南北)战争前的
zydeco	*n.* 柴迪科舞(曲)
accordion	*n.* 手风琴
culinary	*adj.* 烹饪的
sedan	*n.* 大轿车; 厢式轿车
aficionado	*n.* 狂热爱好者; 迷
antidote	*n.* 解毒药; 解毒剂; 矫正方法; 对抗手段
yoga	*n.* 瑜伽
pilates	*n.* 普拉提, 一种健身体操
unwind	*vi.* 放松; 减压; 解开; 展开

Phrases & Expressions

on the rise	在上升, 在增长

Proper Names

the Bigelow Mountains	毕格罗山脉(缅因州)
the Big Island	大岛(夏威夷岛)
Hawaiian Ironman	夏威夷铁人三项赛
Kenai Fjords National Park	基奈峡湾国家公园(阿拉斯加州)
Exit Glacier	出口冰川(阿拉斯加州)
Northern Lights	阿拉斯加北极光
Aurora Borealis	北极光
Chena Hot Springs	珍娜温泉(阿拉斯加州)
Running Reindeer Ranch	驯鹿牧场(阿拉斯加州)
Tabasco	塔巴斯科辣椒酱
French Quarter	法语区(新奥尔良市)
Golden Gate Bridge	金门大桥(美国加利福尼亚州)
Tucson	图森市(美国亚利桑那州南部城市)
Canyon Ranch	峡谷牧场(亚利桑那州图森市)

Cultural Notes

1. Hawaiian Ironman The Ironman World Championship has been held annually in Hawaii since 1978, with an additional race in 1982. It is owned and organized by the World Triathlon Corporation. It is the annual culmination of a series of Ironman triathlon qualification races held throughout the world. For more information, visit https://en.wikipedia.org/wiki/Ironman_World_Championship.

2. Kenai Fjords National Park Kenai Fjords National Park is a United States National Park established in 1980 by the Alaska National Interest Lands Conservation Act. For more information, visit https://en.wikipedia.org/wiki/Kenai_Fjords_National_Park.

3. Chena Hot Springs Chena Hot Springs is a hot spring, resort, and unincorporated community in the Fairbanks North Star Borough, Alaska, United

States, 56. 5 miles northeast of Fairbanks near the Chena River State Recreation Area. For more information, visit https: //en. wikipedia. org/wiki/Chena_ Hot_ Springs, _ Alaska.

4. Golden Gate Bridge The Golden Gate Bridge is a suspension bridge spanning the Golden Gate strait, the one-mile-wide (1. 6 km), one-point-seven-mile-long (2. 7 km) channel between San Francisco Bay and the Pacific Ocean. The structure links the American city of San Francisco, California-the northern tip of the San Francisco Peninsula-to Marin County, carrying both U. S. Route 101 and California State Route 1 across the strait. The bridge is one of the most internationally recognized symbols of San Francisco, California, and the United States. It has been declared one of the Wonders of the Modern World by the American Society of Civil Engineers. For more information, visit https: // en. wikipedia. org/wiki/Golden_ Gate_ Bridge.

Exercises

Comprehension of the Text

I. The following 10 statements contain information given in the text. Identify the paragraph from which the information is derived. Some paragraph may not be used. Each paragraph is marked with a letter.

1. "Butterfield & Robinson"is a perfect choice for those who want to enjoy spiritual relaxation.

2. "Experiential travel", a form of travel favored by millennials, has gained in popularity in recent years.

3. Hawaiian volcanoes and the Volcanic national parks will be unraveled in front of you with "Ride and Seek".

4. By participating in Gondwana Ecotours, you are likely to experience a diversity of natural excursions in Alaska.

5. "Cox and King USA"will take customers back in time, only to be awed by the miraculous adventure through southern Louisiana.

6. Although it is difficult to be found, Maine provides tourists with unforgetta-

ble view of fall foliage.

7. The French Quarter in New Orleans boasts distinctive French flavors.

8. A wide range of sea animals is available to tourists in Kenai Fjords National Park.

9. Vineyards in Northern California never fail to be a sensual paradise for wine lovers.

10. Hawaii will never disappoint those fitness enthusiasts looking for stunning views on bikes.

Vocabulary

Ⅱ. Fill in the blanks with the words given below. Change the form where necessary.

buzzword	immersive	millennial	budding	foliage
fanatic	excursion	gourmet	culinary	kayak
accordion	antidote	yoga	pilates	unwind

1. The sharing economy might seem like a perfect ____________ to environmental and economic difficulties, but it's not without its problems and its critics.

2. Its capital, Chengdu, has a history of more than 3, 000 years and was crowned as the best tourist destination in China by the World Tourism Organization and the China National Tourism Administration. It is the first "Capital of the World's __________ Food" in Asia rated by UNESCO.

3. The jewelers' creations express a highly sensitive interpretation of the beauty of flowers, fruit and ______________ .

4. As Wong grew older and most of his Western-leaning peers were drifting away from traditional folk ways, he ___________ himself in ancient Chinese divination, even while studying architecture at the University of Hong Kong.

5. Playlistism, which means judging a person based on what songs are on the playlist of his or her digital music player, computer or iTunes music library, has become a new ____________, just like baiduren more than a year ago.

6. As chess is a high-stress activity, Tan has found her own way to ______.
"I like staying at home if possible, playing video games and reading fantasy fic-

tions," she said.

7. Family tours, spring ____________ and self-drive tours were, overall, the three main focus points of the Qingming holiday.

8. Once considered a wartime food, wild vegetables are now being thrown into the ____________ spotlight by chefs specializing in Huaiyang cuisine.

9. Dragon's Den is a popular UK reality TV show in which ____________ entrepreneurs pitch their ideas live on television to a panel of celebrity investors, seeking money for their new projects.

10. "When it comes to choosing suitcases, the ____________ generation is not looking for a box to stuff their belongings, but an accessory to go with their styles," said Chen.

Further Reading

TEXT C Traveling in the U. S.

It can shock the visitor to learn that only 14 percent of Americans possess passports. But when faced with such a tempting array of destinations—from the imposing skylines of its major cities, to the jaw-dropping beauty of its national parks—visitor begins to understand why few Americans stray from their own territory. The U. S. A. has a spectacular variety of landscapes, and offers every conceivable activity. Interested in history? Pick up a musket and participate in a Civil War reconstruction in historic Virginia. Need an adrenaline surge? Try back-country skiing in Utah or white-water rafting on the swift Colorado. Want to escape ?Lose yourself in the fantasy land of Disney World or Las Vegas. Simply put, there's enough variety to last a lifetime and the visitor is spoiled for choice.

Travel Documents

The U. S. Immigration and Naturalization Service rigorously scrutinize all travel documents. Visitors are usually required to show a passport, U. S. visitor's visa, and return plane ticket. A visa-waiver program applies t many European and other countries. Longer-stay travelers, such as students, will need a different type of entry visa and proof of finances.

Insurance

You can't predict every eventuality, so it is essential to take out comprehensive travel insurance for your trip. Coverage should include medical treatment, emergency repatriation, travel delays or cancellations, ticket loss, property theft or loss, and personal liability. Check to see if your credit card already covers car rental and/or travel insurance.

Health

The United States is relatively free of health risks but nevertheless visitors should take out the maximum possible health insurance. The multitiered U. S. healthcare system is complex and expensive. Unless it is truly an emergency, a visit to the ER (emergency room) should be avoided. A minimum walk-in fee (up to $300) will be universally applied. Hospitals will request a credit card or proof of insurance coverage before any diagnosis or treatment.

$ $ $

In America, the challenge is not finding an acceptable form of payment, but hanging on to your money in this land of plenty! Traveler's checks are generally accepted in stores and hotels and are refundable if lost or stolen. ATMs are to be found on almost every street corner, and most accept foreign-issued bank cards. Credit cards are essential for making hotel and car rental reservations, Visa and Mastercard being the most widely accepted.

Accommodation

The weary traveler has a huge range of accommodation options catering to different budgets and preferences. The choices range from no-frills youth hostels to luxury resorts and New Age spas, and everything in between.

Even campsites give an insight into the broad spectrum of American vacation habits, with dwellings ranging from humble canvas tents to motor homes on wheels for those who like to take all modern conveniences—including the kitchen sink—on vacation. You can avoid soulless highway motels by hitting the back roads and enjoying the personal touch of moderately priced B & Bs and country inns.

Where's the Restroom?

Visitors are often surprised and dismayed at the scarcity of public lavatories in the U. S. A. Railway, bus, and service stations usually have them but better facilities are to be found in department stores, museums, and restaurants.

The word "toilet" is considered vulgar. Use "bathroom" in a private house, "restroom" in a public facility, and "men's room" or "ladies' room" in a restaurant, theater, or hotel.

Flight Deals

For the savvy traveler, when it comes to domestic flight, it's a buyer's market. The existence of no-frills airlines and regular price wars among carriers make for a wide range of fare options (sometimes even for the same seat!). Securing the best deal means doing your homework, and possibly trading convenience for price. If you can be flexible, either book well in advance or pick up a last-minute discount price. If you're willing to fly during an off-peak season and to make a circuitous route involving changes of plane, you can further reduce travel costs.

Driving

Ever since the first pioneers headed west in covered wagons, the United States has been a country on the move. Today, America still offers plenty of open roads, plus affordable car and gas prices. For the tourist, driving may offer freedom, but distances are so vast that a fly-drive package might be the best option. A driving deterrent for visitors to cities is the high price of parking garages, and the aggressive towing or clamping of cars that violate the sometimes complex street parking rules.

For those who still can't resist the romance of a road trip, they will find American drivers to be neither the most courteous nor the most aggressive (despite highly publicized reports of "road rage"). Americans will also tell you that they don't have to look at the license plate of the car in front to tell which state the driver is from. Apparently, there are great regional variations in styles of driving!

Food and Drink Options

Visitors can be overwhelmed by the array of food options in America. In most towns everything is available from fast food to gourmet restaurants, and from regional specialties to all-American fare. If you are on the road, the major challenge will be to eat healthily and affordably. Avoid hotel coffee shops. Most dinner menus offer homemade soups, salads, and fruit plates along with the inevitable fries and pancakes.

The decision to be made when ordering can seem interminable. Do you prefer 1 percent or 2 percent fat milk in your coffee? Or perhaps soy milk, cream, or "half and half" (half milk, half cream.) Then there are the ten different ways of preparing eggs, an impossible variety of sandwich breads, and a bewildering selection of salad dressings to choose from. It may seem redundant to ask for "lite" maple syrup to accompany that towering stack of pancakes, yet people do.

(Words: 963)

Questions for discussions

1. Is it easy to become a budget traveler in the Unites States? What are some possible ways to save money during the trip?

2. If you were to travel in the United States, would you want to explore one or two regions in depth, or would you prefer to dart from city to city? Why?

3. What road rules do you need to abide by during your stay in the United States?

More to Learn

1. Appreciation

On the Amtrak from Boston to New York City

By Sherman Alexie

The white woman across the aisle from me says, "Look,
look at all the history, that house
on the hill there is over two hundred years old,"
as she points out the window past me

into what she has been taught. I have learned
little more about American history during my few days
back East than what I expected and far less
of what we should all know of the tribal stories

whose architecture is 15,000 years older
than the corners of the house that sits
museumed on the hill. "Walden Pond,"
the woman on the train asks, "Did you see Walden Pond?"

and I don't have a cruel enough heart to break
her own by telling her there are five Walden Ponds
on my little reservation out West
and at least a hundred more surrounding Spokane,

the city I pretend to call my home. "Listen,"
I could have told her. "I don't give a shit
about Walden. I know the Indians were living stories
around that pond before Walden's grandparents were born

and before his grandparents' grandparents were born.
I'm tired of hearing about Don-fucking-Henley's saving it, too,
because that's redundant. If Don Henley's brothers and sisters
and mothers and fathers hadn't come here in the first place

then nothing would need to be saved."
But I didn't say a word to the woman about Walden
Pond because she smiled so much and seemed delighted
that I thought to bring her an orange juice

back from the food car. I respect elders
of every color. All I really did was eat
my tasteless sandwich, drink my Diet Pepsi
and nod my head whenever the woman pointed out

another little piece of her country's history
while I, as all Indians have done
since this war began, made plans
for what I would do and say the next time

somebody from the enemy thought I was one of their own.

MOVIES TO SEE (A) RV

I. Movie Introduction

Director: Barry Sonnenfeld

Starring: Robin Williams
Cheryl Hines
Kristin Chenoweth

Running time: 99 mins

Released: 2006

Plot: The executive Bob Munro is stressed, feeling threatened of losing his job and his lifestyle, since his abusive boss Todd Mallory hired the Stanford's geek Laird to work in their soda's company. Bob has promised his wife Jamie Munro, his teenage daughter Cassie Munro and his young son Carl Munro to spend vacations in Hawaii, but Todd demands him to prepare a presentation and attend a business meeting with the owners of a family company in a merging operation scheduled in the same period. Bob hides the truth to his family, rents a recreational vehicle and tries to convince his dysfunctional family that a road trip to the Colorado Rocky Mountains would be good to bring old values back to their family. After many incidents and while in the trailers parking area, the rookie Bob is helped by the bizarre but friendly Gornicke family. They escape from the Gornickes and initiate a journey of difficulties and leaning, retrieving their forgotten family bonds. For more information, visit http://www.imdb.com/title/tt0449089/?ref_ =nv_ sr_ 1.

Ⅱ. Classic Scenes

Task 1 Study the underlined sentences and expressions in the following classic scenes.

1. In little Cassie's bedroom and in the car to pick up her schoolmate several years later.

Cassie, age 5: Daddy?

Bob Munro: Yeah, baby?

Cassie, age 5: I'm never gonna get married.

Bob Munro: Why not? It's not as bad as it looks.

Cassie, age 5: Because I always want to live here with you.

Bob Munro: Well, you know, one day, you're gonna grow up, meet a wonderful guy, and you're gonna get married. But you and I will always be best friends.

[kisses forehead] Good night, Cassie.

Cassie Munro: [Scene switch] Dad, could you be any more of a dork?

Bob Munro: Cassie, you know where this girl lives or you just think you know?

Cassie Munro: I know where, I just know one way to get there. And you refuse to go that way.

Bob Munro: Because it's a stupid way.

Cassie Munro: Yes, if you consider getting there stupid.

Jamie Munro: Why don't you use the navigation?

Bob Munro: Because your daughter, Sacajawea back there, doesn't know the name of the street. She just knows it as "the one next to the one with the fountain."

Carl Munro: Hey, Dad, Cassie just gave you the finger.

Bob Munro: If we don't find this house in two minutes...

Cassie Munro: There it is.

Jamie Munro: Okay, Honey, hurry up, go get your friend.

Bob Munro: Which friend is this, the nice one?

Jamie Munro: You used to know all her friends. You were funny and charming.

Bob Munro: Well, she is 15. She doesn't want me to be charming. She finds it creepy. Oh, no! It's the "too-nice one."

2. When Bob drives an RV back home and they have a heated discussion about the place for vacation.

Cassie Munro: Mom, some idiot just parked this ugly RV outside our house.

Jamie Munro: What?

Cassie Munro: Oh, my God, it's your husband.

Bob Munro: Oh, hi. [smiling]

Jamie Munro: What is that?

Bob Munro: It's a RV.

Jamie Munro: And why is it in front of our house?

Bob Munro: We're taking it on vacation.

Carl Munro: To Hawaii?

Bob Munro: No, it doesn't float. Colorado.

Cassie Munro: What happened to Hawaii?

Bob Munro: Come on, Hawaii's a winter destination. It's summer. The place I'm taking you is special, and not like Uncle Mike. It's a lake—Lake Nirvana, where I went with my parents as a kid.

Cassie Munro: Is he kidding? Is he being funny? Because I can never tell.

Bob Munro: Oh, come on. You've always wanted to camp, right?

Cassie Munro: Don't you see? This is what he came up with to punish me for Gretchen. I was gonna surf. Nice one, Dad. Thanks.

Carl Munro: The hotel in Hawaii has a weight room. Doesn't anybody respect my lifting schedule?

Jamie Munro: We're not campers. We don't camp.

Bob Munro: Why not?

Jamie Munro: Why...? Why not? For one thing, we like to shower.

Bob Munro: Well, it's got a shower. Come on. You and I will go out right now and take a shower.

Jamie Munro: Bob, do you know where you stay when you take an RV trip?

Bob Munro: Where?

Jamie Munro: RV camps. Honey, try to remember. We're not friendly.

Bob Munro: In Hawaii, we'll never see the kids. This way, we both can spend time with them.

Jamie Munro: (shocked) You need to spend time with them. I spend 9 hours a day with them. And I want Hawaii.

Bob Munro: All right, we'll go to Hawaii. At Christmas. Then it'll just be us and a lot of Jewish people. We'll have all the hams to ourselves.

Jamie Munro: Oh, I'll have to cook every night.

Bob Munro: No, you won't, because I'll cook every night, every meal.

Jamie Munro: We were gonna take naps, hotel rooms, afternoon, lock-the-door naps.

Bob Munro: Oh, good naps.

Jamie Munro: How are we gonna do that in an RV.

Bob Munro: I'll drive slowly.

Jamie Munro: I was gonna get a massage.

Bob Munro: I'll give you a massage.

Jamie Munro: You're gonna do all the cooking. You're gonna give me a massage. And you're gonna spend time with the kids.

Bob Munro: You got it.

Jamie Munro: Did you cancel out Hawaii trip because Todd told you to? Did you volunteer us for some sort of experiment? The family travels around and drinks nothing but Pure Vibe soda, see if our teeth fall out?

Bob Munro: Honey, I'm running out of time with my kids. Come on, baby. Why don't you come out in the wilderness with your big, brawny man? Don't make me call for my mail-order bride.

3. When the family are camping in the Mount Watson RV park.

Cassie Munro: You know if you wore clothes that fit, you wouldn't look like a ten-year-old.

Carl Munro: It's how I roll. [sees some Hip Hop Wannabe playing basketball] Oh sweet.

Hip Hop Wannabe: You say something, Frodo?

Carl Munro: I was just saying how that guy Shaq'd you there. We got two-on-two, right?

Hip Hop Wannabe: Why don't you find an under-2-feet league?

Carl Munro: Why don't you trade that thing in on top of your neck for a face?

Hip Hop Wannabe: I'm gonna floss your rear.

Carl Munro: Let's go, man. Bring it. Come on.

Bob Munro: Yo, my mobile-homeboys, what's tripping in the wood?

Hip Hop Wannabe: This termite belong to you?

Bob Munro: Yo, my man said...

Carl Munro: [gets mad] Don't call him...

Bob Munro: [restraints Carl] Easy! This my man, C. He's small but ferocious. But you dogs, you're hardcore, where you from?

Hip Hop Wannabe: Scottsdale!

Bob Munro: Scottsdale! In the'Zoner, ya'll that's a hardcore hood, but you want take on my man C here, go ahead because you know, he's fierce, he gonna come up in your face he gonna major damage you, you gonna walk away maybe limp but I say talk to the hand, call waiting, ' cause he's out, boy is out...I can't restrains him ' cause I'm conversating you right now to give him a chance to cool down, to get back to a realistic level, as it were because we could be chilling in our crib, not just on this mobile home thing, representing Malibu, and Westwood, you know. Malling it, like we all can, boys to mensch, pimp my Mercedes, call me back, put you on hold, you know what I'm saying?

Hip Hop Wannabe: Er...we gotta go. [leaves]

Bob Munro: Mm-hmm, you better, man, don't make me call my lawyer, ' cause I'll audit!

Cassie Munro: Aren't you glad Dad came? They were about to kick your butt.

Bob Munro: Carl. That's not helpful. Carl!

Bob Munro: Carl, it occurs to me that you and I haven't had too many warm 7th Heaven kind of dialogues in the last year.

Carl Munro: You're busy a lot.

Bob Munro: Yeah, but not too busy to notice that you are sensitive about your size. I'll bet you $1,000 right now you'll grow up bigger than me.

Carl Munro: I've seen pictures of you when you were my age. You were huge. You were shaving already.

Bob Munro: Yeah, well, that's my point. See, I achieved maturity very early. I stopped growing at the eighth grade. But you have the other body type. You're like my friend John Vigoshi. When he was 16, he had a 9-inch summer.

Carl Munro: How do you mean that?

Bob Munro: He grew very tall, very quickly, and so will you. And you've been proactive. You're lifting weights. And when you grow up big, you know what we'll do?

Carl Munro: What?

Bob Munro: We'll enter father-son extreme-fighting competitions.

Carl Munro: All right.

Bob Munro: You'll have to push the wheelchair. But we'll get them high, and we'll get them low.

4. On the way to Lake Nirvana.

Whole family: [sings together] Big rolling turd coming through coming through...Oh, we're on that road. On a big steaming load.

Carl Munro: Hey, Dad, maybe we can go to Yellowstone on the way home.

Jamie Munro: I'd love to go to Yellowstone.

Carl Munro: Yeah, Dad, can we?

Bob Munro: Absolutely. Come on. I wanna show you something wonderful. It's hard to forget this place. My dad was so moved by it. He said: "You know, a snack stand up here would do tremendous." My mom, always supportive, "And who's gonna run it, Allan, you?" My dad: "Why don't you blow it out your big, saggy rear end, Ellen." Can't buy memories like that. Or like this. Hey, you know, I should take the RV to get the emergency brake fixed before we head for L. A.

Jamie Munro: Yeah. Good idea.

Bob Munro: And you guys don't want to hang around some dingy garage. Why don't wait here by the lake, enjoy the view. I'll drive to Boulder, be back in an hour. We'll have a big picnic. How about that?

Jamie Munro: OK. Sounds good. Guys, tell your dad what you wanted to tell him.

Cassie Munro: Thank you for taking us on this trip.

Carl Munro: Kinko that.

Bob Munro: Better than Hawaii.

Jamie Munro: Yeah, better than Hawaii.

5. When Bob was dropping off Gornicke's bus.

Jamie Munro: Are you an idiot? Do you want your children to see their father bouncing down the highway?

Bob Munro: What are you doing with the Partridge Family?

Jamie Munro: What are you doing on top of the bus?

Bob Munro: Because I was chasing you. You win. I blew off my job because I can't live without you. You happy?

Jamie Munro: I never asked you to blow off your job. I just wanted you to be honest with me.

Bob Munro: Honest like, "Todd's gonna fire me if I go to Boulder" honest? "Screw Hawaii" honest.

Jamie Munro: Oh, I see. You think that if you told me you were in trouble and your job was in jeopardy, that I'd give you a hard time about it?

Bob Munro: No crying. That's cheating.

Jamie Munro: You think I'm some horrible witch that doesn't care? I do care! I care a lot! In fact, I hate you, jerk.

Bob Munro: I didn't want you to know I was in trouble. You and Cassie and Carl, you mean everything to me. What you think about me is the most important thing in the world. I didn't want to fail.

Jamie Munro: If you don't know how I feel about you after 19 years of marriage, then I must be a failure as a wife.

Bob Munro: Then you admit you are the problem.

Jamie Munro: Bob. You mean more to me than just a paycheck.

Bob Munro: That's good, because we won't be getting one for a while. I missed that meeting.

Mr. Gornicke: No, you didn't. Come on, Bob, come here.

Task 2 Work in pairs or groups and play the roles in one of your favorite scenes.

Ⅲ. Cultural Notes

1. Sacajawea: Sacajawea was a Lemhi Shoshone woman who helped the Lewis and Clark Expedition achieve each of its chartered mission objectives exploring the Louisiana Territory. With the expedition, between 1804 and 1806, she traveled thousands of miles from North Dakota to the Pacific Ocean, established cultural contacts with Native American populations, and researched natural history. For more information, visit https: //en. wikipedia. org/wiki/Sacagawea.

2. Frodo: Frodo Baggins is a fictional character in J. R. R. Tolkien's legendarium, and one of the main protagonists of *The Lord of the Rings*. Frodo is a hobbit of the Shire who inherits the One Ring from his cousin Bilbo Baggins and undertakes the quest to destroy it in the fires of Mount Doom. For more information, visit https: //en. wikipedia. org/wiki/Frodo_ Baggins.

3. The Partridge Family: *The Partridge Family* is an American musical-sitcom starring Shirley Jones and featuring David Cassidy. Jones plays a widowed mother, and Cassidy plays the oldest of her five children who embark on a music career. It ran from September 25, 1970, until March 23, 1974, on the ABC network as part of a Friday-night lineup, and had subsequent runs in syndication. The family was loosely based on the real-life musical family The Cowsills, a popular band in the late 1960s and early 1970s. For more information, visit https: // en. wikipedia. org/wiki/The_ Partridge_ Family.

Ⅳ. Questions for discussion

1. Would you like to go on an extravagant but expensive trip or an austere but meaningful trip? What are the reasons of your choice?

2. What is the best alternative to strike a balance between work and family?

3. What important lessons can we learn from the movie? Did Bob set a good example for his kids when he was educating them through a family trip into the

wilderness?

V. Movie Review

Task: Write a movie review on *RV*.

MOVIES TO SEE (B) Into the Wild

I. Movie Introduction

Director: Sean Penn

Starring: Emile Hirsch, Vince Vaughn, Catherine Keener

Running time: 148 mins

Released: 2007

Plot: A young man bravely sets out alone on what turns into a majestic journey to explore the beauty and wonder of the world. Throughout his travels, which ultimately lead him into the wild and wilderness, he seeks and ultimately finds pleasure and joy along with a sense of truth and purpose he has been yearning for all his life. Along the way he meets and deeply touches a cast of others who are all in their own ways also looking to escape or move on from the past and enjoy life again.

To Recommend More Movies

- ❖ *Little Miss Sunshine* (2006)
- ❖ *Up* (2009)
- ❖ *Rio* (2011)
- ❖ *Rain Man* (1988)
- ❖ *Couples Retreat* (2009)

Unit Twelve Holidays & Customs

Pre-reading Activities

Answer the following questions before you read this text.

1. What are some most widely celebrated holidays in America? How are they observed?

2. Can you list some American core values displayed through the celebration of holidays?

3. Do different religions, races, and ethnicities enjoy an equal opportunity to observe their holidays? Do you know any traditional Chinese holidays observed in America?

TEXT A Holidays—What They Are And How They Are Celebrated

While most American holidays are observed nationwide, they are in fact **mandated** by individual states, and the way in which they are celebrated is influenced by religious **affiliation**, ethnic background, and regional culture. **In practice**, most states observe the federal public holidays. Those that fall on a Saturday or Sunday are observed on a Friday and Monday respectively. On official holidays, schools, banks, private businesses, and government offices will be closed. Transportation and other services will operate **on** a reduced **schedule**.

Some holidays are uniquely American celebrations, such as Thanksgiving and Independence Day. Others are religious or ethnic festivals that have been imported by immigrants but that have assumed a **distinctively** American identity. **A case in point** is **St. Patrick's Day**, when Americans of all ethnicities place their tongue firmly in cheek, don something green, and claim to be of Irish **descent**!

A **cynic** might say that many of these holidays, particularly religious ones, have lost their original meaning and are kept alive by family tradition and Hallmark marketing. Certainly it seems that **no sooner** has the St. Patrick's Day green beer gone **flat than** the "Kiss me I'm Irish" hats are replaced by Easter eggs in store windows.

Cynicism aside, no one mounts a **parade**, loves the **razzmatazz**, or gets in the spirit of holidays more than Americans. A holiday is an opportunity to exhibit their **patriotism**, a coming together to **reaffirm** their identity and unity. On **Memorial Day**, **Veterans Day**, and **Presidents' Day**, for example, "Old Glory," the American flag, will **be** much **in evidence**. Holidays also mark the rhythm of the seasons. Memorial Day and **Labor Day** "**bookend**" the summer season (the latter holiday weekend often devoted to **frantic** back-to-school shopping!).

In addition to national holidays, there are countless other events ranging from small-town celebrations to countywide affairs. Street parades, often headed by **majorettes** leading a marching band, demonstrate a uniquely American combination of individualism, competition, and team cooperation.

Communities hold festivals to celebrate whatever it is that has put them on the map. Practically every food, dance, and ethnic group is celebrated with a festival. Polka festivals are held in the North, catfish festivals in the South, and **German Oktoberfests** in practically every state!

Fourth of July

This **quintessential** American holiday **commemorates** the signing of the **U. S. Declaration of Independence** on July 4, 1776. America dresses up in the **stars and stripes** to celebrate its birthday. Everything from T-shirt to tablecloths is in red, white, and blue. Family and friends gather to enjoy barbecues and picnics against a backdrop of outdoor concerts and fireworks. Hot dogs, hamburgers, corn, and apple pie are the patriotic foods of choice.

Halloween—October 31

On Hallowmas (the **feast** of All Hallow's Eve—originally the **pagan** festival of Samhain, or "summer's end") people **superstitiously** left out sweets to

appease the souls of the dead, who were rumored to **roam** the earth the night before **All Saints' Day**. In its modern-day American **incarnation**, Halloween is not a national holiday but has become a highly commercialized event. **Wholesome** suburban homes are transformed into **haunted** houses **complete with** spider webs, skeletons, and witches. Children dress up in costumes, teenagers **opting for** the **gruesome** and **gory** while younger ones dress up as their favorite cartoon character or superhero. They will go from house to house "trick or treating" —receiving candy **in return for** not playing a **prank** on the homeowner. Adults can't resist the opportunity to throw a party and indulge their **fantasy** worlds either, although costumes and masks of current politicians and celebrities tend to be favored over **ghouls** and ghosts.

Thanksgiving—Fourth Thursday in November

Thanksgiving is a uniquely North American holiday, **initiated** by early settlers to give thanks for the abundant harvest that allowed them to survive. In the busiest travel period of the year, families reunite and enjoy a feast of traditional, **indigenous** foods, featuring turkey and dressing, cranberry sauce, candies yams, and pumpkin pie. New Thanksgiving traditions have evolved since the days of the **Pilgrims**, and the meal is usually sandwiched in between the national television broadcasts of the **Macy's** (**New York**) **Thanksgiving Day parade** in the morning, and a college football game in the afternoon (much **to the chagrin of** the cook!) . Canadians celebrate their own Thanksgiving on the second Monday of October.

Christmas Day—December 25

Christians celebrate the birth of Jesus Christ on December 25, and for some people this may be the only occasion during the year when they attend church. Even the nonreligious may celebrate, decorating their houses, putting up a Christmas tree, and gathering together with family to exchange gifts and enjoy a special dinner. Unlike Thanksgiving when there are few regional adaptations of traditional **fare**, the Christmas feast is heavily influenced by ethnic origins. Visit four neighboring households and you'll discover that German *pfeffernuesse*, Italian *crostoli*, Southern bread pudding, and American sugar cookies are all considered the traditional Christmas dessert!

Happy Holidays to All

Those from predominantly Protestant or Catholic countries may be puzzled by Americans in movies wishing each other a hearty "happy holidays" against a backdrop of decorated store windows and December snow. Since the country's **inception**, well **before the advent of** political correctness, Americans have always respected the many other holidays observed by those of different religions, races, and ethnicities.

Various nationalities or ethnic groups may celebrate their own holidays. Mexico's Independence Day, *cinco de mayo* (May 5), is marked with parties and street parades in larger cities, including New York and Los Angeles. Chinese New Year is observed in the Chinatown districts of New York and San Francisco. The French quarter of New Orleans is the scene of decorated floats, **elaborate** costumes, and round-the-clock partying in celebration of **Mardi Gras** (or "Fat Tuesday," the beginning of Lent in late February or early March).

(Words: 964)

New Words

mandate	*n.* 授权；任期；委任；命令 *vt.* 托管；批准
affiliation	*n.* （组织之间的）密切联系，隶属关系
distinctively	*adv.* 独特地，特别地，有特色地
descent	*n.* 下降；血统；倾斜
cynic	*n.* 愤世嫉俗者，讽世者；犬儒学派的人
flat	*adj.* （饮料）走了气的
parade	*n.* 游行行列；阅兵式；阅兵典礼 *vi.* 游行；成群结队地行走
razzmatazz	*n.* 喧闹；欢闹
patriotism	*n.* 爱国主义，爱国心，爱国精神

续表

reaffirm	*vt.* 重申，再肯定
bookend	*n.* 书挡，书靠 *vt.* 首尾挡住
frantic	*adj.* （因害怕或担心）发狂的，狂躁的
majorette	*n.* 军乐队队长或指挥
quintessential	*adj.* 精髓的 典型的
commemorate	*vt.* 纪念，庆祝
backdrop	*n.* 背景，衬托
feast	*n.* 宴会；筵席；盛宴
pagan	*n.* 异教徒，非基督教徒，没有宗教信仰的人 *adj.* 异教徒的，非基督教的，无宗教信仰的
superstitiously	*adv.* 迷信地
appease	*vt.* 安抚；抚慰；绥靖（满足另一国的要求以避免战争）
roam	*vt. &vi.* 漫游，漫步
incarnation	*n.* 化身，前身，典型体现
wholesome	*adj.* 有益健康的；健全的；合乎卫生的
haunt	*vt.* 经常出没于；长期不断地缠扰，缠绕，萦绕 *n.* 常去的地方
gruesome	*adj.* 令人厌恶的；恐怖的；令人震惊的
gory	*adj.* 血淋淋的；令人毛骨悚然的；骇人听闻的
prank	*n.* 恶作剧；开玩笑
fantasy	*n.* 憧憬；幻想
ghoul	*n.* 食尸鬼
initiate	*vt.* 开始；创始；发起
indigenous	*adj.* 当地的；本土的；土生土长的
pilgrim	*n.* 朝圣者；朝觐者
fare	*n.* 食物，饭菜
inception	*n.* 开始；开端；初期
elaborate	*adj.* （衣服、布料等）精致的，精巧的，制作精美的

Phrases & Expressions

in practice	实际上；在实践中
on schedule	按预定时间
a case in point	明证，佐证
tongue in cheek	（说话）不当真的，开玩笑的
no sooner…than…	一……就……
be in evidence	显眼，引人瞩目
stars and stripes	星条旗（美国国旗上有13道横条和50颗星）
complete with	包括，具有配套的
opt for	选择
in return for	作为……的回报
to the chagrin of	令某人懊恼
before the advent of	在……出现以前

Proper Names

St. Patrick's Day	圣巴特里克节
Memorial Day	（美国）阵亡将士纪念日
Veterans Day	（美国为纪念两次世界大战中阵亡将士的）退伍军人节
Presidents' Day	总统纪念日，纪念华盛顿诞辰日
Labor Day	（美国的）劳动节（9月首个周一）
German Oktoberfest	德国啤酒节
U. S. Declaration of Independence	美国《独立宣言》
All Saints' Day	万圣节
Macy's (New York) Thanksgiving Day parade	梅西百货感恩节大游行
Mardi Gras	狂欢节（基督教忏悔星期二当天、大斋期前一日的狂欢活动）

Cultural Notes

1. St. Patrick's Day St. Patrick's Day, while not a legal holiday in the United States, is nonetheless widely recognized and observed throughout the country as a celebration of Irish and Irish American culture. Celebrations include prominent displays of the color green, eating and drinking, religious observances, and numerous parades. The holiday has been celebrated on the North American continent since the late eighteenth century. For more information, visit https://en.wikipedia.org/wiki/Saint_Patrick%27s_Day#United_States.

2. Memorial Day Memorial Day is a federal holiday in the United States for remembering the people who died while serving in the country's armed forces. For more information, visit https://en.wikipedia.org/wiki/Memorial_Day.

3. Veterans Day Veterans Day is an official United States federal holiday that is observed annually on November 11, honoring people who have served in the U.S. Armed Forces, also known as veterans. For more information, visit https://en.wikipedia.org/wiki/Veterans_Day.

4. Presidents' Day Washington's Birthday is a United States federal holiday celebrated on the third Monday of February in honor of George Washington, the first President of the United States. Colloquially, it is widely known as Presidents' Day and is often an occasion to remember all the presidents, not just George Washington or Abraham Lincoln, whose birthday is also in February. For more information, visit https://en.wikipedia.org/wiki/Washington%27s_Birthday.

5. Labor Day Labor Day in the United States is a public holiday celebrated on the first Monday in September. It honors the American labor movement and the contributions that workers have made to the strength, prosperity, and well-being of the country. It is the Monday of the long weekend known as Labor Day Weekend and it is considered the unofficial end of summer. For more information, visit https://en.wikipedia.org/wiki/Labor_Day.

6. German Oktoberfest German-Americans are the largest self-reported ancestral group in the United States. Correspondingly, there are hundreds of large and small Oktoberfest celebrations held annually throughout the country, the largest being Oktoberfest Zinzinnati in Cincinnati, Ohio. For more information, visit https://en.wikipedia.org/wiki/Oktoberfest_celebrations#United_States.

7. U. S. Declaration of Independence The Declaration of Independence is the statement adopted by the Continental Congress meeting at Philadelphia, Pennsylvania on July 4, 1776, which announced that the thirteen American colonies, then at war with Great Britain, regarded themselves as thirteen newly independent sovereign states, and no longer a part of the British Empire. Instead they formed a new nation—the United States of America. For more information, visit https://en.wikipedia.org/wiki/United_States_Declaration_of_Independence.

8. All Saints' Day All Saints' Day, also known as All Hallows, Day of All the Saints, Solemnity of All Saints, or Feast of All Saints is a solemnity celebrated on 1 November by the Roman Catholic Church and various Protestant denominations, and on the first Sunday after Pentecost in Eastern Catholicism and Eastern Orthodoxy, in honor of all the saints, known and unknown. For more information, visit https://en.wikipedia.org/wiki/All_Saints%27_Day.

9. Macy's (New York) Thanksgiving Day parade The Macy's Thanksgiving Day Parade is an annual parade presented by the U. S.-based department store chain Macy's. The tradition started in 1924, tying it for the second-oldest Thanksgiving parade in the United States with America's Thanksgiving Parade in Detroit (with both parades being four years younger than the 6abc Dunkin' Donuts Thanksgiving Day Parade in Philadelphia). The three-hour Macy's event is held in New York City starting at 9:00 a.m. Eastern Standard Time on Thanksgiving Day, and has been televised nationally on NBC since 1952. For more information, visit https://en.wikipedia.org/wiki/Macy%27s_Thanksgiving_Day_Parade.

10. Mardi Gras While not observed nationally throughout the United States, a number of traditionally ethnic French cities and regions in the country have notable celebrations. Mardi Gras arrived in North America as a French Catholic tradition with the Le Moyne brothers, Pierre Le Moyne d'Iberville and Jean-Baptiste Le Moyne de Bienville, in the late 17th century, when King Louis XIV sent the pair to defend France's claim on the territory of Louisiane, which included what are now the U. S. states of Alabama, Mississippi, Louisiana and part of eastern

Texas. For more information, visit https://en.wikipedia.org/wiki/Mardi_Gras#United_States.

Exercises

Comprehension of the Text

Ⅰ Answer the following questions according to the passage.

1. What holidays are uniquely American and what holidays are imported by immigrants?

2. Do you agree with the saying that some American holidays have become heavily commercialized and thus lost their traditional meanings?

3. How is Christmas feast in America influenced by ethnic origins?

Vocabulary

Ⅱ. Fill in the blanks with the words given below. Change the form where necessary.

mandate	affiliation	descent	patriotism	reaffirm
frantic	commemorate	superstitiously	appease	haunt
fantasy	predominantly	abundant	initiate	elaborate

1. The film's ____________ musical theme stayed in my head for days.

2. Many publishers are trying to release ____________ education materials to teach citizens to love their motherland and defend it.

3. Cheng Du has historically been regarded as a "heavenly land" due to its livability and ____________ in natural resources.

4. Israeli-Palestinian violence has been marked primarily by Palestinian stabbings and shootings carried out by young Palestinians with no ____________ to militant groups.

5. China has put forward the ____________ of building the Silk Road Economic Belt and the 21st Century Maritime Silk Road, and is working on the 13th five-year plan.

6. A grand ceremony was held in Tian'anmen Square to ____________

the deceased national heroes during wars.

7. The rat and the rabbit, which were part of an ___________ zodiac fountain at Summer Palace in Beijing, were stolen by French and British troops in 1860 at the end of the Second Opium War.

8. Hundreds of representatives including Confucius' ___________ and enthusiasts of Confucianism took part in the ceremony.

9. Her husband died in 1967, although she ________ that he was still alive.

10. Fortune-telling is a very much debased art surrounded by __________.

Translations

Ⅲ. Translate the following sentences into English.

1. 理论上法律规定男女同工同酬，可是实际上，妇女所得的工资比她们的男同事低得多。(in practice)

____

2. 很多情况下，宗教迫害是导致人们逃奔异国他乡的原因。一个典型的例子是殖民统治时期的印度。(a case in point)

____

3. 这位备受尊敬的艺术家刚表演完，三万人的体育场中就爆发出了雷鸣般的掌声。(no sooner…than…)

____

4. 这是一辆附有空调、移动电视和电话的豪华轿车。(complete with)

____

5. 尽管全球的造纸业近年来经历了坚实的增长，但是其在数字技术到来之前的需求还是很缓慢的。(before the advent of)

____

Ⅳ. Translate the following passage into English.

“我认为大多数人经历的是一种担忧情绪，”心理医师戴维·赖特说，“在回去工作之前，他们表现出退缩，并没有好好享受星期天。”赖特说星期天夜晚的压力是很普遍的，各行各业的人都有。“真的，这就像一周有六个工作日，因为你用整整一天想着将要去工作，害怕上班，想象工作时会发生郁闷的事。”赖特说，“我认为人们应该从多方面去认识它，这就跟害怕坐飞机或考试一样。很多时候对事物的想象比事情本身给人的压力更大。"赖特说在星期天多活动会让人们不去想重返工作或者学习的事情。或许，克服星期天夜晚焦虑的最好建议是找一件一直期盼的事情做，并将之固定下来。这件事可以很简单，比如每周收看最喜爱的电视节目。另一个建议是利用星期天夜晚开家庭游艺会。

TEXT B　The Nastiness That Lies Beneath "Have a Nice Day"

(A) I was walking out of a **groovy East Village** bar in Manhattan this week when a man, extending long arms to remove his raincoat, **punched** me in the back. It was a light blow and clearly not **deliberate** so I walked on, but the man pursued me to the door. "Please excuse me, ma'am, "he said. "I am so sorry!"

(B) He was young, **exquisitely** dressed in a **foppish** bowtie, but his manners were more **elegant** still. And I wondered for the millionth time this trip how New Yorkers ever got a reputation for being rude.

(C) Frequently in America I feel like a **lunking**, **ili-kempt** and **sweary** child. In a Boston hairdresser, I dropped my mobile phone, which **shattered** into several pieces, yet when I uttered what Americans call "the brown word"—a minimum response in Britain—I received **reproachful** stares. My apology got a **terse** "That's OK"from the twentysomething cashier: I had clearly done bad.

(D) In New York I **lost count of** the after-yous and the **beaming** you're-welcome, not only from paid **suck-ups** in restaurants or hotels, but busy-looking, fast-walking folks. Long ago I would have mocked "Have a nice day"as an international gold standard of American insincerity. But alone, ill-slept and, most of all, charmed by its contrast with my own country's **default mode** of public **aggression**, I found it **soothing**, even kind.

(E) So what if it isn't truly meant or is **parroted** 1,000 times a day? It oils the **squeaky** old cogs of social interaction, makes it more pleasant for millions of **hard-packed** people to coexist in an often brutal city. Manners keep public space clean and neutral; provide a little much-needed mental distance between us. And yet conversely, like my fellow northerners, New Yorkers are always talking to strangers in lifts or shops. Trying on shoes in Bergdorf's, I was **appraised** with unexpected friendliness by two scarily well-groomed blondes: "Cute! You should buy them."

(F) That American smile is an agent of mobility, social and geographic; it presents your best self, shows you come in peace, bonds a **disparate** nation. As Britain becomes more **diverse** but more unequal, we really need to **crack** a few more. Yet in London we are both **heedless** and **aloof**, which has led to growing, just-below-the-surface violent rage. "What is it with London these days?" asked a British friend, a long-time New York resident, when he last came home. "Why is everyone angry all the time?"

(G) Britain, a nation with a reputation for **reserve** and old-school **etiquette**, dropped formalities to **sweep away snobbery** and inequality. I suppose some kind of **democratization** has been achieved: equal disrespect for all. Beautiful manners are mocked as affected, yet whenever I've come across them, they have the power to **bewitch** and get results without ever seeming to push.

(H) On her *Spectator* blog this week, the writer Susan Hill **laments** how elderly people are no longer addressed by their titles, especially in hospitals, often because when asked what they wish to be called, they feel it would be **stand-offish** to say Mrs Jones rather than Shirley. And so Shirley quickly becomes "Shirl", whether she likes it or not, **infantilized** and **demeaned** exactly when her dignity is most **imperiled**.

(I) So I enjoyed a bit of "yes, ma'am" in New York. Telesales folk here don't cold-call you with **hackle-raising** "How are you today, Janice?" And while in Britain publicists refer to their celebrity clients with first-name **chummery**, in America it's all "Miss Jolie will see you now". A nation of supposed **brash** modernity is now more traditional than the **Old World**.

(J) Yet while I was **basking** in this **courtesy**, the newspaper told a different tale. Republican protests leading up to the passing of the health care bill revealed a violent tone to public **discourse** I cannot recall in Britain. In Columbus, Ohio, a man with **Parkinson's disease**, sitting on the ground outside a "**tea party**", was approached by a crowd and asked **contemptuously** if he was looking for a **hand-**

out, then had dollar bills **flung** in his face as if he were a beggar.

(K) And in Washington outside the Capitol, anti-health care protesters spat in the face of a black congressman and called two others, including a hero of the civil rights movement, "nigger". A gay politician was **taunted** as a "**faggot**". A Democrat who supported Obama's Bill, and who is **anti-abortion**, was branded "baby-killer"by a Republican from Texas.

(L) While our own post-expenses mood towards politicians has **soured into** disgust, and the far Right has gained **traction**, it is hard to imagine **David Lammy, Diane Abbott** or **Ben Bradshaw** being railed at like that outside Parliament. Even our scathing, muscular tabloid would not be as **intemperate** as US **shock jocks** such as Rush Limbaugh, who compared Obama's policies to those of the **Nazis**, and his healthcare logo to a **swastika**.

(M) That American good manners and muffin-basket delivering **niceties** are merely a **patina** of civility masking an **underside** of intolerance and **repressed malevolence** in the stuff of ***Desperate Housewives***. I visited a conservative small town in Ohio during the US election campaign, and **was deluged with** small kindnesses and invitations to dinner, but I wondered whether they'd be so friendly if I'd revealed my true views on Obama or abortion.

(N) In Britain there is no **deception**, no ***politesse***: a medium-strength **misanthropy** runs through us, from our public manners to our political culture. Perhaps that is preferable to America's extremes and **disjunctures**, even if it means if you got punched by a **hipster** in London, chances are he'd never say sorry.

(Words: 936)

New Words

groovy	*adj.* 吸引人的；时髦的；刺激的
punch	*n.* 用拳猛击（或攻击）
deliberate	*adj.* 故意的；蓄意的；早有计划的

续表

exquisitely	*adv.* 精美地；精致地
foppish	*adj.* 衣着浮华的；有纨绔习气的；矫饰的
elegant	*adj.* （人或物）典雅的，雅致的，优美的
lunking	*adj.* 呆头呆脑的
ill-kempt	*adj.* 不整洁的，邋里邋遢的
sweary	*adj.* 爱咒骂的，爱说脏话的
shatter	*vt.* （使）粉碎；（使）破碎；（使）碎裂
reproachful	*adj.* （表情或话语）责备的，责怪的，谴责的
terse	*adj.* （声明、评论）简短的，短促的，无礼的
beaming	*adj.* 眉开眼笑的；笑容满面的
suck-up	*n.* 奉承者，拍马屁的人
aggression	*n.* 好斗性；攻击性；侵略；侵犯
soothing	*adj.* 慰藉的；使人宽心的；镇静的
parrot	*n.* 鹦鹉 *vt.* 机械地模仿；鹦鹉学舌般地重复
squeaky	*adj.* 吱嘎作响的；发出刺耳声音的
hard-packed	*adj.* （结构）紧密的，密集的
appraise	*vt.* 评价；评估；估量
disparate	*adj.* 全异的；完全不同的；异类的
diverse	*adj.* 形形色色的；各式各样的；不同的；迥异的
crack	*vt.* &*vi.* 破裂；打开；（使……）开裂；说（笑话）；开（玩笑）
heedless	*adj.* 不注意的；不留心的；掉以轻心的
aloof	*adj.* 冷漠的；离群的
reserve	*vt.* 储备；保留；预约 *n.* 储备；保护区；保留；替补队员 *adj.* 保留的；有保留的
etiquette	*n.* 礼仪，礼节；行为规范，规矩

续表

snobbery	*n.* 势利态度；势利眼
democratization	*n.* 民主化
bewitch	*vt.* 使着迷；使着魔
lament	*vt.* &*vi.* （为……）哀悼，痛哭，悲伤 *n.* 悲恸，哀歌，挽歌
stand-offish	*adj.* 冷漠的；冷淡的；疏远的
infantilize	*vt.* 使幼儿化，将（成人）当作幼儿对待
demean	*vt.* 降低（自己）的身份；贬低；贬损
imperil	*vt.* 使陷于危险；危及
hackle-raising	*adj.* 生气的，动怒的
chummery	*n.* 友好，亲昵，愉悦
brash	*adj.* 过于自信的；盛气凌人的；自以为是的
bask	*vi.* 沉浸于，尽情享受（赞美、宠爱或崇拜）
courtesy	*n.* 礼貌；谦恭；彬彬有礼
discourse	*n.* 话语；语篇；演讲；论述 *vi.* 高谈阔论；论述
contemptuously	*adv.* 蔑视地；藐视地
handout	*n.* 救济品；施舍物；印刷品；讲义
fling	*vt.* （尤指生气地）扔，掷，抛，丢
taunt	*vt.* 笑话；嘲笑；奚落；羞辱
faggot	*n.* 男同性恋者
anti-abortion	*adj.* 反对堕胎的
traction	*n.* （对车辆的）牵引力，拉力
rail	*n.* 围栏；轨道；钢轨；扶手 *vi.* 责备；抱怨；责骂
scathing	*adj.* 严厉的；尖锐的；刻薄的
intemperate	*adj.* 无节制的；过度的；过激的
nicety	*n.* （尤指好的礼仪或得体的举止方面的）细节，小节

续表

patina	*n.* （物体表面形成的）薄层
underside	*n.* 下侧，底面，阴暗面
repress	*vt.* 压制，压抑，克制（情感）
malevolence	*n.* 恶意，狠毒
deception	*n.* 瞒骗，欺诈，骗局
politesse	*n.* （法）礼貌，客气，礼节
misanthropy	*n.* 遁世；厌世
disjuncture	*n.* 分离，分裂
hipster	*n.* 赶时髦的人；潮人

Phrases & Expressions

lose count of	记不清楚，数不清楚
default mode	默认模式
sweep away	扫除，刮走，冲走；清除
sour into	（友谊、局势、态度等）变坏；（使）恶化
shock jock	（故意口无遮拦的）电台唱片节目主持人
be deluged with	使涌现；使充满

Proper Names

East Village	东村（在美国纽约市曼哈顿）
Old World	旧大陆；旧世界
Parkinson's disease	帕金森病
tea party	茶叶党（美国近年来迅速膨胀、由保守民众建立的草根组织）
Nazi	（德国的）纳粹党员，纳粹主义，纳粹主义信徒
swastika	纳粹党所用的十字记号，万字符号
Desperate Housewives	《绝望主妇》

续表

David Lammy	戴维·拉米（英国黑人工党议员）
Diane Abbott	戴安娜·阿博特（工党左翼人士，英国第一个黑人女议员）
Ben Bradshaw	本·布拉德肖（英国前文化大臣）

Cultural Notes

1. East Village East Village is a neighborhood in the New York City borough of Manhattan. For more information, visit https://en.wikipedia.org/wiki/East_Village,_Manhattan.

2. Old World The Old World consists of Africa, Europe, and Asia, regarded collectively as the part of the world known to Europeans before contact with the Americas. It is used in the context of, and contrast with, the New World (North and South America). For more information, visit https://en.wikipedia.org/wiki/Old_World.

3. Parkinson's disease Parkinson's disease is a degenerative disorder of the central nervous systemmainly affecting the motor system. For more information, visit https://en.wikipedia.org/wiki/Parkinson%27s_disease.

4. tea party The Tea Party movement is an American political movement known for its conservative positions and its role in the Republican Party. Members of the movement have called for a reduction of the U. S. national debt and federal budget deficit by reducing government spending. In addition, they have also called for lowering taxes. For more information, visit https://en.wikipedia.org/wiki/Tea_Party_movement.

5. Nazi National Socialism (German: Nationalsozialismus), more commonly known as Nazism, is the ideology and practice associated with the 20th-century German Nazi Party and Nazi state as well as other far-right groups. For more information, visit https://en.wikipedia.org/wiki/Nazism.

6. swastika The Swastika (as a character: 卐 or 卍) is a symbol that generally takes the form of an equilateral cross, with its four legs bent at 90 degrees. It is considered to be a sacred and auspicious symbol in Hinduism, Buddhism and Jainism. It is known most widely as an important symbol long used in Indian religions, denoting "auspiciousness. "It was adopted as such in pre-World War I-Europe and later, and most notably, by the Nazi Party and Nazi Germany prior to World War II. For more information, visit https://en. wikipedia. org/wiki/Swastika.

7. *Desperate Housewives* *Desperate Housewives* is an American television comedy-drama-mystery series created by Marc Cherryand produced by ABC Studios and Cherry Productions. For more information, visit https://en. wikipedia. org/wiki/Desperate_ Housewives.

Exercises

Comprehension of the Text

Ⅰ. The following 10 statements contain information given in the text. Identify the paragraph from which the information is derived. Some paragraph may not be used. Each paragraph is marked with a letter.

1. Britain, once a nation with good reputation for etiquette, has deteriorated towards unanimous disrespect for beautiful manners.

2. What Americans think of as vulgar language is nothing but a minor overreaction for Britons.

3. Telephone sales representatives pay special attention to their good manners when they want to reach their clients.

4. Good manners make social interaction fluid and smooth for struggling New Yorkers.

5. Obama's policies were coldly greeted and harshly attacked by a US shock jock.

6. During the trip, the writer found it hard to understand why New York earned its reputation for impoliteness.

7. There is a growing tendency for Britain to become vulnerable to rage and violence.

8. The writer used to scoff at the insincere intention of a standard American greeting—"Have a nice day. "

9. While the writer was exuberantly immersed in American etiquette, a newspaper told a different story.

10. In the writer's opinion, British snobbery and cynicism is preferable to America's deception and extremes.

Vocabulary

Ⅱ. Fill in the blanks with the words given below. Change the form where necessary.

deliberate	elegant	shatter	reproachful	aggression
soothing	diverse	reserve	etiquette	lament
imperil	courtesy	repress	deception	contemptuously

1. After three days, the strikers' demands were met almost without ______.

2. Alcoholics are notorious for their ability to ________ themselves about the extent of their problem.

3. For example, one may try to demonstrate the spirit of men who pursue a high quality life by using seawater and abstract Chinese ink painting patterns to express a kind of restrained ________ found in traditional Chinese culture

4. The Chinese people came together, creating a great nationwide force for resistance against Japanese ________ and eventually securing complete victory for the first time in China's modern history.

5. In spite of the ethnic ________ in the county, the challenges have brought a profound sense of community among locals.

6. The conflicts in Syria and Iraq have turned tens of thousands of people into refugees, and thousands of them made a beeline for Europe to escape the civil wars and ________.

7. "My hosts were ________ and made us feel at home," said one foreign student in the culture exchange program.

8. The Deputy Commander has condemned this weekend's protest as ______ provocation.

9. By contrast, Cameron said an abusive corporate culture breeds ______ , diminishes creativity, commitment and loyalty that will impede growth because

employees will leave.

10. It did not take long for the central bank to ______ investors' fears.

Further Reading

TEXT C Valentine's Day

Some people are armed while some people actively embrace it, but no one doubts about its ubiquity in the air. Everyone is susceptible to its power. It is what makes the world turn, breaking hearts but repairing them simultaneously. The most intelligent students cannot comprehend it, Einstein never figured out a formula to calculate its strength, and Pablo Picasso could never put it on canvas. Its evasiveness, however, is what motivates us to run after it.

That's why, of course, we have an entire day to celebrate the one thing that no one can understand.

Love.

In America, Valentine's Day is often referred to as a holiday where either people are delirious with bliss while spending the day with their soul mate or mourning their single status, eating a box of chocolates they bought for themselves. We imagine couples frolicking through parks and meadows, while girls and boys who don't have a boy or girlfriend sit in their bedrooms lamenting their miserable love life. More or less, this is the basic gist of the holiday. However, there are several different types of love to be taken into consideration. Romantic love is important, but not the only type of affection that should be or is celebrated as a part of Valentine's Day. The beauty of this day is the commemoration of all types of loves that dictate all relationships, whether they are romantic or familial.

I've decided to divide the different characteristics of love into three categories.

1. Child's play

This type of affection is apparent in all children under the age of 12, who are silly enough to eat glue but also innocent enough to religiously follow the rule that prohibits them from running with scissors. For these children, Valentine's Day is a day filled with treats and corny but endearing cards that are exchanged. They have no idea what love means, moreover they have no clue what it is. Essentially, this day is all about the treats. A day or two before, children start to prepare their Valentine's Day treats. Although these treats aren't required, they are advised primarily because of one rule: if you don't give, you don't get. And all children want to get.

Furthermore, grocery stores know what to expect. They're stocked with cards and candy just for those children. With a list of children in the class that is usually given to them by their teacher, the kids write the name of each of their classmates on every one of the cards possibly with a note before taping a piece of candy to it. On the day, these treats are passed our and they enjoy the candy while the rest of America spends their Valentine's Day in a different way.

2. A day of mourning

This type of love-sickness is both pitiful but also enjoyable from an observer's perspective. It consists of pubescent teenagers lamenting over the lack of boyfriends or girlfriends. From ages 12—18, both girls and boys are guilty of this practice and they all know it. Many often make an effort of incorporating red or pink into their outfits for a cute touch, but in reality it's a day of mourning for these teens that haven't met anyone special. The entire day, they mourn over the boyfriend they never had, feeling their juvenile hearts break when they see couples strolling the hallways, walking awkwardly with their hands grasped awkwardly together.

To those who feel bad about themselves on Valentine's Day, I have only one thing to say: Don't fret; you'll find the "one".

3. All-encompassing

This type of love is most beautiful. For those who practice the "all-encompassing" way of Valentine's Day, all loved ones are celebrated. A box of chocolates with a card with a heart-warming message is given to their special someone, while chocolate and other small gifts are distributed to their entire family. This way, everyone's happy and feels loved, exactly the feeling this day should elicit.

There are certain holidays that have been desecrated by gifts, shopping, and money and there remain few days that still achieve the purpose they were created to fulfill. It's easy to get caught up with holiday shopping, and spend time and money looking for the perfect gifts to give to family and friends on Christmas. Yet, spending ridiculous amounts of time and money for gifts doesn't seem all that worth it in the end. It's wonderful to spend Thanksgiving Day dining with the family, but the elegance of the day is ruined by black Friday shopping the following day. It seems as if this consumer society has not only brainwashed our minds but also has infiltrated our holidays.

Valentine's Day, however, has managed to keep its integrity. There are no shopping deals or retail store sales that can distract from this joyous occasion. It's simply a day set aside to show gratitude to loved ones. In simpler terms, it's a day of love and chocolate, the two greatest things on earth.

(Words: 830)

Questions for discussions

1. In your understanding, what should be valued most in true love?

2. Do you think that romantic love is the most principal theme for Valentine's Day? Why or why not?

3. Do you know anything about Chinese Valentine's Day (Qixi Festival)? What is the origin of the story and how is old tradition preserved today?

More to Learn

1. Appreciation

Shall I compare thee to a summer's day?

By William Shakespeare

Shall I compare thee to a summer's day?
Thou art more lovely and more temperate.
Rough winds do shake the darling buds of May,
And summer's lease hath all too short a date.
Sometime too hot the eye of heaven shines,

And often is his gold complexion dimm'd;
And every fair from fair sometime declines,
By chance or nature's changing course untrimm'd;
But thy eternal summer shall not fade
Nor lose possession of that fair thou ow'st;
Nor shall Death brag thou wander'st in his shade,
When in eternal lines to time thou grow'st;
So long as men can breathe or eyes can see,
So long lives this, and this gives life to thee.

MOVIES TO SEE (A) Pretty Woman

Ⅰ. Movie Introduction

Director: Garry Marshall

Starring: Richard Gere
Julia Roberts
Jason Alexander

Running time: 119mins

Released: 1990

Plot: Edward is a rich, ruthless businessman who specializes in taking over companies and then selling them off piece by piece. He travels to Los Angeles for a business trip and decides to hire a prostitute. They take a liking to each other and he offers her money if she'll stay with him for an entire week while he makes the "rich and famous"scene (since it doesn't do for a man of his stature to be alone at society parties and polo matches). Romantic comedy (and complications) ensue. For more information, visit http://www.imdb.com/title/tt0100405/?ref_ =fn_ al_ tt_ 1.

Ⅱ. Classic Scenes

Task 1 Study the underlined sentences and expressions in the following classic scenes.

1. When Edward met Vivian for the firs time.

Vivian: Hey, sugar, you lookin' for a date?

Edward: No, I want to find Beverly Hills. Can you give me directions?

Vivian: Sure. For five bucks.

Edward: Ridiculous.

Vivian: Price just went up to ten.

Edward: You can't charge me for directions!

Vivian: I can do anything I want to, Baby; I ain't lost.

Vivian: Man, this baby must corner like it's on rails!

Edward: Beg your pardon?

Vivian: Well, doesn't it blow your mind? This is only four cylinders!

Vivian: Wow! Great view! I bet you can see all the way to the ocean from out here.

Edward: I'll take your word for it. I don't go out there.

Vivian: Why don't you go out there?

Edward: I'm afraid of heights.

Vivian: You are? So how come you rented the penthouse?

Edward: It's the best. I looked all around for penthouses on the first floor, but I can't find one.

Edward: I hadn't exactly planned this.

Vivian: Do you plan everything?

Edward: Always.

Vivian: Yeah me too! I'm actually, no I'm not a planner. I would say I'm a kinda fly by the seat of your pants gal, you know moment to moment. Yeah that's me, that's...yeah.

2. The next morning when Edward told Vivian about his business.

Vivian: You don't actually have a billion dollars, huh?

Edward: No. I get some of it from banks, investors... it's not an easy thing to do.

Vivian: And you don't make anything...

Edward: No.

Vivian: ... and you don't build anything.

Edward: No.

Vivian: So whadda ya do with the companies once you buy'em?

Edward: I sell them.

[Viv reaches for his tie.]

Vivian: Here, let me do that. You sell them.

Edward: Well, I... don't sell the whole company, I break it up into pieces, and then I sell that off, it's worth more than the whole.

Vivian: So, it's sort of like, um... stealing cars and selling'em for parts, right?

Edward: [sighs exasperatedly] Yeah, sort of. But legal.

Edward: I will pay you to be at my beck and call.

Vivian: Look, I'd love to be your beck-and-call girl, but...

Edward: Any questions?

Vivian: Can I call you Eddie?

Edward: Not if you expect me to answer.

Vivian: I would have stayed for two thousand.

Edward: I would have paid four. I'll see ya tonight.

Vivian: Baby, I'm gonna treat you so nice, you're never gonna wanna let me go.

Edward: Three thousand, for six days, and Vivian, I will let you go.

3. When Edward heard Vivian's complaint about her mistreatment doing shopping, he decided to keep her company.

Vivian: The stores are not nice to people—I don't like it.

Edward: Stores are never nice to people. They're nice to credit cards.

Edward: You see this young lady over here?

Hollister: Yes.

Edward: Do you have anything in this shop as beautiful as she is?

Hollister: Oh, yes.

[Edward gives Hollister a look.]

Hollister: Oh, no! No, no! No. I'm saying we have many things as beautiful as she... would want them to be! [babbling] That's the point I was getting at. And I think we can all agree with that. That's why, when you came in here, you knew from the first—

Edward: You know what we're gonna need here? We're going to need a few more people helping us out. I'll tell you why. We are going to be spending an obscene amount of money in here. So we're going to need a lot more help sucking up to us, 'cause that's what we really like.

Hollister: Ohhhh!

Edward: You understand that.

Hollister: Sir, if I may say so, you're in the right store, and the right city, for that matter!

Hollister: Exactly how obscene an amount of money were you talking about? Just... profane, or really offensive?

Edward: Really offensive.

Hollister: [to himself] I like him so much.

Hollister: Mr. Lewis? How's it going so far?

Edward: Pretty well, I think. I think we need some major sucking up.

Hollister: Very well, sir. You're... not only handsome, but a powerful man. I could see the second you walked in here, you were someone to reckon with...

Edward: Hollister.

Hollister: Yes, sir?

Edward: Not me. Her.

[Vivian, smartly dressed and carrying many bags, stops in at yesterday's clothing store.]

Vivian: Do you remember me?

Salesperson: No, I'm sorry.

Vivian: I was in here yesterday. You wouldn't wait on me?

Salesperson: Oh.

Vivian: You work on commission, right?

Salesperson: Ah, yes.

Vivian: Big mistake. Big. Huge! [turns away] I have to go shopping now!

4. At the opera house.

Edward : People's reactions to opera the first time they see it is very dramatic; they either love it or they hate it. If they love it, they will always love it. If they don't, they may learn to appreciate it, but it will never become part of their soul.

Matron: Did you enjoy the opera, dear?

Vivian: Oh, it was so good, I almost peed my pants!

[Vivian walks off.]

Matron: Wha—?

Edward: She said she liked it better than *The Pirates of Penzance.*

5. In the penthouse, when Edward was about to leave for business.

Vivian: What else? You going to leave some money by the bed when you pass through town?

Edward: Vivian, it really wouldn't be like that.

Vivian: How would it be?

Edward: Well, for one thing, it would get you off the streets.

Vivian: That's just geography.

Edward: Vivian, what is it you want? What do you see happening between us?

Vivian: I don't know. When I was a little girl, my mama used to lock me in the attic when I was bad, which was pretty often. And I would… I would pretend I was a princess, trapped in the tower by a wicked queen. And then suddenly, this knight, on a white horse, with these colors flying, would come charging up and draw his sword… and I would wave, and he would climb up the tower, and rescue me. But never in all the time… that I had this dream… did the knight say to me, "Come on, baby, I'll put you up in a great condo."

Edward: I've never treated you like a prostitute.

[He walks away.]

Vivian: You just did.

Task 2 Work in pairs or groups and play the roles in one of your favorite scenes.

Ⅲ. Cultural Notes

1. *Beverly Hills*: Beverly Hills is a city in Los Angeles County, California, United States, surrounded by the cities of Los Angeles and West Hollywood. Originally a Spanish ranch where lima beans were grown, it was incorporated in 1914 by a group of investors who had failed to find oil, but found water in-

stead and eventually decided to develop it into a town. By 2013, its population had grown to 34, 658. Sometimes referred to as "90210", one of its primary ZIP codes, it is home to many actors and celebrities. The city includes the Rodeo Drive shopping district and the Beverly Hills Oil Field. For more information, visit https://en. wikipedia. org/wiki/Beverly_ Hills, _ California.

2. *The Pirates of Penzance: The Pirates of Penzance;* or, *The Slave of Duty* is a comic opera in two acts, with music by Arthur Sullivan and libretto by W. S. Gilbert. The opera's official premiere was at the Fifth Avenue Theatre in New York City on 31 December 1879, where the show was well received by both audiences and critics. Its London debut was on 3 April 1880, at the Opera Comique, where it ran for 363 performances, having already been playing successfully for over three months in New York. For more information, visit https://en. wikipedia. org/wiki/The_ Pirates_ of_ Penzance.

Ⅳ. Questions for discussion

1. Of the two main characters in the movie, who do you admire more and why?

2. Why do you think fairy tales never stop holding a fascination for people over the years?

3. It has grown in popularity that many young girls will choose to marry rich old men. In the materialistic world, what do you think seems to be a touchstone of romantic love?

Ⅴ. Movie Review

Task: Write a movie review on *Pretty Woman.*

MOVIES TO SEE (B) The Truman Show

Movie Introduction

Director: Peter Weir

Starring: Jim Carrey, Ed Harris, Laura Linney

Running time: 103 mins

Released: 1998

Plot: In this movie, Truman is a man whose life is a fake one...The place he lives is in fact a big studio with hidden cameras everywhere, and all his friends and people around him, are actors who play their roles in the most popular TV-series in the world: The Truman Show. Truman thinks that he is an ordinary man with an ordinary life and has no idea about how he is exploited. Until one day...he finds out everything. Will he react?

To Recommend More Movies

- ❖*Roman Holiday* (1953)
- ❖*Big Fish* (2003)
- ❖*Erin Brockovich* (2000)
- ❖*Click* (2006)
- ❖*Yes Man* (2008)

References

1. Brenda Wegmann, Miki Knezevic. Mosaic 1 Silver Edition. New York: The McGraw-Hill Companies, 2007.

2. Counts, G. S. *Education and the Foundations of Human Freedom*. Pittsburgh: University of Pittsburgh Press, 1962.

3. Davis, F. *Fashion, Culture and Identity*. Chicago: University of Chicago Press, 1992.

4. Find Out How to Beat Sunday Night Blues. [N]. 英语学习, 2008 (6): 9.

5. Gina Teague. 文化之旅美国 [M]. 张荣婕注. 北京: 外语教学与研究出版社, 2009.

6. Lim Benjamin. House of Cards. [N]. 英语学习, 2014 (7): 28 ~ 30.

7. On the Amtrak from Boston to New York City. [N]. 英语学习, 2011 (7): 40.

8. Shirley Temple: Our Little Girl Forever. [N]. 英语学习, 2014 (5): 8.

9. The Nutcracker Is America's Most Popular Ballet. [N]. 英语世界, 2001 (7): 104.

10. The Oscar Statuette. [N]. 英语学习, 2014 (6): 54.

1. 常俊跃等主编:《美国历史文化》, 北京大学出版社, 2013 年。

2. 何怀宏:《伦理学专业英语教程》, 北京大学出版社, 2003 年。

3. 李桂兰:《大学英语基础听说教程》, 外语教学与研究出版社, 2009 年。

4. 玛丽安娜·卡尼·戴特斯曼等:《美国文化背景》(第 3 版), 陈国华译, 世界图书出版公司, 2006 年。

5. 王恩铭:《美国文化与社会》, 上海外语教育出版社, 2003 年。

6. 曾鸣, 张剑. 历年考研英语真题解析及复习思路 [M]. 北京: 世界图书出版公司, 2015: 56 ~ 59。

7. 张梦井，杜耀文．中国名家散文精译［M］．青岛：青岛出版社，1999：5~9。

8. 朱永涛：《英美文化基础教程》，外语教学与研究出版社，1991 年。

1. 10 Facts about religion in America.

http://www.pewresearch.org/fact-tank/2015/08/27/10-facts-about-religion-in-america/

2. A Comparative Overview of the Three Main "Western" Religions.

http://catholic-resources.org/Courses/Intro-WesternReligions.htm.

3. American Football.

http://en.wikipedia.org/wiki/American_sport

http://en.wikipedia.org/wiki/History_of_American_football

4. American Geography.

http://beijing.usembassy-china.org.cn/geography.html

http://www.kekenet.com/read/201305/238591.shtml

5. American literature.

http://blog.sina.com.cn/s/blog_58acfbf601015qax.html

6. American Love and Marriage.

http://www.kekenet.com/read/201303/231074.shtml

http://www.kekenet.com/read/201303/231065.shtml

7. American Sports.

http://en.wikipedia.org/wiki/Sport

http://en.wikipedia.org/wiki/American_sport

8. A Survey of American Literature.

http://blog.sina.com.cn/s/blog_48da410e0100sum9.html

9. Best Places to Visit in the USA(Excerpt).

http://travel.usnews.com/Rankings/best_usa_vacations/

10. Black Friday.

https://en.wikipedia.org/wiki/Black_Friday_(shopping) https://blackfriday.com/pages/black-friday-history

11. Common Customs and Etiquette in the U. S. A.

http://www.kwintessential.co.uk/resources/global-etiquette/usa.html
12. Economy of America.
http://beijing.usembassy-china.org.cn/economy.html
13. Education.
http://beijing.usembassy-china.org.cn/education.html
14. Federal government of the United States.
https://en.wikipedia.org/wiki/Federal_government_of_the_United_States
15. Higher Education System.
http://www.Polytech.Poltava.ua/education/America/usa_3.html.
16. Houston. En8848.com.cn 原版英语.
http://beijing.usembassy-china.org.cn/geography.html
17. Ice Age.
https://en.wikipedia.org/wiki/Ice_age
18. Lady Gaga, a Star Surrounded by Controversy.
http://bikinirangerscelebrity.wikia.com/wiki/Lady_Gaga
19. Michael Jordan, basketball-reference.com. Retrieved February 8, 2008.
20. Michael Jordan, National Basketball Association. Retrieved January 15, 2007.
21. Michael Jordan.
http://en.wikipedia.org/wiki/Michael_Jordan
22. Outline of American literature.
http://iipdigital.usembassy.gov/media/pdf/books/outline_us_lit.pdf
23. Philadelphia. En8848.com.cn 原版英语.
http://en.wikipedia.org/wiki/Philadelphia_Museum_of_Art
24. Public Universities in the United States.
https://zh.scribd.com/document/158679550/College-and-University-Education-in-the-US-EJUSA
25. Put a Fork in It.
http://www.slate.com/articles/life/culturebox/2013/06/fork_and_knife_use_americans_need_to_stop_cutting_and_switching.html
26. Raising Children.

http: //www. kekenet. com/read/201303/228234. shtml

27. Streets Of Philadelphia.

http: //www. music. baidu. com

28. The American Two – party System.

http: //www. hjenglish. com/new/p171494/

29. The Best US Guided Tour for Every Personality.

http: //usatravel. about. com/od/Tours – And – Packages/ss/The – Best – USA – Guided – Tour – for – Every – Personality. htm#showall

30. The U. S. Farm Economy.

http: //beijing. usembassy – china. org. cn/economy . html

31. UBS may move US investment bank to NYC.

e – Eighteen. com Ltd. June 10, 2011. Retrieved July 29, 2014.

32. USA History in brief.

https: //china. usembassy – china. org. cn/wp – content/uploads/sites/252/2016/12/historybrief. pdf

33. U. S. Community Colleges: A Gateway to Higher Education for Many.

https: //zh. scribd. com/document/158679550/College – and – University – Education – in – the – US – EJUSA

34. Wall Street.

http: //en. wikipedia. org/wiki/Wall_ Street

35. WFE Market Highlights. World Federation of Exchanges. Retrieved July 20, 2014.

36. What is a Large, Private Research University?

https: //zh. scribd. com/document/158679550/College – and – University – Education – in – the – US – EJUSA

37. What is Passover.

http: //toriavey. com/what – is – passover/

38. Why Do Americans Act Like That. "英语论文大百科"(www. tde. net. cn).

Key for Reference

Unit 1 History

Text A

Vocabulary

Ⅱ. Fill in the blanks with the words given below. Change the form where necessary.

1. flourish	2. provoke	3. hostility	4. intolerant	5. mythical
6. permanent	7. enforce	8. crackdown	9. impose	10. Violators

Translations

Ⅲ. Translate the following sentences into English.

1. It used to be closely tied to Buddhist prayer, but now it's largely secularized in the form of a giant country-wide water and chalk fight, designed to represent spiritual cleansing.

2. Good health is key if older people are to remain independent and to play a part in family and community life.

3. A growing tide of marine litter is harming oceans and beaches worldwide, according to a new report by the United Nations Environment Programme and the Environmental Organization Ocean Conservancy.

4. Whether we should continue to hold the meeting as planned depends in part on when the epidemic disease is curbed.

5. We have organic junk food with organic ingredients flown in from around the globe, disguised as health food by virtue of the organic label.

Ⅳ. Translate the following passage into English.

The frontier experience began when the first colonists settled on the east coast of the continent in the 1600s. It ended about 1890 when the last western lands were settled. The American frontier consisted of the relatively unsettled regions of the United States, usually found in the western part of the country. Here, both land and life were more rugged and primitive than in the more settled eastern part. As on e frontier area was settled, people began moving farther west into the next unsettled area, sweeping aside the Native Americans as they went. By settling one frontier area after another, Americans moved across an entire continent that was 2,700 miles wide. They came to believe that it was their destiny to control all the land, and eventually they did. The Native Americans were given small portions of land, called reservations, to control, but the United States government broke many promises and created much misery for the Indian nations.

Text B

Comprehension of the text

Ⅰ. The following 10 statements contain information given in the text. Identify the paragraph from which the information is derived. You may choose a paragraph more than once. Each paragraph is marked with a letter.

1. B 2. C 3. D 4. D 5. G 6. I 7. M 8. N 9. P 10. T

Vocabulary

Ⅱ. Fill in the blanks with the words given below. Change the form where necessary.

1. imposing 2. grieve 3. encroach 4. coordinate 5. hereditary
6. democratic 7. repealed 8. apprehension 9. radical 10. unanimously

Unit 2 Geography

Text A

Vocabulary

Ⅱ. Fill in the blanks with the words given below. Change the form where necessary.

1. mass 2. folkway 3. multicultural 4. heritage 5. stretch
6. vast 7. fertile 8. reassemble 9. territory 10. distribution

Translations

Ⅲ. Translate the following sentences into English.

1. So this is what he asked them to do: Select four answers to the question "What should a reader be to be a good reader?" — "The reader should belong to a book club."

2. "But if we speak of human rights and what happens in China, it also happens in many other countries," he said.

3. However, such cooperation must base on trust, negotiation, equality and mutual benefits. It must proceed from actual facts, rather than deductions.

4. People must be taught to appreciate Earth as not only their home, but also the home of our children and grandchildren, as well as all other plants and animals.

5. One day, she waited for her parents to leave the house so she could take apart the television and reassemble it before they returned.

Ⅳ. Translate the following passage into English.

Throughout their history, Americans have been people on the move. The early immigrants had to travel to get to the New World. Once they arrived, they settled along the East Coast. But they weren't content to stay there. Explorers and traders journeyed to the unknown western territories. Later, settlers moved west to develop these new areas. As a result of this westward migration, Americans eventually occupied the whole continent—from the Atlantic to the Pacific. Even today, Americans seem unable to stay put. Research says that the average American moves every five years.

Text B

Comprehension of the text

Ⅰ. The following 10 statements contain information given in the text. Identify the paragraph from which the information is derived. You may choose a paragraph more than once. Each paragraph is marked with a letter.

1. E 2. F 3. G 4. J 5. K 6. A 7. K 8. H 9. D 10. G

Vocabulary

Ⅱ. Fill in the blanks with the words given below. Change the form where necessary.

1. historic	2. availability	3. diversify	4. dominate	5. boosted
6. year-round	7. humid	8. prosperity	9. elevated	10. Underwent

Unit 3 Government and Politics

Text A

Vocabulary

Ⅱ. Fill in the blanks with the words given below. Change the form where necessary.

1. ambiguous	2. lobbying	3. autonomous	4. liberate
5. successor	6. appoint	7. disproportionate	8. delicate
9. conservatively	10. excessively		

Translations

Ⅲ. Translate the following sentences into English.

1. Find out ahead of time what regulations apply to your situation.
2. A health diet should consist of fresh fruits and vegetables.
3. Energy security will also drive China's shift away from coal and oil.
4. He will appeal to the state for an extension of unemployment benefits.
5. The conference may help to focus attention on the economy.

Ⅳ. Translate the following passage into English.

The ethnical judgments of the Supreme Court justices have become an important issue recently. The court cannot maintain its legitimacy as guardian of the rule of law when justices behave like politicians. Yet, in several instances, justices acted in ways that weakened the court's reputation for being independent and impartial. Justice Antonin Scalia, for example, appeared at political events. That kind of activity makes it less likely that the court's decisions will be accepted as impartial judgments. Part of the problem is that the justices are not bound by an ethics code. At the very least, the court should make itself subject to the code of conduct that applies to the rest of the federal judiciary. This and other similar cases raise the question of whether there is still a line between the court and politics.

Text B

Comprehension of the text

Ⅰ. The following 10 statements contain information given in the text. Identify the paragraph from which the information is derived. You may choose a paragraph more than once. Each paragraph is marked with a letter.

1. B 2. F 3. A 4. G 5. H 6. C 7. E 8. D 9. H 10. F

Vocabulary

Ⅱ. Fill in the blanks with the words given below. Change the form where necessary.

1. exaggerate	2. overturn	3. statistics	4. inevitable	5. candidate
6. classic	7. monopolize	8. moderately	9. assaults	10. community

Unit 4 Economy

Text A

Vocabulary

Ⅱ. Fill in the blanks with the words given below. Change the form where necessary.

1. dramatically	2. nurture	3. enhanced	4. profoundly
5. regulate	6. Nonetheless	7. succession	8. abundant
9. substitute	10. advocacy		

Translations

Ⅲ. Translate the following sentences into English.

1. As I said at the beginning, shared responsibility, solidarity, and a commitment to fairness and social justice are among the most important qualities for health leadership today.

2. Employees will take pride and be engaged in their work if they understand how their efforts impact the organization.

3. Owing to graft, the manager of this company was discharged from his post

and prosecuted.

4. So the term "middle class" covers a multitude of differences.

5. Russian roads are notoriously dangerous and drivers still rarely give way to pedestrians.

Ⅳ. Translate the following passage into English.

The unemployment rate probably won't fall quite as rapidly in 2015, according to economists, especially if more people enter the labor force because jobs are easier to find. Yet another large spate of hiring similar to the gain in 2014 would make the low unemployment rate more believable. "By the end of next year we will be at the point where the unemployment rate is between 5% and 5.5%, and it will truly feel legitimate," Faucher said.

Text B

Comprehension of the text

Ⅰ. The following 10 statements contain information given in the text. Identify the paragraph from which the information is derived. You may choose a paragraph more than once. Each paragraph is marked with a letter.

1. C 2. E 3. G 4. B 5. D 6. E 7. F 8. A 9. C 10. B

Vocabulary

Ⅱ. Fill in the blanks with the words given below. Change the form where necessary.

1. rival 2. revenue 3. downturn 4. intertwined 5. capitalization
6. signify 7. restructuring 8. rebound 9. catastrophic 10. inextricably

Unit 5 Arts

Text A

Vocabulary

Ⅱ. Fill in the blanks with the words given below. Change the form where necessary.

1. supplementary 2. debut 3. triggered 4. philanthropy 5. provoked

6. boost 7. sturdiness 8. muse 9. bubble 10. reveal

Translations

Ⅲ. Translate the following sentences into English.

1. The meeting was called in response to a request from U. S.

2. Some restaurants are modifying the recipes of British dishes to breathe new life into the classics, while others are using better quality ingredients but remaining true to British traditions and tastes.

3. In the aftermath of the hurricane, many people's homes were destroyed.

4. Contrary to popular belief, moderate exercise actually decreases your appetite.

5. In view of the present situation, we'll have to revise our original plan.

Ⅳ. Translate the following passage into English.

The first performance of Tchaikovsky's *The Nutcracker*, in St Pertersburg in 1892, was a flop. Wrote one critic the next day: "For dancers, there is rather little in it; for art, absolutely nothing, and for the artistic fate of our ballet, one more step downward." Two decades passed before another production was attempted. A century later, the ballet constitutes the single biggest fine-arts moneymaker in the United States, which has claimed the ballet as its own. In 1996, box-office receipts for some 2,400 American performances of the work by more than 20,000 dancers totaled nearly US $50 million. Despite the ballet's popularity, however, few Americans are aware of its history—or of some of the twists and turns of fate that have changed it from its original form.

Text B

Comprehension of the text

Ⅰ. The following 10 statements contain information given in the text. Identify the paragraph from which the information is derived. Some paragraphs may be used twice. Each paragraph is marked with a letter.

1. D 2. F 3. H 4. G 5. B 6. A 7. C 8. E 9. G 10. C

Vocabulary

Ⅱ. Fill in the blanks with the words given below. Change the form where necessary.

1. insulation 2. expressive 3. fatigue 4. reject 5. definition
6. obstinate 7. compulsorily 8. anguish 9. illuminated 10. heritage

Unit 6 Religion

Text A

Vocabulary

Ⅱ. Fill in the blanks with the words given below. Change the form where necessary.

1. fundamental 2. Protestant 3. diversified 4. eternally
5. sin 6. persecution 7. denomination 8. consequence
9. solely 10. seminar

Translations

Ⅲ. Translate the following sentences into English.

1. Our mission is to find ways for people to live in harmony with nature.

2. One of the things I love about travel is the chance to break away from daily routines and form some new ones.

3. The fact is that the overwhelming majority of scientists say that the earth is in peril, if we do not act now.

4. This can happen for a variety of reasons, and these reasons can be unintended as well as deliberate.

5. We have been called pessimistic but we like to be referred to as realists.

Ⅳ. Translate the following passage into English.

The fundamental American belief in individual freedom and the right of individuals to practice their own religion is at the center of religious experience in the United States. The great diversity of ethnic backgrounds has produced religious pluralism; most of the religions of the world are now practiced in the United States. Ninety percent of Americans say that they believe in God, although not all of them participate in traditional religious organizations. About 80 percent of Americans are Christians, about 2 percent are Jewish, and another 4 percent belong to other religious faiths such as Islam, Buddhism, and Hinduism.

Text B

Comprehension of the text

Ⅰ. The following 10 statements contain information given in the text. Identify the paragraph from which the information is derived. You may choose a paragraph more than once. Each paragraph is marked with a letter.

1. C 2. D 3. E 4. F 5. H 6. I 7. J 8. K 9. L 10. L

Vocabulary

Ⅱ. Fill in the blanks with the words given below. Change the form where necessary.

1. aggregated 2. affiliation 3. occurrence 4. well-documented
5. discrimination 6. supportive 7. division 8. diversity
9. predictor 10. ethnically

Unit Seven American Values

Text A

Vocabulary

Ⅱ. Fill in the blanks with the words given below. Change the form where necessary.

1. deferentially 2. dignity 3. recreating 4. individualistic
5. utmost 6. self-defeating 7. destructive 8. thought-provoking
9. superstition 10. devalue

Translations

Ⅲ. Translate the following sentences into English.

1. I did this film because I believe that if we as a country are going to cause such disorder we must also be prepared to face the horrendous images that result from these events.

2. They are concerned with the training curriculum, but not the details of each course.

3. To a large extent these problems lie beyond the direct control of the health sector.

4. Animals are not inferior or superior to humans; we are only different.

5. We can engage in gardening, writing, painting, walking, baking bread or simply spending time in contemplation.

Ⅳ. Translate the following passage into English.

American hospitality begins at home especially when it involves food. Most Americans agree that good home cooking beats restaurant food any day. When invited for a meal, you might ask, "Can I bring anything?" Unless it's a potluck, where everyone brings a dish, the host will probably respond, "No, just yourself ". For most informal dinners, you should wear comfortable, casual clothes. Plan to arrive on time, or else call to inform your hosts of the delay. During the dinner conversation, it's customary to compliment the hostess on the wonderful meal. Of course, the biggest compliment is to eat lots of food!

Text B

Comprehension of the text

Ⅰ. The following 10 statements contain information given in the text. Identify the paragraph from which the information is derived. You may choose a paragraph more than once. Each paragraph is marked with a letter.

1. E 2. G 3. I 4. G 5. A 6. D 7. F 8. B 9. I 10. C

Vocabulary

Ⅱ. Fill in the blanks with the words given below. Change the form where necessary.

1. permission 2. contract 3. compose 4. commitment 5. mingle
6. vowed 7. newlywed 8. engagement 9. counsel 10. bouquet

Unit 8 Education

Text A

Vocabulary

Ⅱ. Fill in the blanks with the words given below. Change the form where necessary.

1. regulations	2. prestigious	3. navigation	4. magnet
5. modestly	6. trustees	7. mandate	8. dynamically
9. orientation	10. intercollegiate		

Translations

Ⅲ. Translate the following sentences into English.

1. The costs of the nationality verification process, which can amount to two or three months of salary, are unacceptably high for these migrant communities.

2. The poor are hungry and malnourished not because there is no food, but because they cannot afford to buy the food that is available.

3. The key is to do a variety of targeted reading and writing activities with your child that are appropriate and fun for his phase of development.

4. In almost all these cases, health officials have determined that the individuals became sick because of exposure to infected birds.

5. The couple run a toy company, working at the cutting edge of robot technology for 30 years.

Ⅳ. Translate the following passage into English.

Educational institutions in the United States reflect the nation's basic values, especially the ideal of equality of opportunity. Americans believe that everyone deserves an equal opportunity to get a good education. American schools tend to put more emphasis on developing critical-thinking skills than they do on acquiring quantities of facts. American students are encouraged to ask questions, think for themselves, and express their own opinions in class, a reflection of the American values of individual freedom and self-reliance. The goal of the American education system is to teach children how to learn and to help them reach their maximum potential.

Text B

Comprehension of the text

Ⅰ. The following 10 statements contain information given in the text. Identify the paragraph from which the information is derived. You may choose a paragraph more than once. Each paragraph is marked with a letter.

1. F 2. G 3. H 4. H 5. H 6. B 7. B 8. C 9. F 10. B

Vocabulary

Ⅱ. Fill in the blanks with the words given below. Change the form where necessary.

1. flexibility 2. collaborate 3. thematic 4. intensify 5. distinctive
6. inquiry 7. constraint 8. nimble 9. foster 10. aspiration

Unit 9 Literature

Text A

Vocabulary

Ⅱ. Fill in the blanks with the words given below. Change the form where necessary.

1. indigenous 2. staunch 3. thematic 4. culminate
5. ethical 6. triumph 7. sufficient 8. endeavor
9. inadvertently 10. eminent

Translations

Ⅲ. Translate the following sentences into English.

1. By virtue of her individual drive and competitiveness, she has already ascended to the apex of the major leagues.

2. TV and the Internet alienate people from their friends, since modern people lack the face-to-face communication with friends.

3. But for now suffice it to say that we're already seeing this happen in social networks.

4. But they deserve credit for their concrete efforts to make peace.

5. But today, there is increased recognition of the fact that China must exer-

cise positive influence on international affairs.

Ⅳ. Translate the following passage into English.

William Shakespeare, an eminent English poet and playwright, was born in a charming little village in Warwickshire. Within about 32 years of his writing career, Shakespeare gave to the world nearly 40 plays, not two of which invoke the same feeling or image among the audience. Shakespeare took his plots from Greek legends and Roman history, from Italian stories and English chronicles. But whatever he touches sparkles with a peculiar beauty of his own and an old story is thus turned into a superb work of dramatic art. Though his characters are often clothed in old, foreign dresses, their thoughts and feelings belong to the age of Shakespeare and so his drama becomes an expression, a monument of the English Renaissance.

Text B

Comprehension of the text

Ⅰ. The following 8 statements contain information given in the text. Identify the paragraph from which the information is derived. You may choose a paragraph more than once. Each paragraph is marked with a letter.

1. A 2. B 3. F 4. G 5. I 6. I 7. D 8. J

Vocabulary

Ⅱ. Fill in the blanks with the words given below. Change the form where necessary.

1. fetter 2. recurrent 3. obsessed 4. dilemma 5. epochal
6. strenuous 7. bustling 8. embedded 9. deliverance 10. substantial

Unit Ten Sports

Text A

Vocabulary

Ⅱ. Fill in the blanks with the words given below. Change the form where necessary.

1. trailing 2. respective 3. classification 4. boycott
5. tournament 6. competitive 7. substantial 8. preclude
9. simultaneous 10. overall

Translations

Ⅲ. Translate the following sentences into English.

1. In this phase, you aim to reduce differences between you and the organizational environment by changing either the environment or your behavior.

2. Only by reporting in this way can a news medium be regarded as responsible to society.

3. And so over the years, protein tended to be associated with animal-based foods.

4. To some extent, this is due to the nature of the world around it.

5. He eventually conceded to write a thank-you note instead.

Ⅳ. Translate the following passage into English.

Adults who emphasize good sportsmanship, however, see winning as just one of the several goals they'd like their kids to achieve. The help young athletes take pride in their accomplishments, so that the kids see themselves as winners, even if the scoreboard doesn't show the numbers going in their favor. The best coaches—and parents—encourage their kids to play fair, to have fun, and to concentrate on helping the team. Remember the saying, "Actions speak louder than words"? That's especially true when it comes to teaching your kids the basics of good sportsmanship. Your behavior during practices and games will influence them more than any pep talk or lecture you give them.

Text B

Comprehension of the text

Ⅰ. The following 10 statements contain information given in the text. Identify the paragraph from which the information is derived. You may choose a paragraph more than once. Each paragraph is marked with a letter.

1. B 2. F 3. I 4. G 5. A 6. I 7. H 8. D 9. C 10. B

Vocabulary

Ⅱ. Fill in the blanks with the words given below. Change the form where necessary.

1. prolific	2. deemed	3. assist	4. recruit	5. effectively
6. rigorously	7. consensus	8. rival	9. Abruptly	10. emerged

Unit 11 Travel

Text A

Vocabulary

Ⅱ. Fill in the blanks with the words given below. Change the form where necessary.

1. boasts	2. cuisine	3. chaotic	4. cutting-edge	5. seclude
6. permeated	7. zealous	8. austerity	9. flourishing	10. embellish

Translations

Ⅲ. Translate the following sentences into English.

1. John and other teachers considered it foolish to weigh in on such an important decision.

2. No one article can ever do justice to the topic of fraud.

3. Keaton comes here once or twice a year to soak up the atmosphere.

4. Holidaymakers continued to pour down to the coast in search of surf and sun.

5. Then disappointment sets in as they see the magic is no longer there.

Ⅳ. Translate the following passage into English.

On 4th last November, I went to New York, one of the world's greatest metropolitan cities. In the evening, I stayed in a hotel in Manhattan, located in the busiest part of New York. At night I took a stroll along the street which was crowded with banks, companies, department stores and agencies. The high buildings rising against the night sky looked like precipitous cliffs. The walls, made of transparent glass, were like a world of crystal palace. The colorful street lamps twinkled far and near, high and low, distinct and dim. Walking along the street as though I were floating in the sky with millions of stars around. The car swept along like dragons in the wind and their tail lights stretched in the far distance like countless red ribbons. Here in the brightly-lit shop windows were displays of shining gold and silver kitchen vessels, red agate and green jade pieces. The gold and diamond pieces glittered and the ancient copper utensils were also attractive. Over there, lofty palaces stood guarded by policemen in uniforms at their gates, with beautifully-colored curtains draped behind the windows. On the pavement, men with different skin colors were miscellaneously decorated and hurrying to and fro. Wandering along the busy street, and looking around at the glorious, brilliant flowers, I could not, however, find its beauty. I was just a casual and hurried passer-by.

Text B

Comprehension of the text

Ⅰ. The following 10 statements contain information given in the text. Identify the paragraph from which the information is derived. Some paragraph may not be used. Each paragraph is marked with a letter.

1. T 2. A 3. F 4. L 5. O 6. C 7. P 8. H 9. R 10. E

Vocabulary

Ⅱ. Fill in the blanks with the words given below. Change the form where necessary.

1. antidote 2. Gourmet 3. foliage 4. immersed 5. buzzword
6. unwind 7. excursions 8. culinary 9. budding 10. millennial

Unit 12 Holidays and Customs

Text A

Vocabulary

Ⅱ. Fill in the blanks with the words given below. Change the form where necessary.

1. haunting 2. patriotic 3. abundance 4. affiliation 5. initiative
6. commemorate 7. elaborate 8. descendants 9. fantasized 10. superstition

Translations

Ⅲ. Translate the following sentences into English.

1. The laws demand equal pay for equal work between genders in theory, but in practice, women receive much lower wages than their male colleagues.

2. In many cases religious persecution is the cause of people fleeing their country. A case in point is colonial India.

3. No sooner had the honorable artist completed his performance than the capacity crowd of 30,000 at the stadium burst into thundering applause.

4. This is a luxurious car complete with air conditioning, portable TV and telephone.

5. Though the global paper making industry has experienced solid growth over recent years, it has seen slower demand before the advent of digital technology.

Ⅳ. Translate the following passage into English.

"I think what most people experience are thoughts of dread," said psychotherapist Dr. Wright. "Before going back to work they experience withdrawal behaviors, they don't enjoy their Sundays." Wright said Sunday night stress is very common and it hits all walks of life. "Really it's like having a six-day workweek because you spend the whole day thinking about going to work and dreading going to work and anticipating things happening at work that may be stressful," said Wright. "I think people can identify it many different ways. It's the same as the fear of flying or the fear of taking a test. Often times the anticipation of the event is much more stressful than the event itself." Wright said keeping active on Sunday will keep people's minds off heading back to work or school. Perhaps the best advice for beating Sunday night anxiety is to create a ritual you really look forward to. It can be as simple as watching a favorite TV show each week. Another suggestion is to make Sunday family game night.

Text B

Comprehension of the text

Ⅰ. The following 10 statements contain information given in the text. Identify the paragraph from which the information is derived. Some

paragraph may not be used. Each paragraph is marked with a letter.

1. G 2. C 3. I 4. E 5. L 6. B 7. F 8. D 9. J 10. N

Vocabulary

Ⅱ. Fill in the blanks with the words given below. Change the form where necessary.

1. reservation 2. deceive 3. elegance 4. aggression 5. diversity
6. repression 7. courteous 8. deliberate 9. contempt 10. soothe